D0421035

Contemporary Color
Theory & Use
Second Edition

Contemporary Color
Theory & Use
Second Edition

By Steven Bleicher

DELMAR
CENGAGE Learning™

Australia • Brazil • Japan • Korea • Mexico • Singapore • Spain • United Kingdom • United States

Contemporary Color: Theory & Use
Second Edition
Steven Bleicher

Vice President, Editorial: Dave Garza

Director of Learning Solutions: Sandy Clark

Senior Acquisitions Editor: Jim Gish

Managing Editor: Larry Main

Associate Product Manager:
Meaghan Tomaso

Editorial Assistant: Sarah Timm

Vice President, Marketing: Jennifer Baker

Marketing Director: Deborah Yarnell

Marketing Manager: Erin Brennan

Marketing Coordinator: Erin DeAngelo

Senior Production Director: Wendy Troeger

Senior Content Project Manager:
Kathryn B. Kucharek

Senior Art Director: Joy Kocsis

Technology Project Manager: Chris Catalina

© 2012 Delmar, Cengage Learning

ALL RIGHTS RESERVED. No part of this work covered by the copyright herein may be reproduced, transmitted, stored, or used in any form or by any means graphic, electronic, or mechanical, including but not limited to photocopying, recording, scanning, digitizing, taping, Web distribution, information networks, or information storage and retrieval systems, except as permitted under Section 107 or 108 of the 1976 United States Copyright Act, without the prior written permission of the publisher.

For product information and technology assistance, contact us at
Cengage Learning Customer & Sales Support, 1-800-354-9706

For permission to use material from this text or product,
submit all requests online at **www.cengage.com/permissions**
Further permissions questions can be e-mailed to
permissionrequest@cengage.com

Library of Congress Control Number: 2010940071

ISBN-13: 978-1-111-53891-0

ISBN-10: 1-111-53891-3

Delmar
5 Maxwell Drive
Clifton Park, NY 12065-2919
USA

Cengage Learning is a leading provider of customized learning solutions with office locations around the globe, including Singapore, the United Kingdom, Australia, Mexico, Brazil, and Japan. Locate your local office at: **international.cengage.com/region**

Cengage Learning products are represented in Canada by Nelson Education, Ltd.

To learn more about Delmar, visit **www.cengage.com/delmar**

Purchase any of our products at your local college store or at our preferred online store **www.cengagebrain.com**

Notice to the Reader
Publisher does not warrant or guarantee any of the products described herein or perform any independent analysis in connection with any of the product information contained herein. Publisher does not assume, and expressly disclaims, any obligation to obtain and include information other than that provided to it by the manufacturer. The reader is expressly warned to consider and adopt all safety precautions that might be indicated by the activities described herein and to avoid all potential hazards. By following the instructions contained herein, the reader willingly assumes all risks in connection with such instructions. The publisher makes no representations or warranties of any kind, including but not limited to, the warranties of fitness for particular purpose or merchantability, nor are any such representations implied with respect to the material set forth herein, and the publisher takes no responsibility with respect to such material. The publisher shall not be liable for any special, consequential, or exemplary damages resulting, in whole or part, from the readers' use of, or reliance upon, this material.

Printed in Canada
1 2 3 4 5 6 7 15 14 13 12 11

Table of Contents

Preface

Color is the single most important design element. No other formal design component has its unique power. Color stimulates the eye and brain and creates an immediate unconscious response from the viewer. It can move the soul and sway emotions. It can physically affect the viewer's feelings of temperature; raise or lower pulse rate, blood pressure, and respiration; and make items appear lighter or heavier, near or far, cheap or expensive. The right color can make or break a work of art or design.

Intended Audience

Contemporary Color: *Theory & Use, Second Edition*, has been developed and designed to teach the effective use of color across the areas of art and design. The text covers in detail fundamental studio elements along with a historical perspective to give the reader a deeper insight and understanding. The book has been designed with the awareness that artists and designers are visual learners. The pictures, images, and illustrations reinforce the text and bring the material to life. In addition, the book contains the most comprehensive and up-to-date information on color psychology.

Understanding the intrinsic power of color and its relationship with all of the other design elements is important for every artist, designer, and student. *Contemporary Color* may be used by both introductory and intermediate level art and design majors from community colleges to universities and professional art institutions and academies.

Emerging Trends

Digital and other new technologies are now a part of every art and design student's education. It is vital that students understand them as well as they do traditional materials and methods of working with color. To this end, *Contemporary Color,* as its name suggests, includes all forms of new technology, including digital imaging and animation, Web creations, virtual entities, lasers, and holography, to prepare today's students for a future in art and design.

Background of this Text

This book has been developed sequentially. Each chapter builds upon the information in the previous chapter to give the reader a complete understanding of this most complex of design elements. *Contemporary Color* bridges the areas of theory and practical application with its use of illustrations and professional examples from great design to outstanding works of art by emerging artists as well as modern masters.

While most books on color treat digital and other new forms of art as an afterthought, *Contemporary Color* integrates all forms of art throughout the text. This enables the reader to understand that these are not separate entities, but are all a part of the world of art and design. The theory and use of color is not handled one way on canvas and another on the computer; the same overriding principles apply for both. Only the medium changes, not the underlying concepts. Therefore, there has been a conscious effort to select images that span the scope of contemporary art and design.

In addition, the illustrations and images used in the text are predominantly contemporary art and design. I found throughout twenty years of being a practicing artist and teaching that this approach makes much more sense to students—using examples of art and design they can relate to and that are a part of their lives. This allows a fresher perspective because students are not studying the distant past and trying to figure out how this might relate to what they are doing or may want to do. They are studying the recent past and present to understand how their contemporaries are using these concepts today.

This book was written to bring the material on color up to date not only in visual terms, but also in terms of the new philosophies, concepts, and media currently in use. The aim was to integrate all forms of contemporary art and design to show our common concerns and practices. This book is an attempt to bring sometimes divergent areas together, showing that with respect to color, we use one common language.

Since this book is solely about color, it is assumed that students have had some previous background in design. However, the text has been designed and developed to present the information in a clear, logical, and concise manner and to enable anyone to read and understand the materials, regardless of background.

Textbook Organization

This book is organized and structured so that readers are introduced to the fundamental elements of color in a logical order. Each chapter builds on the previous one to give the reader a solid foundation, increasing their knowledge about and ability to use color effectively.

Chapter 1: Color Perception

Color exists in and is as much a component of the function of the brain as it is the eye. This chapter explains the biology and physiology of vision, how a person sees and perceives color. It also presents an overview of the various modes of perception. Understanding how color is perceived is as important as how it can be used.

Chapter 2: Color Theory—Making Sense of Color

From the dawn of time, mankind has tried to make sense of color. The theories that evolved have shaped our ideas and use of color. This chapter highlights the major theorists and their contributions, including contemporary theories of color from the palette to the swatch.

Chapter 3: Color Psychology

We don't approach color in a vacuum. We carry with us a lifetime's worth of ideas, experiences, and preferences. These affect how we relate to color in everything from the products we buy, to the food we eat, to the color of our homes, to the clothes we wear, and they may even reveal aspects of our personality. Depending upon our age, sex, and socioeconomic background, our responses to color will vary accordingly.

This chapter helps the artist and designer understand these issues in order to use color more effectively.

Chapter 4: Color Harmonies

This chapter visually explains color harmonies: what they are, why they are important to both artists and designers, and how to use them effectively. The full scope of color harmonies and their interactions are examined in a variety of media and styles.

Chapter 5: Pigments, Colorants, and Paints

Not only is understanding color harmonies and their interactions necessary, but it is also equally vital to understand the composition of the materials or media used.

There are two types of colorants—traditional and digital. This chapter looks at traditional media including pigments, colorants, and dyes and explains their formulation and usage.

Chapter 6: Digital Color

Today, learning about pigments is not enough. Nearly every image in any magazine, advertisement, product, and package has been digitally processed. It has become so much a part of our daily lives, we now take it for granted. This chapter explains digital color, from the most elemental level of the pixel to its complex digital elements.

Chapter 7: Color and 3-D

The world we live in is not a two-dimensional space, though most of the art and designs created are two-dimensional. From sculpture to product design to new forms of dimensional art, color can be used to enhance or deny the dimensionality of a form or object. This chapter examines all aspects of color as it relates to working with forms and objects that are fully three-dimensional.

Chapter 8: Color in Fine Art

Beginning with impressionism, this chapter reviews the trends and movements in modern art that have placed color at the forefront of their aesthetic philosophies. Pioneering movements from the Fauves, to expressionism, color-field painting, and op art are reviewed. Also, contemporary uses of color in environmental, installation, and conceptual art are examined.

Chapter 9: Color in Design

Color is used to emphasize and accent a design or product and usually influences our buying decisions. This chapter shows how designers use color in graphics, advertising, packaging, industrial design, and animation to communicate their ideas effectively.

Chapter 10: Global Color

Throughout the world people view and employ color differently. It is seen in relation to one's national origin, religion, cultural upbringing, and more. Color and its usage may distinguish a people and can be used for its symbolic nature. It can quickly identify a faction or a single individual. Since color has an instantaneous subliminal human response, it can trigger a whole host of associations. This is, in part, why groups—whether they are religious, political, or cultural—use identifying color markers. This chapter examines how color is used and its differing meaning around the world.

Chapter 11: The Future of Color

Color doesn't stand still. It is always changing, developing, and transforming our lives. New technologies are allowing us to work with an ever-increasing array of colors and hues. This chapter examines new products, theories, concepts, and modes of expression. It also looks at the law and our legal system, one of the newest arbiters of color use.

Features

The following list provides some of the salient features of the text:

- An innovative and contemporary approach to the introduction to color theory for students and a skill-sharpener for professionals.
- Equally focuses on traditional and digital color and their practical applications in contemporary art and design.
- Integrates digital and other new forms of art throughout the text.
- Clear, concise illustrations and images are used to supplement the text and encourage visual learning.
- Includes a comprehensive segment on the psychology of color.
- Color and 3-D are thoroughly explored, including types of media, colorants, and their uses.
- Colorants and pigments are examined to assist the artist and designer in choosing and using the correct medium to convey the concept or idea in the most effective manner possible.

New to This Edition

- An entire new chapter on global color and issues of multicultural color use.
- Extensively revised chapter on the future of color in light of recent trends and theories, including the impact of green design on color choices, making this thought-provoking content even more timely and relevant for today's students.
- Thorough updates to the chapter on digital color include coverage of cutting-edge concepts and the latest technology, including HDTV; CD, DVD, and Blu-ray discs; LCD, LED, and plasma displays; megapixels; motion gaming and animation; and Web 2.0 applications such as Second Life.
- New contemporary and fine art examples throughout the text.

Ancillary Package

The ancillaries for this new edition are designed to enhance both the instructors' and students' use of the book. The Instructor Resources have been fully updated to meet new and revised content in the text. There is also a new CourseMate product that correlates with the book and provides helpful features for both students and instructors.

Instructor Resources

The Instructor Resources were developed and fully revised to assist instructors in planning and implementing their instructional programs and are available online. They include sample syllabi for using this book for either an 11- or 15-week semester. They also provide chapter review questions and answers, comprehensive studio exercises, and assignments. PowerPoint slides that highlight the main topics are an additional instructor resource.

All these features have been updated to the new content in the book and can be found at **http://login.cengage.com.** At the CengageBrain.com home page, search for the ISBN of your title (from the back cover of your book) using the search box at the top of the page. This will take you to the product page where these resources can be found.

CourseMate

Contemporary Color: Theory & Use, Second Edition includes a Media Arts and Design CourseMate, which helps you make the grade.

This CourseMate includes:

- an interactive eBook, with highlighting, note taking, and search capabilities
- interactive learning tools including:
  - ✔ Quizzes
  - ✔ Flashcards
  - ✔ PowerPoint Lecture slides
  - ✔ and more!

Go to login.cengagebrain.com to access these resources.

Steven Bleicher, sitting in front of sculptures on the rooftop garden of Antonio Gaudi's Casa Mila in Barcelona, Spain. © Steven Bleicher

of Technology. He has been a member of the College Art Association's Education Committee and is a board member of Foundations in Art Theory in Education (FATE). He serves as an educational consultant in foundation curriculum and program design. In addition, Steven has presented papers and lectured on his innovative approaches to foundation studies and art education throughout the United States, Canada, Europe, and Asia.

Most recently, Steven has been developing a new book on Color Psychology. In conjunction with this effort he has become a highly sought-after consultant working with industry and speaking at colleges, universities, and professional organizations around the globe.

Steven is also a highly accomplished artist whose work is included in many major collections. His artwork is widely exhibited both nationally and internationally in numerous solo and group exhibitions. His artwork has also been reproduced in several books on art and design, and his approach to the artistic creative process was featured in Robin Landa's book, *The Creative Jolt*.

About the Author

Steven Bleicher is a Professor of Visual Arts at Costal Carolina University. He received both his Bachelor of Fine Arts and Master of Fine Arts degrees from Pratt Institute in New York. Steven has worked and taught at the New York Studio School of Drawing, Painting and Sculpture; the State University of New York, Brooklyn College; Marian College; and The Art Institute of Fort Lauderdale, in addition to serving as the Assistant Dean of the School of Art and Design at The Fashion Institute

Acknowledgments

I would like to thank all of the artists, designers, and others who freely contributed their work to this book. Your work is what this book is all about.

I would like to thank Robin Landa who suggested to Jim Gish and the editors at Delmar that I should be approached to write a book on color.

My appreciation and thanks also go out to Jim Gish and Meaghan Tomasso, my editors at Delmar, for all of their patience, support, and direction. In addition, I would like to thank the rest of the professional staff at Delmar, including Kathy Kucharek, Senior Content Product Manager;

Joy Kocsis, Senior Art Director; and Sarah Timm, Editorial Assistant, who have made this book a reality.

I would also like to thank all my students and my colleagues' students who volunteered their work for the Instructor Resources.

Delmar Cengage Learning and the author would also like to thank the following reviewers for their valuable suggestions and expertise:

Brett Baker, MFA
Chair, Media Arts
Art Institute of Fort Lauderdale
Fort Lauderdale, Florida

Dick Bjornseth, MFA
Professor
Savannah College of Art and Design
Savannah, Georgia

Marcia Cohen
Professor
Savannah College of Art and Design
Atlanta, Georgia

Amanda Farrar, MFA
Senior Instructor
The Art Institute of Las Vegas
Henderson, Nevada

Anthony Fontana
Instructor
Bowling Green State University
Bowling Green, Ohio

Amy Gibson, BFA, MA
Instructor
James Sprunt Community College
Kenansville, North Carolina

Ron Green, Ph.D.
Assistant Professor
Coastal Carolina University
Conway, South Carolina

Rosemary E. Gould, MFA
Adjunct Professor
North Central Michigan College
Petoskey, Michigan

Douglas Heinlein, BFA, MFA
Academic Director
The Art Institute of Seattle
Seattle, Washington

Juan Juarez, MFA
Assistant Professor
Syracuse University
Syracuse, New York

Matt Klos, BFA, MFA
Instructor
Anne Arundel Community College
Arnold, Maryland

Una Charlene Langer, BFA, MPM
Instructor
The Art Institute of Pittsburgh
Pittsburgh, Pennsylvania

Lindsay McCulloch, MFA, BA
Lecturer
Anne Arundel Community College
Arnold, Maryland

Lisa Rasmussen, BFA, MA
Instructor
The Art Institute of Pittsburgh
Pittsburgh, Pennsylvania

Kelly Wheelis
Instructor
The Art Institute of Phoenix
Phoenix, Arizona

Steven Bleicher, 2011

Questions and Feedback

Delmar Cengage Learning and the author welcome your questions and feedback. If you have suggestions that you think others would benefit from, please let us know and we will try to include them in the next edition.

To send us your questions and/or feedback, you can contact the publisher at:

Delmar
Executive Woods
5 Maxwell Drive
Clifton Park, NY 12065
Attn: Graphic Arts Team
800-998-7498

Or the author at:
Coastal Carolina University
Visual Arts Department
PO Box 261954
Conway, SC 29526
stbleicher@aol.com
stevenbleicher@gmail.com

Introduction

At the start of every term, I open up the windows and ask my class to look at the trees that cover our campus. I ask them what colors they see. I usually receive one response—green. I ask them to look again at the trees, at every leaf, and write down every single color or aspect of the color they can see. The responses I get the second time around are much more varied. This is an exercise in sensitizing their eyes to color, to really see all of the color that is there. I want them to see the variation of greens that are there. I want them to realize just how many different greens there can be and the infinite variety of hues. This is the majesty and poetry of color.

Color is, in some sense, most closely related to music. They both have rhythm and harmony and are used to add emphasis and feeling. They can play directly on our senses and emotions and bypass our conscious minds, or they can be used for purely intellectual pursuits. There is a poetic aspect to each that can be hard to define. The goal of this book is to give the reader an understanding of color and an approach to such an ephemeral subject.

Our physiology, religious background, cultural heritage, and personal inclination determine our sense of color. Perceptual, psychological, and pictorial concerns can also affect the way we choose and work with color. Understanding how these elements influence our judgments and choices allows us, as artists and designers, to use them more effectively.

This book sets out to address all of these issues in a friendly, open manner. I have tried to write the book in the same way that I speak to my students—using a positive and upbeat approach—to pass on my excitement, enthusiasm, and passion for the subject. My hope is that you will learn to appreciate the tremendous variety, power, and sheer sensuous pleasure that is created with color.

Dedication

To Helaine, my wife, partner and best friend, and who brings color into my life.

1

Color is not real. It changes, fluctuates and is transitory by its very nature. Color is poetry.

Why do we study color? Why is it important? Color may be the most underrated of all of the fundamental elements of design and yet it may be the most important and powerful. A single patch of color can communicate more than words themselves. That single hue can represent joy or sadness.

Color is one of only two design elements that have an unconscious response from the viewer's brain. The other is texture. Viewers will respond to the color used before they can read a label or make sense of the imagery. This is the power of color.

More has been written on imagery than color, because it is the most elusive and enigmatic of all of the elements of design. There are no absolutes. This is why many schools separate out color from the other parts of design in their curriculum. A work of art can be about color alone without having any specific imagery, as in the work of Katharina Grosse (Figure 1-1).

Philosophers have said that the world is colorless and that our perceptions of hues are nothing more than illusions. This is like the old question: If a tree falls in the woods and no one is around to hear it, does it still make a sound? You could ask a similar question about color. If you close your eyes, does the world retain its color or is it only in the eye of the beholder?

We can never know if our friend or neighbor sees exactly the same color in exactly the same way as we do. Color is a uniquely personal experience. This is another of color's mysteries. We can compare our thoughts and feelings, but as yet there is no measurable objective way to get a definitive answer. Standards are hard to come by. The most we can do is mix color by a specific formula to achieve a standardized result, but the perception of the hue is as varied as the shapes of snowflakes on a winter's day.

Figure 1-1.
Katharina Grosse, *Ohne Titel*, 2008, acrylic and soil on aluminium honeycomb panel, 227 × 94 cm.
An artwork does not have to have a specific subject matter. It can be realistic, abstract, or solely about color and the application of color. Using acrylic, soil, and aluminum on a honeycomb panel, Grosse creates an array of textures that captivate the viewer with their rich, intense hues.
© VG Bild-Kunst, Bonn, and Katharina Grosse. Photo courtesy of Galerie nächst St. Stephan Rosemarie Schwarzwälder, Vienna. Photo: Olaf Bergmann.

Color is a part of our daily life. Everything within our world is comprised of color. We take it for granted, never giving it a second thought. The human eye and brain are marvelous organs—they allow us to experience our surroundings and take pleasure in that experience. Color can be enjoyed for its own sake. When we sit and look at a sunset, we are drawn by the magic of nature's palette. But this ability to revel in the beauty of a sunset is a uniquely human experience.

Do Animals See Color?

Relatively few animals have the ability to see color in the same way we can. Many use other means of perceiving their environment, including the ability to see infrared wavelengths of color not visible to humans. Among those that can see color are the higher primates, and new data suggests that dolphins and whales may also be able to see color. Most pets such as your dog and cat cannot see color. They see only shades of gray. So that bright yellow bone or pink squeak toy are nothing more than shades of light gray to Fido. In the same way, your cat is not reacting to the color of the toy mouse but is more likely reacting to the catnip imbedded in the toy (Figure 1-2). In our human zeal and love for our pets we imbue them with our own characteristics and traits that they could not physiologically possess. As research continues, new information regarding how animals perceive their environment is being discovered. This knowledge adds to our own understanding of the sense of sight and color vision.

Color Perception

We must understand how we see color before we can use it effectively. A better word may be *perceive* rather than *see*, because we do more that just observe color. How we perceive it—feel it, sense it, taste it, and are influenced by its ways—is still not completely understood. We are just beginning to scratch at the surface of this most powerful of all of the design elements.

The first step in sight and color perception is the response to the visual stimulus of light. This response or reaction to a stimulus is known as **sensation**—to the activation of light receptors that are the basic foundations of perception. **Perception** is the attempt to understand and make sense of the stimuli received. It does us no good to respond in some fashion if we don't understand what the stimulus is. The scientific term for the minimum amount of stimulus energy needed for perception is **absolute threshold**. In terms of sight, the minimum amount of light

Figure 1-2.
The image on the right is what you see, a brightly colored cat toy mouse. The image on the left is what your cat (or dog) would see. The color is for the owner and not the pet. The cat notices and may be drawn to the areas of high contrast but it is the catnip inside that may be the real lure.
© Steven Bleicher

required to produce a visual entity is a candle flame at 30 miles on a clear night. While we would not be able to see any color from this distance, we would be able to perceive the light. Therefore, our visual acuity is much greater than we might initially imagine.

Light and Color

Without light, there would be no vision or color, because light and color are inseparable. Light is considered visible energy. To make matters more complex, as the amount of light varies (increasing or decreasing), so does the amount of color. The images in Figure 1-3 show a landscape at different times during the same day. Notice that the color is not constant, but changes with the varying amount of light throughout the day. As the type of light changes from sunlight to artificial light, the quality of the color will also change. This total inconsistency of color makes it one of the most intriguing, poetic, and transitory elements to work with.

To fully understand this concept, pick a spot outside your window and look at a tree or any other object on a daily basis. Look at this item every day, at different times of the day from morning, noon and evening, and watch how the color changes. The item that you thought was consistent in hue, value, and intensity is not; it changes as the amount and quality of light varies. For a more immediate example, just turn off the lights in the room you are in. You will see that as the amount of light changes, so does the color of everything in the room.

What we are really seeing when we look at color is the action and reaction of light. White light, or the visible spectrum, is composed of wavelength, amplitude, and saturation. This may also be referred to as visual stimulus. Wavelengths, the length of light waves, are measured in nanometers. The shorter wavelengths include X-rays and the visual spectrum of color and white light; the longest lengths include infrared, as seen in Figure 1-4. Different wavelengths are also associated with different hues. Shorter wavelengths indicate violet and blue, and longer wavelengths indicate yellows, oranges, and reds.

Newton's Theory of Color

Sir Isaac Newton was one of the first to understand what we now consider our modern concept of the relationship of light and color. His experiments in the seventeenth century using a prism demonstrated that white light contained or was composed of the visible colors of the spectrum.

As shown in Figure 1-5, when white light enters a prism, it is refracted or bent as it comes out the other side, and the visible spectrum of colors is displayed.

The spectrum can also be seen as part of a naturally occurring event in a rainbow (Figure 1-6). The raindrops act in the same manner as a prism, refracting and bending the light to create a multicolored arc. Newton devised that the spectrum was composed of seven separate, discernible hues. The acronym ROYGBIV that most of us learned in kindergarten stands for these: red, orange, yellow, green, blue, indigo, and violet. However, most people can discern only six of these hues; they have trouble telling the difference between indigo and violet. It has been surmised that either Newton had great color acuity and could see a wider range of colors than the majority of people, or that he picked the number seven since it is considered a holy number. We must remember that, previously, Newton got into a great deal of trouble with the authorities and the church with his earlier theories of gravity, and was imprisoned for a time. So, this may have been his way of ameliorating his past transgressions with the church and thereby avoiding prison again.

Figure 1-3.
Notice how the color changes in the landscape at different times of the day as the amount and quality of the light changes. Top row: 7 a.m. and 9 a.m.; middle row: noon and 2 p.m.; bottom row: 5 p.m. and 6:30 p.m.
© Steven Bleicher

GAMMA RAYS   X-RAYS   ULTRAVIOLET LIGHT   VISIBLE LIGHT   INFRARED LIGHT   MICROWAVES   RADAR   TELEVISION

Figure 1-4.
A diagram illustrating the electromagnetic spectrum. We can only see a small portion of the entire spectrum. Some animals and insects can see infrared color wavelengths.
© Steven Bleicher

Figure 1-5.
An illustration of
Newton's principle of
white light being broken
down into the colors
of the spectrum after it
passes through a prism.
© Steven Bleicher

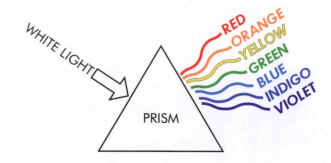

Figure 1-6.
A rainbow is created
when light hits the
falling raindrops and is
refracted like a prism.
Newton may have been
inspired by these natural
events. The colors of a
rainbow are the same
spectral hues produced
by a prism.
© Steven Bleicher

Sources of Light

When we look at an apple and observe its
bright red color, what we are seeing are the
reflected light waves. There are two parts that
make up a reflection or the bouncing of light
waves from a given surface (Figure 1-7). The
incident beam comes from the light source
hitting the object. The **reflected beam** bounces
off the object and allows us to see its particular
hue. When the surface is smooth, these light
waves bounce off or are reflected in an even
manner. With a rough surface, the reflected

beams bounce off and are scattered in many
different directions.

Artists such as Alyson Shotz are interested
in the intersection between art and physics
(Figure 1-8). Her current work is based on the
theory of electromagnetic waves that remain
in a constant position, known as **standing
waves.** She uses dichroic or interference
acrylic filters, which allow her to introduce
color into the structure as a physical part of
the object or sculpture. These filters use the
principle of interference, producing colors

WHITE LIGHT INCIDENT BEAM

ORANGE REFLECTED BEAM

Figure 1-7.
As white light hits the orange, all of the spectral hues are absorbed except for the orange hue, which is reflected, giving the fruit its color and name.
© Steven Bleicher

in the same way as oil films on water or the reflection off a CD by subtracting color from the spectrum. The hues produced are a product of the physical structure and acrylic filters. Because some of the light reflecting travels a slightly longer path than others, some light wavelengths are reinforced by this delay, while others tend to be canceled, producing the colors seen in her work.

Another factor in determining color is the light source used to view any given object.

Different light sources will affect the color perceived. The best light source is sunlight because it is the most accurate in color reproduction. While you can get light bulbs that equal the brightness and intensity of sunlight, they tend to be very expensive, last only a few hours, and burn very hot, which can cause injury. When speaking about traditional light bulbs, they are more correctly referred to as lamps. A light fixture is actually called a **luminaire**, although

Figure 1-8.
Alyson Shotz, *Wavelength 2*, 2008. The interference filters within the acrylics used in the structure produce the color. The acrylic elements are actually clear; the color seen is a visual phenomenon.
Photo courtesy of Derek Eller Gallery, New York.

the term has fallen out of common usage. There are several types of lamps, including neon, tungsten, fluorescent, and halogen. Halogen lights are most commonly used in automobile headlamps because they give off a very bright light that can illuminate a large area. By far the most widely used lamps are fluorescent and tungsten. They are used in both home and industry and offer the best in affordability, ease of operation, and overall illumination. All bulbs or lamps are sources of radiant light, which means that the light is directly emitted from an energy source. The other sources of radiant light are the sun, lamps of all types, and other hot objects. Reflected light is the light cast back and is caused by the light waves bouncing off an object.

Metamerism

Since there are so many different types of lamps and light sources, understanding their effect on color perception is essential. Tungsten, or incandescent bulbs, tend to give off a warm light and bring out the warmer range of hues including yellows, oranges, and reds. Fluorescent lights, on the other hand,

burn much cooler and create a cool cast to objects by bringing out a greater range of green, blue, and violet hues. Therefore, an object may appear to be one shade of a hue under one type of lamp and look drastically different when viewed with another light source (Figure 1-9). This occurrence is called **metamerism**. Many art students learn firsthand about this phenomenon when they complete a color assignment at home, normally under incandescent light, and then bring their work to class where it is usually viewed under fluorescent light. The resulting shift in value and intensity in their projects causes frustration and concern among students and grading nightmares for their instructors. In many cases, students and teachers must agree in advance which light source should be used to create and then view the color assignments. Only then can consistent results be achieved.

The Human Eye

Now that we understand how light affects color, the other major factor in perceiving color is the eye. While the eye has often been referred to as a camera, it is much more than that. It is a very complex receptor that sends its information as electrical impulses to the brain, which in turn makes sense of these various stimuli. The brain interprets the data sent to it and in many respects the visual images and colors we see are really a function of the mind and not the eye.

The human eye is actually a receptor for light. Light passes through the cornea, which helps to focus the light waves (Figure 1-10). It also functions as a protective covering.

The light then passes through the aqueous humor, a fluidlike substance that supplies nourishment to the organ, and continues through the lens, finally striking the retina. Located in the back of the eye, the retina has several layers of cells that are specialized to interpret different aspects of

Figure 1-9.
An example illustrating the concept of metamerism. As the type of light changes from daylight to tungsten light the quality of the hue perceived changes. The sunlight makes the hue appear to be lighter and more saturated.
© Steven Bleicher

SUNLIGHT   TUNGSTEN LIGHT

this incoming data. These visual receptors make up the photoreceptor layer, which includes the rods and cones.

Rods and Cones

Rods and cones are aptly named due to their specific shapes (Figure 1-11). Rods are long, thin, and cylindrically shaped. Their sole purpose is to read lights and darks, or value. They cannot perceive color at all. This is why as something comes into your field of vision, you make out its shape long before you can make out its color. The rods can operate in extremely low light, which is many hundred times less than the cones. Cones are fat, bulgy-shaped receptors that perceive color. They require much more light to process information. Some feel that because they require much more light to process color, that this is the reason we see so little color at night. Another reason is that the greater the amount of light, the brighter the color that can be seen. Therefore, it makes perfect sense that at night when there is so little light, we would only be able to perceive small amounts of color, regardless of physiology. It becomes another question of which came first—the chicken or the egg. Is it because the cones need more light to process information that we see very little color at night, or is it because it is dark and with less light very little if any color can be seen?

In total, there are more than 100 million rods and only

about 6 million cones in each eye. The rods and cones are massed together in three groups. The first group is composed of all rods, the next is a combination of rods and cones, and the last group is made up only of cones. This area comprised of only cones is found in the **fovea**, a depressed spot in the center of the retina. To

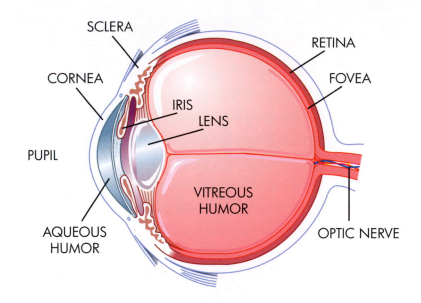

Figure 1-10.
A diagram of a cross-section of the human eye. Light enters the pupil and hits the retina at the back of the eyeball, which contains the rods and cones. These photoreceptors translate light into electrical impulses. This information is transmitted to the brain via the optic nerve.
© Cengage Learning, 2012.

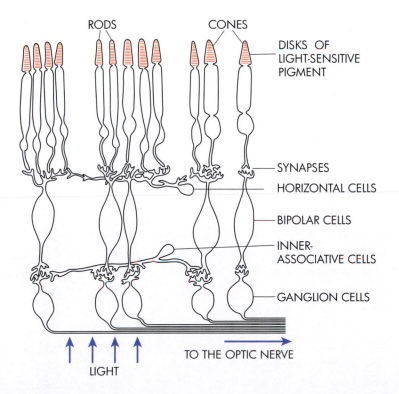

Figure 1-11.
A diagram illustrating the rods and cones that are the actual photoreceptors in the retina. Rods are long and thin and cones are bulgy. Light activates the light-sensitive pigments in the rods and cones.
© Cengage Learning, 2012.

Figure 1-12.
Finding your blind spot. Hold the book up at arm's length. Keep your left eye closed and look at the four-leaf-clover-shaped squiggle. As you move the book toward yourself, you will find that the spot on the magenta background has disappeared. You have just found your blind spot. Flip the book over and close your right eye this time to find your other blind spot. Everyone has two—one for each eye.
© Steven Bleicher

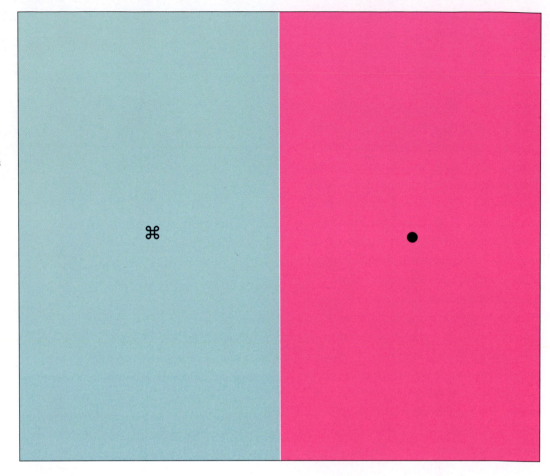

put this into perspective, the fovea contains 350,000 cones and is smaller than the head of a pin. Because of this, we only see color as a very small area of our field of vision. The area of the highest color acuity is only about a two-degree area directly in front of our vision field. Subconsciously our eyes zoom in on this area when we want to examine the color of an area or object.

Located just below the fovea is the optic nerve, which consists mainly of fibers derived from the ganglionic cells of the retina. It carries the information from the eye to the brain where it is converted to the images we see. At the point where the optic nerve passes through the optic disk, there is a hole in the retina where there are no photoreceptors. Consequently, the brain receives no visual information from this area of vision. This area is your "blind spot." Actually you have two,

one in each eye. This area is fairly large, as you can see in the illustration in Figure 1-12.

University of Rochester researchers led by Dr. Heidi Hofer (now at the University of Houston) have been able to photograph the human retina. The cones cells that detect color are buried in the deepest part of the retina, which make photographing them difficult. The images, while slightly blurry, are the best that current technology will allow. They clearly identify the individual color receptor cells or cones. These can be seen as the red, green, or blue dots within the photograph (Figure 1-13). The colors correspond to the electromagnetic wavelengths of light the cells perceive: blue-violet for the shortest range, green for the middle, and red for the longest wavelengths.

The research found that the variety and amount of each type of cones cells differ greatly from person to person. However,

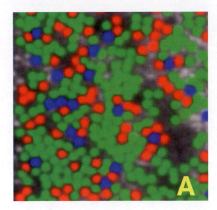

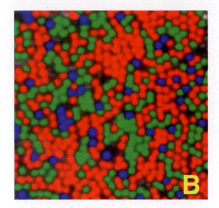

Figure 1-13.
Photographs of cone cells.
The amount and type of color receptor cells vary from person to person as demonstrated in these two images. Person A has more middle wavelength sensitive receptor cells while person B has more long wavelength sensitive receptor cells. Yet both have normal color vision and perceive color in much the same way.
Images courtesy of Dr. Heidi Hofer. Data from H. Hofer, J. Carroll, J. Neitz, M. Neitz, and D. R. Williams, "Organization of the Human Trichromatic Cone Mosaic," *Journal of Neuroscience*, 2005; 25: 9669–9679.

despite these differences people identify colors in a nearly identical fashion. Researchers theorize that this indicates the brain may play a greater role in color identification and recognition than previously thought.

Even today, scientists are not completely sure how cones work. They contain a light-sensitive pigment called **iodopsin**. While much of how the iodopsin works is still not known, it's believed that there are three types of cone pigment each for sensing a different wavelength of light: blue-violet for short range, green for middle range, and red for the longest wavelengths. This generally accepted theory is known as the **trichromatic theory**, but much research must still be done to know for sure.

Rods also contain a light-sensitive pigment called visual purple or **rhodopsin**. As light hits this pigment, it burns or bleaches it, and thereby changing the electrosignal for darkness transmitted by the rods to the brain.

In low light, rods have very high amounts of unbleached visual purple. This allows us to see in these conditions.

Afterimages

Another theory of color vision states that cones are grouped together in pairs: red with green and blue with orange, and so on. As one fires off, the other is inhibited or stopped from firing. This **opponent–process theory** accounts for color processing in the bipolar cells and thalamus. But this process is important to us because it may be responsible for color afterimages. Color **afterimage** is the perception of a color that isn't really there and is seen as the complement of the color being viewed. Seeing an afterimage can make many people dizzy and sick.

Look at the red airplane in Figure 1-14. Stare at it for a minute or so, then look at the black dot next to it. You will see a green afterimage. This is why all hospital

Figure 1-14.
Stare at the red airplane for at least 30 seconds. Then quickly turn your gaze to the black dot. What do you see? This is an afterimage.
© Steven Bleicher

operating theaters are painted a pale green. Think about a surgeon performing an operation staring into an open body cavity filled with blood. As the surgeon looks up, he would see green spots which could make him nauseous or feel ill, which is the last thing a patient would want a surgeon to feel in the middle of a procedure! But the spots are mitigated by the light green hue of the walls. Remember, you must have some of the color's complement to relieve afterimage.

Color Perception Deficiencies

There are many things that can affect color perception. These can include accidents and injuries, aging, disease, drug use, or even heredity. A physiologic response, but one not so easily remedied, is color blindness. There are only a very few people who are truly color blind, and we call them **monochromatics**. These people have only one type of cone: it treats all wavelengths of light the same and sends the brain faulty information, so that they only perceive shades of gray. If you want to experience this condition, dim the lights in a room until you can no longer see any hues, just shades.

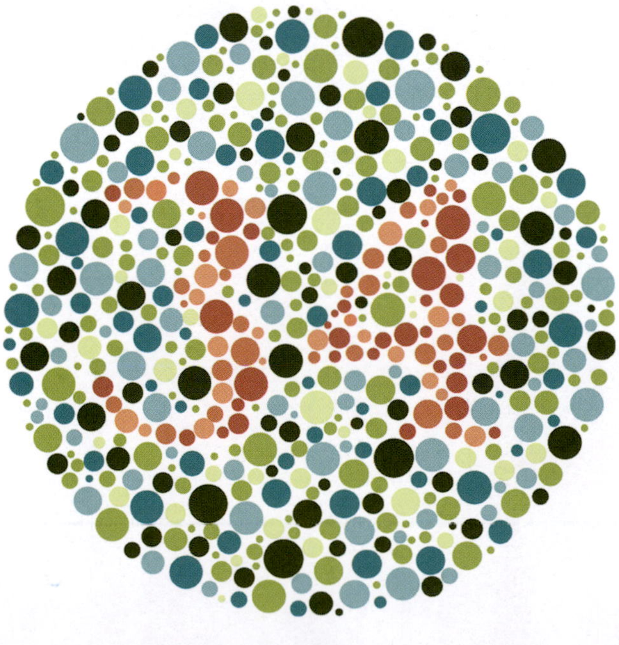

Figure 1-15.
An example of one of the plates from the Ishihara Color Test. What number do you see? If you do not see a number, you may want to have yourself tested to see if you have a color deficiency.
Illustration by Nash Design and Color Vision Store.

The more apt name used for people who suffer some form of color insufficiency is color deficiency. The Ishihara Color Test (Figure 1-15) is the diagnostic tool used to test color deficiency and diagnose specific insufficiencies. The most common color deficiency is dichromatic, or the inability to see one of the three primary colors (Figure 1-16). The person lacks one type of cone and therefore has problems seeing opponent colors such as red and green or blue and yellow. Most commonly found in men, it's believed that there is a genetic or hereditary basis. It is estimated that 7 percent of the men in America, or nearly 10 million men, are color deficient, while only .04 percent of women are affected.

Certain physical ailments such as diabetes and vitamin B12 deficiencies can also affect the lens and impair color vision. As people age, the lens can also yellow and thereby decrease the ability to discern hues. This can lead to color confusion, and with so many elderly people taking several medications on a daily basis, this condition could be life threatening. In a study in 1984, Peter Hurd and Julia Blevins found that many senior citizens with these conditions experienced difficulties in differentiating between blue and green capsules, as well as many shades of green and yellow. This has led to many instances of people mistaking medications and taking the wrong prescription, which caused serious complications.

Recently, however, there have been remarkable advances in correcting color deficiencies. There are now a few companies making corrective lenses and even one company that makes a Web-browsing utility. ColorMax offers a specialized lens that reflects the light waves in such a way as to compensate for the color deficiency. A company called Solarguard makes sunglasses that not only filter out harmful ultraviolet rays, but also aid in

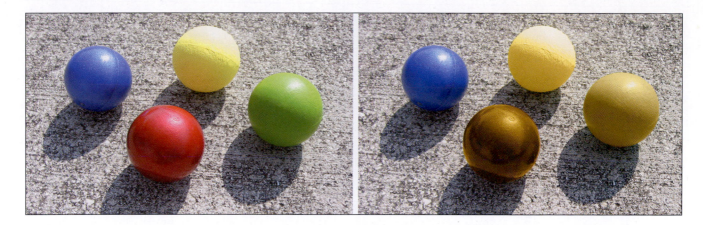

color correction. The newest technology developed by a software manufacturer is a product that adjusts the color on your monitor to compensate for color perception deficiencies. With these and other recent advancements, color insufficiencies are no longer the problem they once were and may one day be a thing of the past.

Synesthesia

Another form of color perception is **synesthesia**. Synesthetes, people who have this perception abnormality, perceive their environment by using a peculiar combination of two or more senses to understand and relate to the world around them. For them, sounds have color, shapes may have flavors, and scents may have color counterparts. This is not a metaphoric relation, but a true and real way of experiencing the world. For example, a synesthete would not see the letters on this page in black and white, but in color, as pictured in Figure 1-17.

There are three basic types of synesthesia: developmental, which starts in early childhood and is not learned, but an involuntary response; acquired, which may occur as a result of a tumor, injury, or accident; and drug induced, caused by taking LSD or another hallucinogenic drug. The main differences between these three types are that in both the acquired and drug-induced states, the resulting visualizations are unorganized and random. For example, if a developmental (or true) synesthete sees the letter R as red, they will always see it as red. Their visualizations are constant and never vary.

Artists and designers have long been interested in this form of perception and have tried to use it as a means of enhancing their sensory awareness and artistic sense.

Figure 1-16.
In this split image, the picture on the left is how a person with normal color vision would see the four brightly colored rubber balls. The picture on the right is what the same scene would look like to someone with a red-green color deficiency, which is the most common form of color insufficiency.
© Steven Bleicher

This is not a metaphoric relation but a true and real way of experiencing their world.

Figure 1-17.
An example of how a synesthete would see a page of text. They see each letter as a separate hue for a total of 26 different color variations, one for each letter.
© Steven Bleicher

One exercise regularly used by many artists and teachers is to play a piece of music and have the listener draw or paint the feelings they experienced. There are many such examples of this including David Hockney's *Ravel's Garden with NightGlow* and Vasily Kandinsky's *Impression III*. *Impression III* was painted a few days after Kandinsky attended a Schoenberg New Year's concert in Munich. Hockney listened to the Ravel's music and painted his impressions trying to approximate the snyesthesic experience (Figure 1-18). Probably the most famous artist who tried to combine the concept of art and music was Walt Disney in the movie *Fantasia*. Disney took several classical pieces of music and animated them to combine the viewer's senses and bring the music to life. This was his attempt to allow viewers to see the music and hear with their eyes.

Our contemporary concept of multimedia is an attempt to combine both sound and visuals to express an idea, convey a message, or even sell a product. Virtual realities also rely on the use of multiple sensory inputs to allow users to suspend their sense of what is real and accept the illusions set before them. Scientists have also discovered that people make a better connection to material when more than one sense is involved or stimulated. By combining auditory and visual stimuli, the brain produces more synaptic pathways that create solid links to the material and make it easier to recall when tested. Music videos are another form of the application of this concept. The aim of a music video is to visualize the lyrics, mood, and melody of the song and to enhance the listener's appreciation and enjoyment.

Figure 1-18.
David Hockney, *Ravel's Garden with Night Glow from L'Enfant et les Sortileges*, 1980, oil on canvas, 60 × 72". Hockney often listened to music as a means of inspiration for some of his work. The color and images in this painting were Hockney's interpretation of Ravel's music. He wanted to capture in paint the feel and "color" of the music.
Photo © David Hockney.

Color and Health

Color and light have long been known to possess healing qualities. While not thoroughly understood, they have been used in both traditional medicine and alternative therapies. For example, hospitals use phototherapy on infants born prematurely who often suffer from jaundice. This and other forms of light and color therapies are used in treating dermatological ailments including psoriasis and acne. Researchers at Cornell University reported that applying blue light to the back of the knees can reset the body's internal clock and alleviate sleep disturbances that accompany shift work. New areas including the use of these treatments for AIDS-related tumors are also being explored.

In clinical studies, an Italian physician, Dr. Ponza, painted rooms (including their windows) one hue so that the occupants were literally bathed with colored light. For example, it was found that when patients were placed in a green room, their capillaries dilated. On the other hand, red increased muscle tone and had a stimulating effect. But the most striking conclusion from these studies was that the colored environments had an effect on both sighted and blind patients. The blind participants were affected in the exact same manner as the sighted. When blind patients were placed in a green room, even though there was no way they could "see" the color, their blood vessels dilated in the same way and to the same degree as sighted patients. When blind patients were moved to a room with another hue, they responded in the same manner as the other patients. This led to the conclusion that there must be other color receptors in the body. While experiments of this type have been repeated with similar results, it is still a mystery as to the location and physiology of these color receptors.

Another area of study on alternative color perception is known as **dermo-optic vision**.

In this form of perception, the person quite literally feels the color. There have been a number of theories regarding how it works, including the hypothesis that there are sensors in the skin that pick up the energy field or wavelengths of the color. It has been noted that the ability to detect colors by touch increases under bright light and decreases in low light. This is the same as our ability to see color with our eyes: the less light, the more limited range of hues we are able to distinguish. Another interesting side note was that respondents sensed warm and cool hues in much the same manner as sighted people respond to color temperature. This may suggest that this aspect of color perception may be more innate and depends more on biology than environment or education.

Chromatherapy

Chromatherapy is another use of color; it is the science of healing with colors. This treatment can range from bathing patients in colored light to having them meditate on a specific hue. Kirlian photography, named after its inventor, is a photographic process in which a current is passed through an object (or person) and the corona or discharge is recorded onto film. The exposed paper shows the electromagnetic field and glowing aura of the subject. It is believed that the auras correspond to the seven major energy centers or "chakras" in the body and can be read to diagnose certain ailments or even one's spiritual equilibrium. Figure 1-19 shows a Kirlian photograph of the tip of a finger. The red and blue aura radiates out from the orange center, or fingertip, and the white lines show that the electromagnetic field is present.

Some believe that this aura exists in everyone and everything and is the energy field within all physical objects. This electromagnetic field produces a variety of colors, where red is considered the densest and follows the sequence of the spectrum to violet,

Figure 1-19.
A Kirlian photograph of a fingertip showing the person's aura. Some people believe that all things, animate and even inanimate objects, have auras. These electromagnetic fields are made up of the same energy as light waves and produce the colors seen in the photograph. Photo courtesy of Jerry Muehe, Marin County, CA.

which is said to have the highest frequency. The size, shape, and colors displayed in the image will vary from individual to individual.

There are eight colors normally used in chromatherapy. They include white and the seven spectral hues. It is believed that each has its own special healing properties.

White—contains all of the colors in the spectrum and is used to relax and soothe.

Red—enhances energy and stimulates the production of red blood cells.

Orange—increases sexual stimulation and increases pleasure. It also represents youth and curiosity.

Yellow—may have antibacterial properties, and is associated with wisdom and clarity.

Green—used to treat bacterial infections and in healing stomach ulcers; is also considered calming and since it is also in the exact middle of the spectrum, brings balance to the individual.

Blue—decreases toxins in the body and is said to promote knowledge and self-assuredness.

Indigo—aids in intuition, inspiring the individual, and also has a sedative effect.

Violet—is used for calming the nervous system and promoting creativity and spiritual awakening.

Many companies have jumped on the chromatherapy bandwagon. Kohler, a major manufacturer of kitchen and bath fixtures, offers a line of tubs that includes a color-therapy feature (Figure 1-20). This allows the bather to be totally immersed in a combination of colored water and light. "By enhancing the bathing experience with chromatherapy, Kohler has created a welcome refuge within the home, away from our stress-laden, busy lives," said Michael Moldenhauer, marketing manager of bathing products for Kohler. "Again, we are trying to raise the bar on what embodies the ultimate bathing ritual."

Luminotherapy

Even white light can have a therapeutic effect. Seasonal affective disorder, or SAD, produces anxiety and depression in some people who live in areas with little natural sunlight during the winter months. Luminotherapy, or the use of lights with the same photosensitivity as sunlight (about 55,000 K), has proven to be an effective treatment. The patient is required to sit in front of the special lamps for 30 minutes or more, usually on a daily basis. The light stimulates the pineal gland and increases the production of melatonin, a hormone involved in regulating the body's internal clock. Melatonin is also an antioxidant, which may also increase the body's ability to fight infection and disease.

The field of color therapies and other uses of color and light as healing agents is still at an infancy in Western medicine. Eastern

Figure 1-20.
Kohler Chromatherapy tub with magenta light. An example of Kohler's new line of chromatherapy bathtubs. The bather is immersed in water and colored light to help relieve stress, creating a unique bathing experience. Photo courtesy of Kohler Plumbing.

traditions have long accepted the role of color in a person's well-being and continued health. Practitioners of Feng Shui use various hues in the home and workplace to produce an optimum balance of the energy forces. In Figure 1-21, the hues of the Feng Shui compass show the eight types of "chi"—the subtle flow of electromagnetic energy, which

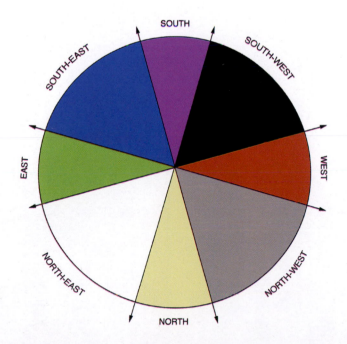

Figure 1-21.
In the Feng Shui compass north is at the bottom and south is at the top. Each color relates to a force of nature, just as some of the early color theories that will be studied in the following chapter.
© Steven Bleicher

is said to exist in everything and link the universe. The colors of the compass also correspond to the time of day, season of the year, and birth order, as well as parts of the body. What role these various color and light therapies will play in the future is still under study, but one thing is certain—we are only now beginning to understand the healing and curative powers that are associated with color.

Summary

Light is the basis for all color. For this reason, color and light are inseparable. The amount and quality of the light will determine the strength and brightness of the color we perceive. In the seventeenth century, Sir Isaac Newton demonstrated what we now consider to be our modern concept of the relationship of light and color—that white light contains all of the spectral hues. What we actually see is the reflected color of an object. Light, and therefore color, is captured by the photoreceptors in the eye and transmitted to the brain via the optic nerve. Therefore, we are discovering that the brain may be the real color perception organ.

There are many types of color perception, from dermo-optic vision, the concept that there are other color receptors in the body, to synesthesia, the concept that in some individuals two or more senses are needed to perceive and understand the world. All of these enhance the color experience and are used by artists and designers in the creative process. From auras and medical uses of light in luminotherapy, we are still exploring the ways in which our bodies perceive light and color. New scientific breakthroughs will continue to expand our notion of color.

Color Theory—Making Sense of Color: Chapter 2

2

Mankind has been trying to make sense of color and its use since the dawn of time. Our artist ancestors, the cave painters, used a limited range of hues made from natural elements to express representations and images of their world. For example, in the buffalo shield pictured in Figure 2-1, the red circles symbolize sun haloes—the circles that can be seen around the sun prior to a storm. The small black dashed lines represent pieces of the warrior so tiny that his enemies would not be able to harm him.

Figure 2-1.
A Crow war shield made from buffalo hide. The symbols and colors used by each tribe represented their concepts of the meaning of color. Photo © 1989 The Field Museum, #A111351c, Photographer D.A. White & June Bartle.

As far as we can tell, there was little thought as to how the various hues cave painters used related to each other and to their primitive world. Throughout time, each culture and tribal group have had their own various symbolic uses of color. However, it wasn't until Aristotle that thoughts of how colors were formed and how they might be used together in some harmonious way began to evolve. And they have been evolving and changing ever since. The one thing that can be said about color theory is that it is ever changing. As digital and other new technological applications are invented, our conception and thoughts about color will change with them.

Many early theories were highly subjective, with moral overtones. Others showed the personal bias of the author. They speculated on how and why we see the various hues around us. Color theories assist the artist and designer in finding a logical and reliable method of dealing with color. These theories also were developed to help communicate ideas about color to other artists, designers, and manufacturers. Moreover, they helped to answer the most basic questions about color—how it was formed and how it could be used. Theories changed as man's basic understanding of science and technology evolved. Even today, new theories of color in a digital or computational age are being addressed and rediscovered. But before we can understand where we may be going, it is important to know where we have been and how we arrived at our contemporary understanding of color.

Today, more is written about imagery than color. With the widespread use of digital and other new technologies in both fine art and design, there is a resurgence in theorizing about color and its role in new media and as a vehicle for communication. The field may be more wide open than ever with new developments taking place on an almost daily basis. No contemporary artist works from a single color theory. They can mix and match the best of all theories, using what works and discarding what does not.

Naming Color

After the first six hues—red, blue, yellow, orange, green, and violet—there has been little agreement about the names for any given color. Names have more to do with language and culture than hue or chroma. Originally, names had to do with the pigment content of the paint. The names were descriptive of the minerals, plants, and other things that made up the colorants or pigments. As far back as the eighteenth century, hues still had simple direct names, such as sky blue, and primary yellow. During the nineteenth century and with the ever-increasing explorations and colonialism of the west, there was a shift that gave the various hues more romantic sounding names such as canary yellow, Tahitian green, and so on. But it was the boom of the 1950s and on that changed the naming of color. Hues took on descriptive names such as bubble gum pink and fire engine red. Colors were being named by manufacturers to boost the sales of their products. During the 1960s and 1970s, the names of colors became synonymous with commercialism and consumerism. When we think of names such as harvest gold or avocado, we automatically think of kitchen appliances including refrigerators and stoves. Color names are developed by an industry to fit their particular need. The names used by a cosmetics company would vary widely from the names given to hues used in the automotive industry. There is no uniformity or

convention. Hue names keep changing with the times to reflect the culture and society and fads of the day.

The Color Circle

Most color theories are based on a circular arrangement of the hues in a chromatic order or sequence. They may be viewed as a circle, wheel, or sphere, as in Figure 2-2. This circular format allows relationships between each hue to be expressed in a concise visual manner. In this type of arrangement, each hue can be viewed individually or in relation to one another. The ring-shaped format also works the best for showing the relationships in subtractive color theory. There are several types or versions including additive, subtractive, process, and pigment-oriented color wheels. Philosophically, the circle represents a continuum: we don't think of color as ending, but as being ongoing, so the circle adds to the poetic notion of color.

Contemporary artists continue to use the circular format as a means for formalistic paintings about color and color interactions. Karina Peisajovich uses this spherical design

Figure 2-2.
Color is usually portrayed in a circular format as wheel, sphere, or simple circle.
© Steven Bleicher

Figure 2-3.
Karina Peisajovich, *Expanded Munsell,* 2010.
This drawing is one image from her recent series *Color Theory.* Each image within the series focuses on a major color theorist including Gothe, Chevreul, Ostwald and Munsell.
© Karina Peisajovich

to explore color relationships related to the Munsell 3-D Color Wheel. In *Expanded Munsell*, several arcs of the three-dimensional color wheel are exploded depicting a specific set of color relationships (Figure 2-3). The arcs, which are composed of individual color bricks or blocks, set up an underlying progressive rhythm. This clear configuration allows for experimentation in an organized fashion.

Aristotle

Aristotle may be considered the grandfather of color theory by virtue of having written the first known book on the subject, *DeColoribus*. He wrote that all colors were derived from different mixtures of sunlight, firelight, air, and water (Figure 2-4). Blacks, as well as the darker hues, were a result of the lack of one or more of these elements.

A dark shade of a hue, for example, might be caused by a unique combination of blackness and either sunlight or firelight as they mixed in the atmosphere. He developed these concepts based on observation and experience and believed this explained why we see fiery reds at dawn and dusk. His basic color palette included red, yellow, blue, green, and violet, as well as white, black, and brown. But in the end, he felt that art was really all about line and that all the rest, including color, was merely ornamental.

da Vinci

Leonardo da Vinci was not only one of the most accomplished artists of his day, but he was also a scientist and inventor. His notebooks are filled with new inventions,

Figure 2-4.
Aristotle's color palette was based on natural phenomena. He believed that it was the combination of two or more of these elements that produced the colors we see.
© Steven Bleicher

WATER

FIRE

AIR

SUNLIGHT

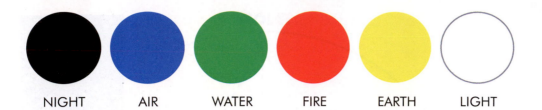

NIGHT   AIR   WATER   FIRE   EARTH   LIGHT

Figure 2-5.
A diagram illustrating da Vinci's color palette that was based on his religious convictions. Notice how each of the colors relates to a physical manifestation of the natural world.
© Steven Bleicher

such as the helicopter, and anatomical studies of cadavers. He brought these same powers of investigation and observation to color in his *Treatise on Painting* that was published posthumously in 1651, more than a hundred years after his death. He proposed a basic set of six hues, as seen in Figure 2-5. Each color held a direct relationship to the natural world. In his color set, white related to light, yellow stood for the earth, green for water, blue for air, red for fire, and black for night or darkness. As a highly religious person, these associations of hues to the natural world were a spiritual manifestation in paint of his devout convictions. It would not be for another fifty years that the study of color would be treated in a scientific manner and that the influence of religion would not play a dominant role in its treatment.

Newton

If Aristotle is the grandfather, then Newton surely must be considered the founding father of color theory. As we have seen previously, he was the first to bring a scientific method of investigation to the study of color. He endeavored to find a basic truth behind the nature and science of color. In his 1701 book, *Opticks,* he experimented with the defraction of light through a prism to devise a spectral color range of hues. He realized that the prism broke down the white light, showing the seven hues that make up the spectrum. He was also the first to place hues in a circular arrangement,

a format that is still used today. Newton's color circle or wheel (Figure 2-6) is based on light and not pigment so that the center is white and indicates the combination or mixing of all the colors. A few years later, J. C. Le Blon would adopt much of Newton's research in creating his own color ideology. It could be said that Newton laid the groundwork for all who followed and that for the rest of time, theorists were either railing against or basing their work on his experiments.

Le Blon and Harris

In 1703, J. C. Le Blon developed the theory of the primary color system. His concept was that three hues—yellow, red, and blue—could not be reduced or broken down any further and therefore were the primary or basic hues (Figure 2-7). He also stated that these hues could be mixed or blended in varying combinations to make up all of the other colors. From

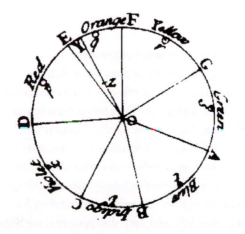

Figure 2-6.
A reproduction of Newton's color wheel containing seven hues, the colors of the spectrum that he saw as a result of his experiments with a prism. Notice that all of the color spaces are not equal in size.
This item is reproduced by permission of the Henry E. Huntington Library, San Marino, California.

Figure 2-9.
Vincent Van Gogh.
Night (After Millet),
1889.
Van Gogh read Goethe's
color theory and used
it in this painting
creating the colored
shadows. The blues in
the shadows of the man
are complementary to
the oranges used in the
figure. The lines of
the shadows also act as
a pictorial device to
lead us into the center
of the picture.
Photo © Van Gogh Museum
Amsterdam (Vincent Van
Gogh Foundation).

Figure 2-10.
Wayne Thiebaud,
Rosebud Cakes, 1991–95.
Thiebaud uses
complementary hues of
yellow on the cakes and
balances it against the
violet and blues in the
shadows. His interest
in detail extends to the
shadows of the frosting
leaves on the cake, each
having their own cool
colored shadows.
Art © Wayne Thiebaud/
Licensed by VAGA, New
York, NY.

Chevreul, Rood, and Pointillism

A contemporary of Goethe, Michel Eugene Chevreul was a French chemist and head of one of the leading dye houses in Paris. In his early work with dyes and colorants, he verified much of Moses Harris's work that all hues could be derived or created from the three primaries. He distinguished and described three main elements or attributes to color: purity (saturation), value (luminosity), and hue (Figure 2-11). But his major contribution was in developing color harmonies or color schemes. He wrote that two or more hues next to each other on the color wheel will optically blend and work with each other, and that strongly contrasting hues were placed opposite each other on the color wheel. While many of the Impressionists such as Monet rejected his ideas, these concepts were embraced by French painter Georges Seurat and became central to his concept of visual color mixing.

Another major influence on Seurat was the work of Ogden Rood. Rood was trained as both an artist and scientist. Using spinning disks, he proved that pigments could be optically or visually combined as the disks turned to simulate the effect of the mixing or blending lights. On a still plate or picture, the same effect could be achieved if dots or points of paint were very small and placed next to each other. The dots must be so close as to actually touch each other. Otherwise, if there was any space in between them, the eye would not visually mix the hues, but would read them as separate and distinct colors (Figure 2-12).

Figure 2-11.
An illustration of Chevreul's basic concept of hue, purity and value. The center circle shows the represented hue of green. The vertical axis represents purity or saturation with the most saturated version of the hue at the top and the most desaturated at the bottom. The horizontal axis represents value with left side showing a tint of the middle color and the far right expressing a shade of the same hue.
© Steven Bleicher

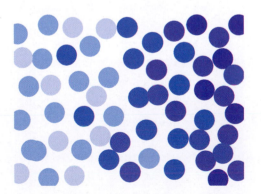

Figure 2-12.
An example of how the pointillist style of visual color mixing works showing that if the dots or dabs of color are touching one another then the colors will blend in the viewer's eye. On the right you can see that when there is space between the dots we read them as separate colors.
© Steven Bleicher

Figure 2-13.
Seurat, Georges (1859–1891). Study for "A Sunday on La Grande Jatte." 1884–1885. Oil on canvas, 27 ¾ × 41 in. (70.5 × 104.1 cm). Bequest of Sam A. Lewisohn, 1951 (51.112.6). Seurat did numerous small and full-size studies for this painting. This one clearly illustrates how he used the leading scientific theory of his day in developing his pointillist style of visual color mixing basing it on the writings of Chevreul and Rood. Look closely at the image and you can begin to see the dabs of color that make up the gradients. This style of painting is a very slow and methodical way of applying color. Image copyright © The Metropolitan Museum/Art Resource, NY

Seurat was the leading exponent of visual color mixing. He applied and used this theory as the basis of his pointillist style, as seen in Figure 2-13, *Study for Sunday Afternoon on the Island of Grande Jatte*. Other artists including Camille Pissarro and Vincent Van Gogh also began using Rood's color concepts in their painting. But Rood was not flattered by their adoption of his theories. Quite the opposite, he was appalled at the way his theories were put in practice by Seurat and others. He once said to his son that if that was what he had contributed to modern art, that he wished he had never written *Modern Chromatics*. He could never come to terms with the way his concepts had been applied by the artists of his day.

Albers, Itten, and the Bauhaus

Probably the most influential of all of the various groups on contemporary art and design was the Bauhaus. Johannes Itten and Joseph Albers (Itten's former student) taught at the school prior to its closing by the Nazis. Itten developed his color sphere and star, which was a flattened version of the sphere (Figure 2-14). Itten favored rectilinear design in a grid format because he believed that the most evident reaction of hues was at their edges where colors meet. These academic color studies were at the heart of the Bauhausian tradition. The shortcoming to all of the Bauhaus research was that it looked at color in a vacuum, as an independent element without any relation to imagery, function, or psychology.

Albers refined his teacher's work and continued these formal investigations of how colors interact with one another. He studied the optical illusions of color, making one color appear like two different colors, depending upon which color ground it was placed. He also found that two different hues could be made to look the same, depending upon which color ground they were placed. These were very formalistic color experiments usually done in simple geometric shapes such as squares and rectangles. In these studies, color was the key to the complete exclusion of imagery. He felt that throughout art history, color had been relegated to a minor role in

Figure 2-14.
An illustration of the
12 hued Itten color
star. The star is really
a flattened out sphere.
Expanding out from the
pure white center are
tints of the various hues
leading to the points of
the star where the purest
most intense form of the
hue is located.
© Steven Bleicher

place of imagery and abstraction. And as a result, during his tenure at Yale, Albers narrowed the scope of his work to very academic studies of the interactions of colors to one another. He began his Homage to the Square series exploring the full range of color interactions and relationships. In *Homage to the Square: Beaming* (Figure 2-15), the radiance of the center square is created by the pale desaturated shades of the two outer squares. This creates a frame that intensifies the center square and makes it appear more luminous and brilliant. These works had a great deal of influence on the artists of the minimalist movement, many of whom were Albers's students at Yale. The minimalists were so-named because they sought to refine form to its most basic elements; they regularly worked with simple geometric shapes and forms. This group, which included Carl Andre, Sol Lowit, and Donald Judd, used very flat planes of highly saturated color in their work.

Munsell

Albert H. Munsell might be considered the father of modern color classification. He was frustrated with the myriad of names for hues and the lack of ability to standardize color. Peach could be anything from a slight tint of red-orange to a strongly tinted hue of yellow-orange and anything in between. There were no formulas for mixing and

and bright. But in the end she must leave the world of color and return to gray: family and home, and the boring sameness of daily life on the plains. Other films, such as *Pleasantville, Memento,* and *Wings of Desire,* use this motif as a way of creating a counterpoint between reality and fantasy or a dream state. Reality is always shown in black and white as if it is missing something, while the fantasy or dream world is in vivid color.

More importantly, Batchelor also speaks about the difference between color in the tube and the can. Starting in the 1950s and into the 1960s, artists abandoned the traditional tube of paint and turned to the hardware store and premixed cans of house paint. It is the hand versus the machine or "ready-made." Throughout the history of art, the artist was connected to the palette—the place where color was mixed by the artist's hand and applied to the canvas. There was a direct relationship between the palette and color mixing, color mixing to traditional color theory, and color theory to the color circle. And the circle has dominated color theory from Newton to Munsell. But with the move to the can, artists moved from the circle to the color chart. The color chart (Figure 2-20) is nothing more than a simple list in which every color is equivalent to every other color and independent of every other color. No great hierarchies exist, only random selections of color. The color circle is analogical and the color chart is digital; therefore, it refers directly to contemporary modernity.

With current printing technology, digital color is apt to be flat, shiny, and intense. The intensity of digital color tends to localize it unlike the broad generalized color created on the artist's palette. Muted colors that are considered more tasteful appeal to those in a higher socioeconomic bracket, while bright saturated hues may be considered more common, popularist, and egalitarian. The computer, especially the personal computer,

democratized color. In addition, these flat saturated hues keep the viewer at a distance, giving off a more industrial or mechanical look to the work.

Digital color is not only visually flat, it also lacks any true physical texture. The tactility of traditional paint mixed on a palette and applied by a brush is gone. Virtually all printers (laser or inkjet) lay down a thin microlayer of colored ink or pigment. This creates a smooth texture-free surface. Texture, or more correctly, the simulation of texture, can be created only within the virtual confines of the software package or computer. For example, in the latest version of Photoshop, the new "brushes palette" now has a texture mode or option. The user can decide on an array of simulated textures, such as canvas. Otherwise, texture is absent in today's technology and gone with it is the "hand" of the artist, or so some would say. This has become one of the great debates raging at art conferences and gatherings all over the world.

Color Forecasting

Color forecasting is another form of color theorizing, not for classification and categorization but for purely aesthetic use by designers and artists. CAUS (The Color Association United States) may be one of the oldest color-forecasting services. Others include the Color Council and Trend Union. These color forecasting services began when manufactures and designers cut off by World War I could not get dyes, fabrics, fashion style directions, and other information from Europe. Since then, they have become industry staples in fashion, interior, industrial, product, and graphic design. The services work in pretty much the same manner. A group of experts from both the design and manufacturing areas meet to discuss all aspects of product sales and development. Based on these factors, color forecasters

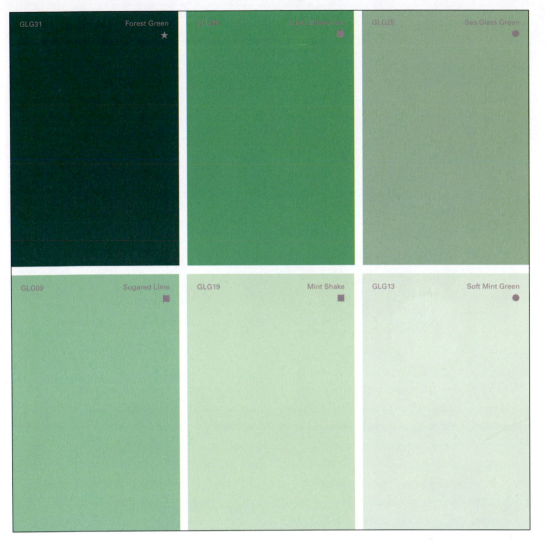

| GLG31 | Forest Green ★ | GLG23 | Lucky Shamrock | GLG25 | Sea Glass Green ● |
| GLG09 | Sugared Lime | GLG19 | Mint Shake | GLG13 | Soft Mint Green ● |

Figure 2-20.
Glidden Paint color swatches. Glidden, an ICI Paints Brand. Batchelor believes color swatches represent a break from the traditional color wheel and are more representative of contemporary color philosophy. No longer is the artist mixing colors on a palette but is selecting color from a premixed swatch. These color swatches also have a direct relationship to the way colors can be selected on a computer. Courtesy of Glidden™ Paint, An AkzoNobel Brand.

make predictions or develop themes for the coming seasons. They may develop specific palettes for different industries or economic groups. These palettes represent trends that may come into the market in the next eighteen to twenty-four months (Figure 2-21). Color forecasting services always make their predictions several seasons in advance to allow for manufacturing time. Designers are always working well ahead of what is happening in the current market.

Forecasting services and associations allow designers to have an understanding of the future direction of color including trends from movies and music, as well as the development of new colors and buying trends. If these were not available, designers would have to either do all of the market research on their own or make guesses, which could be very costly if the choices turned out to be poor ones. Few students realize that while in school they may be able to choose their favorite colors for their design projects, but that in the professional world colors are selected through intensive market research. Color forecasting services give the designer up-to-date information in these areas.

Ellen Lynch-Goldstein, designer and Chair of the Accessories Design Department at the Fashion Institute of Technology, explains how designers use color forecasting in the fashion industries.

Figure 2-21.
Dory Designs,
Color Board.
Forecasting services
develop style boards
to depict color trends
and their influences.
This board produced in
2009 illustrates Dory
Designs' 2011 product
development.
Photo courtesy of Dory
Ventures, LLC/Photograph
by Steffen Knudsen Allen.

"The industry uses color-forecasting services as a barometer to see what's predicted and to develop their own ideas. Forecasts that are primarily international are not as important to the American market as they are to Europe. For example, if a forecast predicts that yellow will be a hot color in accessories, American designers will incorporate that color into other colors to give just a hint of yellow while the European market will use full yellow bags and shoes as a 'basic' color." This is a good explanation of how the designers, as whole, view these services. The forecasts are used as guides and not strictly adhered to. They give the design community an idea of the directions color may take in the coming seasons (Figure 2-22).

Figure 2-22.
Sarah Mullins, *Gold Bag
with Weather Leathers,*
2009.
Fashion-forecasting
services predicted that
metallic hues would
become a dominant
fashion trend. Mullins
created a handbag
using two weathered
metallic gold leathers
with textured pin tucks
fitting nicely into this
schema. Mullins feels
that designers must
stay on top of new
trends and forecasting
services play an essential
role in planning her
upcoming lines.
Photo courtesy of Sarah
Mullins/Photograph by
Steffen Knudsen Allen.

Summary

All of the myriad of theories that have been developed have one thing in common: they all try to make sense out of what is arguably the most complex of all of the design elements—color. All artists and designers have been influenced by this work. Each theorist built on his predecessor's work, either incorporating it into his own work or in the case of Goethe, outright rejecting Newton's ideas. Some, like Seurat, based their entire life's work on the theory of one person or another. These theories gave us the concepts of the primary and secondary hues and tried to place them in some sort of context.

As technology and manufacturing became more prevalent, the theories shifted to developing a common language or method for the application of color. Contemporary theorists such as Batchelor and others are trying to make sense of new mediums and their relationship to color. As new strides in technology create new applications, so too will contemporary theories be developed and presented to help us make sense of these new color spaces and to use them to their fullest.

Color Theory Time Line

350 BCE	Aristotle	*DeColoribus* (the first book on color theory)
1500	daVinci	*Treatise on Painting* (published posthumously in 1651)
1701	Newton	*Opticks* published
1703	LeBlon	Develops concept of primary hues
1766	Harris	*Natural System of Color* published
1810	Goethe	*Theory of Colors* published
	Chevreul	Develops concept of color harmonies or color schemes
1879	Rood	*Modern Chromatics* published
1905	Munsell	*Color Notation* published. Three-dimensional color wheel developed.
1920	Itten	*The Art of Color*—Itten develops color star
1931	CIE	CIE develops chromaticity chart based on wavelengths, not actual color.
	Ostwald	*Color Science* published
1960	Albers	*Homage to the Square Series* begun
2001	Batchelor	*Chromophobia* published
2003	Nadin	*Anticipation* published

Have you ever felt blue? We use color in our language on a regular basis to describe feelings and emotions. People are said to be "green with envy," "in the pink," or "seeing red." They can be "true blue," "white as a ghost," or a "yellow-bellied coward." Even our medals for bravery and heroism have a color: the Purple Heart honors the wounded in combat.

Color and emotions are so closely related that we use these terms as descriptions for concepts and feelings that go beyond words and language.

Color plays a vital role in culture and daily life and may be the single most important aspect of a painting, product, or design. It is not enough for an artist or designer to produce a particular product in any color of their choosing: they must be aware of how their choice will affect the viewer. In design, the simple act of choosing a color can make or break a product. Even a vast knowledge of color harmonies, such as how two or more hues may be mixed to create an infinite number of new hues, will not ensure that viewers derive the artist's intended message. Why do people favor one color over another and what does it all really mean?

When we look at anything from a painting to a package or even a simple product, we bring a lifetime's worth of memories, experiences, and psychological baggage that impacts and affects our perception. Color psychology and market research go hand in hand, but these two areas have had an uneasy relationship or alliance since the days of Sigmund Freud. Psychologists and psychiatric professionals are concerned with pure academic scholarship and the need to understand and make sense of the psyche. Their research may result in new diagnostic tools and therapies, as well as a better understanding of the human mind. Market research, on the other hand, might be considered the application of this knowledge for commerce and industry.

Whichever your primary focus, the goal is understanding this complex relationship of color, psyche, and emotion that enables artists and designers to produce effective works of art and designs. Artists must have more than the technical knowledge of creating and mixing color, they must also understand its impact on the viewer. This knowledge enables the artist and designer to intentionally create a work that will elicit the specific desired response from the viewer.

Innate Responses

Our reaction to color and the color of an item or object is determined by two factors. There are inherited or innate responses to color, ones that we all share as human beings and those that are taught to us from infancy. We are born with certain "wired in" responses to color. These are reactions that are common to all people regardless of their place of birth, cultural upbringing, or social status. One of the most primal and innate responses to is our reaction to the combination of yellow and black (Figure 3-1). They are the colors of poison and danger. Bumblebees, wasps, police caution tape, and road hazard warning signs all contain these two colors. So while they are easy to recognize and read they are not inviting and rarely used in design.

Learned Color Responses

Our response to color is not purely unconscious or intuitive; it is learned. Blue for boys and pink for girls is a cultural response to color

Figure 3-1.
Picture of a Bumblebee.
The yellow and black
strips of a bumblebee
signal danger. Even if
you did not know that
bees could sting, you
would still be wary of
anything or animal with
these colors or markings.
Photo © PictureNet/Corbis.

taught to us by our family and reinforced in the marketplace (Figure 3-2). Infants and young children if given their choice would select bright simple saturated primary hues, with red topping the list for both sexes. Colors are also cultural, having religious connotations. For example, in India red is used for weddings and white for funerals; neither would be acceptable in the western cultural view.

For years, fire trucks have been painted red, hence the name "fire-engine red." But several years ago it was discovered that this red hue is hard to see at dawn and dusk when there is little light. Today, yellow-green is used for fire trucks and hydrants because it can be seen from farthest away, regardless of the light and time of day. Years from now when schoolchildren are asked what color fire trucks are, they will answer "yellow-green."

Color and Psychoanalysis

Psychiatrists have long been interested in perception and color and their combined effect on the psyche. While Sigmund Freud was one of the first to begin to discuss the use of color and its relationship to psychology in his monograph on Leonardo da Vinci, it was Carl Jung in *Man and His Symbols* who began to see color as a primal element that needed to be addressed. He saw the artist's use of color as a manifestation of the unconscious. Laurie Schneider Adams sees a close relationship between art and psychology, and she believes that the artist's use of the color, form, and imagery are autobiographical in nature.

The Luscher Color Test

In 1960, Dr. Max Luscher developed a color test to determine personality traits and disorders. The Luscher Color Test has become the standard and is considered the most reliable of all of the color personality insight tools because it held its results even for those with color vision impairment or color blindness. The simple and most widely used version of the test contains eight colors. The four psychological primaries—dark blue,

Figure 3-2.
Portia Munson, *Pink Project*, 1994.
In this installation, Munson's has assembled a collection of pink items specifically marketed to women and girls. Her work reflects the deep social conditioning regarding color preference that people undergo daily.
Photo courtesy of Portia Munson.

yellow, red-orange, and green—make up the first group of the color test, with violet and neutrals of brown, gray, and black (the absence of all color) making up the second or auxiliary group. These auxiliary colors require a bit of an explanation: black and gray are not actually colors at all because they represent the negation of all color. Violet is a mixture of dark blue and red-orange, while brown is actually a mixture of red-orange and black. By placing these colored swatches in descending order of preference, it revealed aspects of personality, including anxieties, conflicts, and compulsions.

Look at the eight color swatches in Figure 3-3 and choose the one you like the most. Don't think about what your favorite color is, but rather which one of these

particular patches you prefer. In the full color test, you would then rate each of the eight swatches in order from most to least favorite. Position one is the color you most prefer and represents what you want most or covet. It is your greatest desire. The color picked in position eight is the least preferred and represents what you seek to avoid. This order would give insight into your personality and psyche. The number of possible combinations that are detailed in Luscher's book gives a more complete picture of the subject's personality. Look in the following and find your first choice. How well does it match up to your personality?

Dark blue represents total calm, tranquility, harmony, and comfort, and relates to one's need for contentment and fulfillment. When picked in the first position, it represents a need for emotional stability, for rest, relaxation, and the desire to recharge. The person choosing blue wants a calm and orderly environment. If it is a person's first choice, it is usually chosen for itself and not as a rejection of another color.

Blue-green used in the test contains a small amount of blue. It is an expression of steadfastness—standing up tall and firm like a tree. People who choose green in the first position can be assertive and demanding, primarily concerned with themselves and their personal gains. It could be called the "me" color of people who want to add to their own personal fortune. It is no accident that this is also the color associated with money and wealth. Green, like the street light, stands for "go" and represents those who want to push ahead to succeed.

Red-orange is not a pure red. It has some yellow in it thereby giving it a bit of an orange feel and with it the feeling of energy. It represents vital forces of desire, appetite, and hunger and, as we will see, is the favorite of fast-food restaurants. It also represents activity, and the person choosing this hue will

Figure 3-3.
An illustration of the 8 color swatches that make up the Luscher Color Test. Pick your favorite color from among the samples and then match your choice to the corresponding explanation. How accurately does the statement reflect your personality?
© Steven Bleicher

be active and participate in sports and other physical activities. People choosing red in the first position want their own personal activities to be intense and want to experience life to the fullest and live it on the edge. It is also a color of strong sexual desire, but the ability to satisfy one's needs may be difficult. It is an intense hue and could be considered the "extreme color" as in extreme sports.

Bright yellow is the most saturated intense hue in the test and stands for sunny, bright, and happy thoughts. It represents the subject's desire for happiness. It may also represent someone who is going through a major personal crisis and wants and desires a happy outcome. Yellow is the color of haloes and gold and may have a religious significance or connotation. It represents the future, and the person who picks it is someone looking forward to the future and all it can bring.

Violet is composed of both red and blue and holds some of each color's association. Violet can represent someone who wants or sees a magical identification to the world with intimate and erotic overtones. When it is the first choice of children, it may mean they still find the world a magical place. An adult who chooses it in the first position may be both sensitive and unrealistic in their desires or goals.

Brown is a shade of orange representing sensations of the body and bodily functions. It is an earthy tone indicating the importance of home and feeling of belonging. It also may denote that the person selecting this shade may have feelings of unease and the desire to remedy a problem or situation.

Black is the darkest of all the colors in the test and is the negation or absence of all color. It represents the color of anarchy and protest; the person picking it wants to rebel against anything and everything. Those who choose black are those who do not to give up anything and may feel that things are not as they want them to be. It also denotes someone who may be pushing against fate and may do so just to be different and not do what everyone else is doing—the dissenter and agitator. Black has an intense effect on the other colors chosen after it and is most normally picked in the last position.

Gray is a neutral; it is not a hue and is the midpoint in between black and white. It is not one thing or another and is free from all stimuli. It could be considered the DMZ color choice—not part of one thing or another. People selecting gray in the first position want to separate themselves from everyone and everything, walling themselves up. These people watch themselves go through the motions of

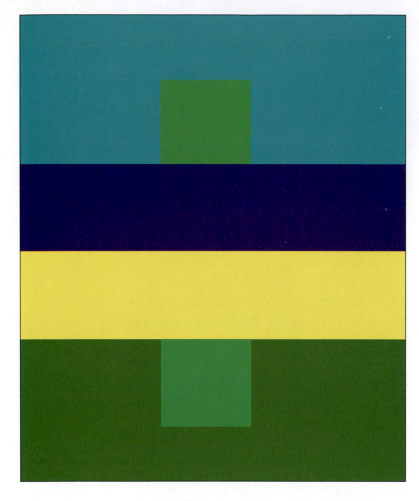

Figure 3-4.
An example of the Retinex Theory Color. The green stripe running down the center is actually the same color. It looks like two different hues of green due the lightness or darkness of the corresponding background hues. We perceive color in relationship to the amount of light and the other hues surrounding it. © Steven Bleicher

daily life and are not involved. They prefer to stand alone stoically. Gray is statistically most often picked in sixth place in the test.

The Brain and Cortex

We must remember that we do not pick out or decide on a color in isolation. Edwin Land, the inventor of the Polaroid camera, took this idea a step further with his **retinex theory**. Retinex is a combination of the words *retina* and *cortex*. He stated that colors are not determined in isolation and that colors change in relation to one another. We can take two swatches of the same color (in Figure 3-4, the chosen color is green), and depending upon the background color they are placed on, radically change their visual appearance. Johannes Itten and Joseph Albers demonstrated this theory in their works and were part of the traditional Bauhausian approach to teaching color theory.

Color Constancy

As a part of his research, Land concluded that cognitive function and our learned responses to objects played a dominant role in our color recognition and the consistency with which we viewed an objects' color. He said that even in the dark, we expect an object to retain its color. For example, we expect lemons to be yellow when we turn the lights off because we think we still see yellow even though the light has changed. This is another example of a learned response to color. Through a lifetime of experience, limes have always been green; therefore when we see a lime, we expect it to be green. No matter how the light changes, or the color surrounding the lime may change, we know the lime is green and that is exactly what we see. The brain and psyche ignore the reflected wavelength light impulses, overriding the incoming data, and decide based on years of knowledge of the color of the item. When we think of how we see, our first thought is of our eyes, but the mind and subconscious play a much more significant part in how we perceive color than we can imagine. The brain, in the end, may be the real arbiter of color.

Color Function and Cognition

By changing the color of an object, we can drastically alter its function and use. We tend to recognize objects such as signs by their color as much as by their shape or lettering. Red is the color of a stop sign and whether it is the octagonal shape as in America or a circular format as in Europe, the color red automatically signals us to stop. What would happen if you painted the sign green? Would people stop? In several psychological studies over the years in controlled situations, stop signs were

Figure 3-5.
Green Stop Sign.
Would you stop for a
green stop sign?
© Steven Bleicher

changed from red to green (Figure 3-5). Everything else about the signs remained exactly the same. Drivers would regularly go right through the intersections without stopping. When pulled over by the researchers, the people in the car would say, "Yes, I saw the stop sign." When asked why they failed to come to a complete stop, their answer invariably was "But the sign was green and green means go." The drivers were more influenced by the color of the sign than the printed word or the shape of the sign.

What other objects can you think of that are always a specific color and never vary?

Something as simple as changing the tint or shade of a particular color can impact its meaning and function. If we look at the logos for any of the major sports organizations—the National Football League, Major League Baseball, etc.—they are in saturated hues of red, white, and blue. One underlying psychological meaning is the association with American national patriotism. The bright, saturated hues also reference the vitality of the sports played. If we took any of these logos and substituted tints of blue and red would they still have the same meaning or would they lose much of their power and attraction? In another example, would the logo for the American Red Cross (a red cross) hold the same meaning if its was replaced with a tint making it a pink cross?

A History of Blue

Color associations can change and be as relative as the application of color itself. Blue can stand for being "true blue," loyal, and steadfast. These identifications with the hue go as far back as 1340 B.C. to the Egyptian civilization and the reign of King Tut. In western culture, the color blue dates to 431 A.D. when the church began to associate specific colors with the saints and religious figures to bring the stories of the Bible to life. The gem, lapis lazuli (a deep blue), was ground into pigment and used to paint the clothing of the Virgin Mary. It quickly became associated with her

Figure 3-6.
Gentile Da Fabriano, *The Adoration of the Magi*, 1423.
The Virgin Mary's robes of deep blue evolved into navy blue and with it all of the associations of qualities of truth and honesty.
Photo © Scala/Ministero per i Beni e le Attività culturali/Art Resource, NY.

traits of piety, truth, and goodness (Figure 3-6). The contemporary, mass-produced equivalent is navy blue, which is still associated with truth, honesty, and confidence. Certainly no businessman or politician would be without a navy suit!

Blue is America's favorite color, reminding us of peaceful easy times. It may be a toss-up whether navy or denim is number one. The blue jean is uniquely American, invoking the West and era of the cowboy (Figure 3-7). The name *jean* is derived from the Italo-English *genoese,* meaning from Genoa where the fabric style, originally

linen and cotton, was originally developed. The pants became known by the name of their material in the 1850s. What makes jeans so special is their denim fabric, which is very dense and will not completely absorb all of the indigo dye. The colorant fades out little by little through continued washing, producing a unique look for each pair of pants. Some feel the color is almost alive as it continually changes. This has become part of their mystique and their rugged appeal.

Blue is also associated with water and sky; the earth is often referred to as a "big

Figure 3-7.
Denim has become
synonymous with
the west. It's hard to
imagine a cowboy out
on the range not wearing
denim. The fabric
has become an iconic
American emblem.
Photo © Comstock/Getty
Images.

blue marble." Lighter blue hues do not have the same impact or meaning as the darker varieties. Unlike the statement of authority in navy-blue, a light blue hue has a more calming and peaceful feel. This may be in part why the United Nations uses this hue as the identifying color (helmets, flags, etc.) for their peacekeeping forces (Figure 3-8).

Picasso's Blue Period

The very same hue that is associated with peace, virtue, and truth is also the color we use to describe someone who is depressed and sullen. There are wonderful anecdotal stories that Pablo Picasso used this color predominately, in what is now referred to as his "Blue Period," because he was very poor and could only afford blue paint. While these stories make great copy, and have become part of the Picasso legend, we know that this period in his work starts with the death by suicide of his closest friend, Casagemas.

The death of his best friend started a serious bout of depression that lasted several years. It just so happens that these years

correspond to the Blue Period, a time in which Picasso primarily uses the color blue in all of his paintings. Picasso created several paintings of his friend lying in state. In one

Figure 3-8.
United Nations'
Peacekeeping Forces.
The light blue used
is a soft tint and is
not aggressive or
authoritarian. This color
selection is in keeping
with the mission of
the United Nations'
peacekeeping forces.
Photo © UN Photo/Saw
Lwin.

of the first paintings, *La Mort de Casagemas,* the hues used are bright and hot and give a warm glow to the figure (Figure 3-9). We see the backlit head of Casagemas, and the yellow highlights in the face, which still has the soft warmth of life. Only the mark of the gunshot wound belies the fact that he is dead and not sleeping.

Juxtaposed to this is what might be considered the first of the Blue Period paintings, *Casagemas in His Coffin* (Figure 3-10), which shows his friend cold and dead, lying in his casket. The features are gaunt and the color is completely desaturated. The flame of the candle, a metaphor for life, in the previous work has long been extinguished and is absent in this picture. In this later painting, Picasso used blue because it summed up his mood and conveyed to the viewer his sense of emptiness and sorrow. This is the power of color.

Psychological Perception

Beyond a poetic use of hue and pigment, as we have seen in the previous chapter, colors have a physiological effect on our bodies and well-being. The color red will increase skin temperature and raise blood pressure and respiration, while blue will lower skin temperature, blood pressure, respiration, and pulse. Mink ranchers use blue lights to keep the normally vicious and ill-tempered animals calm and to allow them to handle the animals more easily. Color can also affect our perception of objects as well. On the English waterfront, dockworkers complained that a product packed in very dark pigmented containers was too heavy and a strike nearly ensued. The shippers replaced the dark containers with containers colored a soft-tinted hue. The new "lighter" boxes pleased the dock workers and talk of a strike passed without issue. The size and weight of the boxes remained the same; only the color changed and with it the perception of their heft and manageability.

Mood and Emotion

Mood and disposition can also influence our perception of color. As an experiment on color and emotion, the U.S. Navy painted its holding cells in the "brig," its military jail, pink. They found that even the most hostile and agitated sailors became docile and calm while in the pink holding area. Why did this happen? One might think that it would have just the opposite effect. The color pink was emasculating and made the prisoners feel withdrawn and less manly and made them easier to control. However, the study also revealed that if the prisoners were left in the pink holding cell for more than a short period of time, they become even more aggressive and violent. The color that at first subdued and quieted, over an extended period of time, irritated and aggravated the sailors so much that they became uncontrollable.

While pink may be questionable to use in certain situations, green, on the other hand, can be a very welcoming hue. People adjust well to new surroundings under the influence of green (Figure 3-11). If you paint the interior of a cabin at a sleep-away camp green, there will be fewer incidences of homesickness among the children. Green interiors are also frequently used in bed-and-breakfast inns to create a warm and inviting atmosphere for the guests.

Color and Appetite

While the U.S. Navy's experiments with color may have failed, fast-food restaurant chains have perfected the use of color to sway emotion. Think about your favorite: McDonald's, Burger King, or Wendy's. All use the same basic color scheme of hot hues of yellow, orange, and red. These colors increase the appetite. Not only do you order

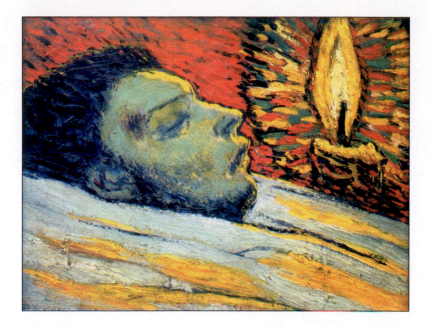

Figure 3-9.
Pablo Picasso, *La Mort de Casagemas,* 1901. The color palette used contains warm hues and gives the viewer the feeling that the person lying in the coffin has only recently passed away. The candle is a visual metaphor for life—when the candle is extinguished, so is life. It might be Picasso's way of holding on to his friend's memory.
© 2010 Estate of Pablo Picasso/Artists Rights Society (ARS), New York. Photo courtesy of Réunion des Musées Nationaux/Art Resource, NY.

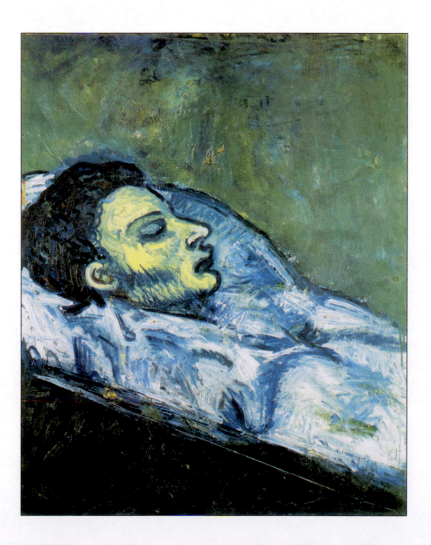

Figure 3-10.
Pablo Picasso, *Casagemas in His Coffin,* 1901. Now the colors are blue and cold. The colors give us a feeling of emptiness and complete stillness. The cool palette also helps distance us from the figure.
© 2010 Estate of Pablo Picasso/Artists Rights Society (ARS), New York. Photo courtesy of On-Line Picasso Project (Dr. Enrique Mallen).

Figure 3-11.
People adjust better to new surroundings in a green room. The bed-and-breakfast inn uses this underlying psychology in its choice of colors for its rooms to make their guests feel welcome and more at home.
Photo courtesy of Lifton Hall Hotel.

and eat more under the influence of these hues, you eat faster. The idea is to get you in, stimulate your appetite, and get you out of there as fast as possible so that the next customer can come in and take your place. The brightly colored, hard plastic seats in these establishments are not just for sanitation and easy cleaning, but are to keep you from getting too comfortable and lingering. Time is money. On the other hand, upscale restaurants use soft lighting, and dark subdued hues of greens, blues, and violets. They want you to relax, to take your time and linger over another after-dinner drink. Here, more time means more money, a higher bill, and more profit to the proprietor.

Color and Flavor

In food stores, bread is normally sold in packaging decorated or tinted with golden or brown tones to promote the idea of home baked and oven freshness. Rarely will you see it sold in a green wrapper because the cast color on to the product would remind buyers of mold. Adding yellow to the

wrapper will boost bread sales bread sales and give the product a sunny bright appeal. When margarine first was introduced there were laws in the dairy states preventing manufacturers from coloring the product yellow, the color of butter. Initially it came with a separate packet of yellow dye; the consumer would have to mix it in to make the white pasty substance resemble the natural product.

In fact if you are on a diet, replace the normal light bulb in your refrigerator with a blue bulb. The food will look unappetizing and can help to reduce the amount of food consumed. The "blue plate special" made famous in the 1930s used this same concept. The color of the plate affects the look of the food and thereby causes the patron to eat less, feeling full faster—another dieting tip.

If you still have any reservations that color affects flavor, take a look at the ingredients on most food products and you will see that one or more of the items listed is a coloring agent or dye. Without the addition of caramel color, Coke would not be a rich brown, but would be a clear colorless liquid such as Seven Up. The color pink will enhance the taste of sweetness in any food product. This is one reason why many bakeries use pink boxes for their cakes and cookies. When we see bright purple edibles or drinks, we expect them to taste like grapes and so on.

The most recent entry into the food-coloring fray is blue (Figure 3-12). In the past, blue was not considered edible because it was not a color found in fresh, natural food products; rather, it reminded customers of mold and decay. Even today, the blue that is used is a very saturated bright hue and never a blue green. These new products are mostly directed to a younger market who have not yet formed negative color associations and usually it is used in candy, soft drinks, and sports drinks.

Packaging and Products

The exact opposite of this approach would be the way food and beverages are packaged. Here color is used to signify the object as well as to enhance the flavor or taste. We recognize specific brands of food, cigarettes, and even magazines by their trademark colors. We reach for a product by recognizing the color of the package before we have even consciously read the name of the product. Shoppers scan the shelf and recognize the product they wish to purchase in 0.03 seconds. We recognize the color yellow of the Cheerios box (Figure 3-13) long before we see or read the name of the product.

What other products do you recognize solely by their color?

In market research studies it has been determined that 60 percent of acceptance or rejection of a product is based on its color. That decision is also made very quickly. Within 90 seconds, a person will make a choice to accept or reject a purchase. Any discussions after that initial

time period will rarely change the person's mind but will be used to reinforce the decision for or against. But by far the most important aspect is the color of the item. If the color is not right, people will not purchase the product.

If you don't think the color of an item is this critical, consider the role it plays in the purchase of a major ticket item such as a car. You go to the dealership and order your dream car including all of the options and extras and wait for it to arrive from the factory. A few weeks pass and the salesman from the dealership calls and says the car is in, but there is just one small problem—there

Figure 3-12.
A blue soft drink.
All of the new blue foods on the market have a bright intense color. For soda and sports drinks the color reminds the consumer of something cold and refreshing. What flavor do you think the drink is?
© Steven Bleicher

Figure 3-13.
A box of CHEERIOS®. We see the color yellow before we read the label. We quickly learn to associate the color of the package to our favorite products and reach for them based on recognizing the specific hue as we shop. CHEERIOS® is a registered trademark of General Mills, Inc. and is used with permission.

was that consumer research studies showed that the public felt the dark gray color was richer, more businesslike, and more astute. Consumers also thought that dark gray gave the product a more compact look. Then, in the late 1990s, Apple came along with the iBook and iMac and revolutionized the world of home computers.

Today, the computer is a fashion accessory and decorative home item. It is now considered a part of the room like furniture, and color is used to accent and decorate it. Other companies such as Dell have followed Apple's lead in creating colorful home computers. This same styling is also being featured in other items, from the George Foreman grill to microwave ovens and a whole host of other products.

Socioeconomic Aspects of Color

Your color choices are determined by many factors. There are socioeconomic aspects that affect your choice of favorite hues and that determine which hues you feel more at home or comfortable with. The higher your economic status, the more you will favor darker, less saturated, complex hues. People in the lower economic brackets tend to prefer and respond favorably to simple, bright, pure hues. This can be seen in everything from department stores to hotels. For instance, Target, a discount department store, uses bright red, while Tiffany's, an ultra high-end retailer, is known for their use of a muted turquoise palette. This color has become so synonymous with Tiffany's that people only have to see the soft blue box to know where the item was purchased. Socioeconomic factors influence everything, including the choice of color for your car, says Carlton Wagner, a color consultant. Someone buying a Ford may be comfortable choosing brown, while another person in a higher economic bracket who is buying a Lexus will not respond well to brown.

was a minor mix up and the color is slightly different. Instead of the deep intense red you ordered, it is bright orange with pink stripes. Orange and pink are close to red, the color you ordered. Would it make a difference to you? Of course it would.

Color is important. The choice of color will have many determining factors such as age, sex, and socioeconomic class of the intended customer. Colors that work for one group of buyers may not work for another, and colors that may be acceptable for one product may not be appropriate for another.

Apple Changes Everything

One of the newest products to be sold in a variety of colors is the computer. Traditionally, they came in the standard gray or putty color. They had an institutional generic look without any thought to the color or style. The one exception to this was the laptop computer, which was generally a dark gray tone. The reason for this

Instead, this person will choose sable, a deeper more complex shade of the same color. The one group that Wagner says does not fit this model is the so-called yuppie (young urban professional). Yuppies tend to pick color choices based on where they want to go, and they look ahead to the next higher economic bracket for their color choices.

The use of orange opens up a product or service to the widest audience (Figure 3-14). It is not an exclusive color and is never used for high-end goods or services. Orange declassifies and may be considered the lowest common denominator in color usage. Whether it's used in a logo, on the product itself, or in the décor, it signifies that the company or products presented are being marketed to a mass audience. Begin to look at all of the companies using orange in their logos and products. What you will find are companies (most that are good solid companies with quality products) trying to reach the largest possible target audience.

Oppenheim's Blue Shirt

Further indication that colors have socioeconomic connotations is evidenced in how we relate color to the names given to certain occupations. "White-collar" workers are executives and others engaged in office work. "Blue-collar" denotes manual labor and has undertones of negative associations of the working class as unskilled and undereducated. Such was the controversy that swarmed when Milwaukee's General Mitchell Airport announced

Figure 3-14.
The color orange automatically signifies products for the mass market. This has nothing to do with the quality of the product or service. Southwest Airline is one of the leading low priced air carriers. Their no frills friendly service has made them an industry leader.
Photo courtesy of Southwest Airlines.

plans to erect a new work of art, Dennis Oppenheim's *Blue Shirt* (Figure 3-15). When the piece was first unveiled to the public, it was felt that it was derogatory and a slap in the face to the city's working class. But the artist felt that the piece was positive and

Figure 3-15.
Dennis Oppenheim, *Blue Shirt*, 2003. Proposal for the General Mitchell International Airport, Milwaukee, Wisconsin. There was protest against the work because many people thought Oppenheim was making fun of the blue-collar workers, which he was not. He felt the piece was a monument to their work ethic.
Photo courtesy of Dennis Oppenheim.

Figure 3-16.
Albert Bierstadt, *In the Mountains*, 1867. Wadsworth Atheneum, Hartford. Gift of John J. Morgan in memory of his mother, Juliet Pierpont Morgan. Bierstadt's painting is a good example of atmospheric perspective. Notice how the color in the foreground is light and bright, while the background is gray and desaturated. As things blend into the background, they also lose detail and become hazy.
Photo © Wadsworth Atheneum Museum of Art/ Art Resource, NY.

exalted the working class that is the core of the city. He also felt that the piece dealt with the human anatomy and how inherited traits and the choices we make through our purchases become a part of our personalities. Here the color and item fused together to imbue the image with many meanings, opening it up to vast interpretations. Only time will tell if this work becomes synonymous with Milwaukee as the St. Louis Arch and the Washington Monument have to their respective locales.

Artists' Use of Color

It is not only the hue that is important in our perception of color; saturation and brightness are also essential elements. Warm, bright, fully saturated colors appear to advance—they make objects seem larger and closer to us. Intense and highly saturated hues are normally used in the foreground and bring the viewer into the painting or work of art. Tints will also create a similar optical boost and open up the space, which makes objects appear larger and closer to the viewer. These will also imbue the image with a positive, uplifting feeling.

On the other hand, cool, dull, low saturated dark colors make objects look smaller and appear to recede in space. They have a restrained feeling and evoke emotions such as sadness, depression, loss, and longing. As objects move back into space, they lose color and saturation and blend or melt away into a middle or light gray. This effect is called **atmospheric perspective** (Figure 3-16).

As items move into the background, there is less light falling on them and subsequently there is less color, detail, and texture. This is why when we look at a mountain range, for instance, the peaks seem to dissolve into thin air and fade away. It is a more realistic and natural way of using color to enhance depth and distance.

When working in a representational manner with color, it is referred to as working with **local color**. Local color and value are synonymous with the exact appearance of the object. In Pat Rosenstein's painting, *The Ack Bassward Painting,* the colors used accurately reflect the natural colors of the objects portrayed (Figure 3-17). This style of painting is also known as photorealism. This use of color to mimic objects and their surroundings can act as a type of camouflage and is also known as **trompe l'oeil**, which means, "to fool the eye."

Color as a Means of Expression

Another method of using color as visual expression is the use of **heightened color**. Heightened color makes elements of a painting or image stand out. In France, the Fauves (or "wild beasts," as the name translates) used this theory of color to make their images stand out (Figure 3-18). This was also a liberating idea that an artist could paint an object—for instance, a tree—any color he wanted. And by making the tree blue or red or violet, force the viewer to stop and rethink just exactly what a tree is and what its true meaning may be. Further, it gave the object a power and intensity it would not normally have. Color could be used for color's sake alone without any relation to the natural world. To the artists of the early 1900s, this was a powerful liberating force.

Prior to this, all art had to relate back to the natural world in both color and form. Even the Impressionists, as radically new as

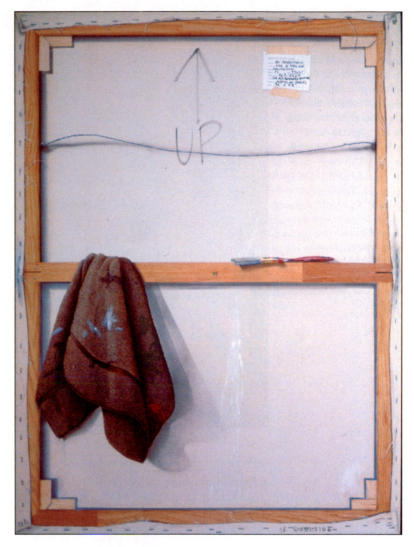

Figure 3-17.
Pat Rosenstein, *The Ack Bassward Painting,* 1998.
At first glance it looks like a photograph of the back of a canvas. Rosenstein's captures the local colors accurately and correctly in this photorealistic work. The shadow of the wire running across the back of the canvas appears to be protruding out into space while it reality it is flat.
Photo © Pat Rosenstein, courtesy of Mary & Sheldon Cooper.

they were for their time, still maintained this naturalistic link—a tree trunk was brown, the sky various shades of blue, and so on. The Fauves made a distinct break with the past and all forms of naturalism and realism, and their work foreshadowed the advent of abstraction.

Outlasting the Fauves during this time period were the German artists of The Bridge (Die Brucke) and the Blue Rider (Der Blaue Reiter), more commonly known as German Expressionists. They used identical concepts of enhanced and elevated color to imbue their paintings with strong emotional and psychological content. Artists began to

Artists or designers rarely, if ever, work with one color alone, or dedicate themselves to only one hue. A few, like Picasso, may work with one dominant color for a period of time as he did in his Rose and Blue Periods (Figure 4-1). But this is the exception. Most work with many hues, and therefore need to know how these various colors will interact with one another. Color harmonies, schemes, and color ways are synonymous terms, meaning the same thing. Rather than an artist trying different hues and having hit-or-miss results, color schemes are formulas or combinations that can be used to create a cohesive unified picture. These formulas are time-proven methods of using color to create a pleasing harmonic balance.

Figure 4-1.
Pablo Picasso, *Le vieux juif*, 1903.
Picasso's use of blue was a physical manifestation in paint of his mental and emotional state. The major themes of the Blue Period paintings are all depressing subjects, including the blind, mental patients, madness, hunger, and melancholia. The canvas is cropped tightly to the figures, which produces a cramped, condensed space and adds to the bleak feeling of the painting.
Photo © 2010 Estate of Pablo Picasso/Artists Rights Society (ARS), New York. Photo courtesy of Scala/Art Resource, NY.

Figure 4-2.
An example of an achromatic or value scale also known as a gray scale.
© Steven Bleicher

ACHROMATIC SCALE

The terms *hue*, *chrome*, and *color* are all names for the same thing. A **hue** is the actual, or proper, name of any given color. Today these words are interchanged with abandon, but as artists and designers, we must be more careful and accurate in our use of terminology. The term color tends to be more universal, while hue tends to be more specific and refers to a color found in the spectrum or on the color wheel.

Shades of Gray

If all color is eliminated entirely, then what we would be left with is an **achromatic** range (Figure 4-2). We would be working with pure value or the lightness and darkness only without any hint of hue. In its most exacting definition, the prefix *a-* is from the Greek meaning not and "chroma" meaning color. In other words, it is without color or not colored. For something to be considered a hue or a color, it must have its own place or position on the color wheel. In theory, if you mixed all the hues on the color wheel, you would get black; however, it does not have its own place anywhere on the wheel. Using this definition, then black and white are not considered colors or hues. Along with the full range of grays, black and white are neutrals. Therefore, they are not hues or colors and should never be referred to as such. This sometimes gets confusing because in daily life people often refer to black, white, or even gray as colors. Artists and designers need to be specific in their use of language. In my own work, as seen in Figure 4-3, I combine digitally created images that have been altered and worked into with graphite to produce an achromatic image. The only addition of color is the added mixed media souvenir items. Their spot color adds a visual contrast and counterpoint to the black-and-white images and aids in establishing a focal point in the artwork.

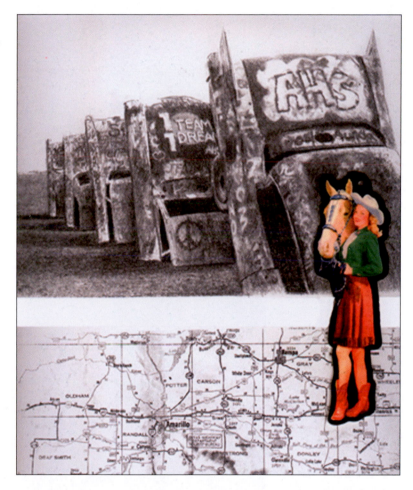

Figure 4-3.
Steven Bleicher, *Cadillac Ranch (from the Route 66 Series)*, 2006. Graphite, digital image and mixed media on paper.
Color acts like a magnet, even limited color. The viewer's eye is first drawn to the colored souvenir item, which then leads into the rest of the work.
© Steven Bleicher

Figure 4-4.
An example of a relational hue and value scale. If you squint your eyes, the line between the hue and its relative value should begin to disappear.
© Steven Bleicher

Each hue has its corresponding, or related, value. This is known as **inherent value.** Understanding this relation of each hue and its corresponding value assists the artist and designer in developing and setting up color harmonies. There is no direct correlation of white to a hue. It is too light in value and even the most bright intense yellow would be darker, which is why yellow starts off our relational value and hue scale as a light gray, as seen in Figure 4-4. As we move up the scale, red and green tend to match each other in their relative value at middle gray. Blues and violets make up the darker end of the scale as deep grays. Just as white has no equivalent hue, neither does black. It's too dark. Even the deepest violet would still be lighter in value than black. In essence, black is the absence of all color and is the darkest value possible.

Tints, Tones, and Shades

The most simple color harmony possible is a **monochromatic** scheme. *Mono–* comes from the Greek for one, meaning that it is a schema that is comprised only of a single hue. As shown in Figure 4-5, it is the full range of a color from its lightest tint to its deepest shade and everything in between, but it is always one very specific hue. A **tint** is

Figure 4-5.
An example of three monochromatic scales: blue, yellow, and orange. The pure hue is at the center and the shades of each are shown on the left, while the tints are displayed on the right. Notice that, depending upon the hue, the addition of black creates surprising results. If black is mixed with yellow, the shade appears to have a greenish cast, while if black is mixed with orange, it creates brown.
© Steven Bleicher

MONOCHROMATIC SCALES

the hue plus the addition of white. We often think of tints as pastel colors, soft and full of light. If a hue is mixed with gray, a **tone** is created. The base gray mixed with the hue can be very light to extremely dark and everything in between the full range. It may be the widest range of the three components that comprise a monochromatic scheme. Mixing black with the hue will produce a **shade** of that color. You can vary the intensity of the shade depending upon which type of black paint is used in its creation. Ivory Black creates a transparent warm shade, while Lamp Black will produce an opaque warm shade. On the other hand, Mars and Oxide Black produce cool shades. So even in something as simple as this, there can be great complexity.

MAROON – SHADE   RED – HUE   PINK – TINT

To illustrate this point more clearly, Figure 4-6 shows what can happen if one specific hue, such as red, is made into a tint and shade. If red is mixed with white to make a tint, the resulting color is pink. On the other hand, if black is added to the hue, maroon is the result. Yet it is still red—the hue has not changed and remains constant. Various tints and shades of red are used in Angelo Filomeno's *Poison* (Figure 4-7).

Figure 4-6.
An illustration of the range of a monochromatic red hue. The base hue is red and when mixed with white, it creates a tint, in this case pink. If the same red hue is mixed with black, a shade is created, namely maroon. Regardless of whether it is a tint or a shade, the hue is still red.
© Steven Bleicher

Figure 4-7.
Angelo Filomeno, *Poison*, 2004.
A single hue of color can be used for its emotional content. Here the red textile embroidered with garnets and Swarovski crystals creates a rich and vibrant image. This intense color palette goes with the evocative nature of the imagery.
Photo courtesy Galerie Anne de Villepoix, Paris.

The shades create depth and contrast giving the visual elements their form. The tints are used in contrast to focus the viewers' attention on the head and body of the rooster in the upper portion of the image. Filomeno uses garnets and crystals as a focal point for the work. The darker values visually recede into the background while the tints appear to advance to the foreground in what is a very shallow depth of field.

Many artists have worked with monochromatic compositions, though Pablo Picasso may be the most famous. His decision to use blue was not because (as some stories have suggested) he could only afford blue paint, but was directly related to the severe depression he sank into after the death of his best friend. However, not all use of blue represents sadness or depression. Mark Tansey, a well-known contemporary artist, uses a monochrome blue range in his oil painting,

Push/Pull (Figure 4-8). Here the blue hue is used to produce an ethereal mood. The imagery alternately looks like the arctic and desert, each having poetic similarities. The photo-realistic nature of the work adds to confusion of the juxtaposed imagery as well as the convincing alternate reality.

Hue, Value, and Saturation

There are three components that artists consider when working with color. They are hue, value, and saturation. Each can be controlled and will have a significant impact on how the hue may be viewed. When choosing a hue from a color wheel or spectrum, an artist is making a specific color choice. For example, blue is a different hue than blue-green or blue-violet. The value of the hue can be changed or adjusted as needed, and more white or black can be added as required.

Figure 4-8.
Mark Tansey, *Push/Pull*, 2003.
Not all blue compositions are depressing. Here the mood here is odd and a bit disquieting. The imagery Tansey uses are of the Sphinx and what appears to be an arctic scene, both considered deserts. Notice that none of the figures look directly at the viewer, adding to the distanced nature of the work.
Photo © Mark Tansey.
Courtesy of Gagosian Gallery.

Figure 4-9.
An example of the desaturation of the hue green. As the color becomes increasingly more desaturated, it loses its green color and becomes more gray and washed out.
© Steven Bleicher

The final component is **saturation** or the intensity and purity of the given hue. Another way to think of saturation is as the brightness or dullness of a color. Brighter, more intense colors usually denote a purer saturation of the particular hue. Any hue can be desaturated to make it appear more gray, drab, and dingy in appearance (Figures 4-9 and 4-10). When looking at the hues on the color wheel, we are seeing the purest most saturated form of the hue. Altering the saturation can drastically change our perception of the image and even make it hard to look at (Figure 4-11). Bright super-saturated hues can be great attention grabbers but can be hard to look at for any length of time.

Figure 4-10.
Franz Gertsch, *Dominique*, 1988. Gertsch uses a desaturated green hue in this portrait. It creates an eerie ghost-like image in that it appears the figure could vanish into the gray-green haze at any moment.
Photo courtesy of Museum Franz Gertsch, Burgdorf, Switzerland.

Figure 4-11.
The center image of the flower is shown at its normal hue and saturation. Its even tones of red and green create a normal-looking picture and are pleasing to the eye. The image on the left is desaturated. It has lost most of its color and there is only a hint of color peeking out of the gray. The picture on the right is super-saturated. Using Adobe Photoshop, the color saturation of the image was enhanced, increasing the intensity of the hues. The colors are so intense they begin to vibrate and jump off the page and are hard to look at for any length of time. Pumping up the saturation of an image can be used to grab the viewer's attention or to create a focal point.
© Steven Bleicher

The Color Wheel

The circular format of the color wheel will now become more useful and meaningful. The specific placement of the hues along the circumference of the wheel will help illustrate the relationships or harmonies. First, each hue is spaced an equal distance from each other. A color wheel can have as few as six hues and then doubles itself as more hues are distinguished. The next and most commonly used would be the twelve-step color wheel (Figure 4-12), but you could also have twenty-four- and forty-eight-step versions as well. Color wheels must always have an even number of hues and that number must be divisible by three. Any other combination would not be a true and accurate color wheel.

The color wheel is comprised of three primary colors, or **primaries:** yellow, red, and blue. Primaries are so named because they cannot be broken down any further and are the principal ingredients that make up all other colors. If you mix equal parts of two primary hues, a **secondary** hue is created. There are only three secondaries: orange, green, and violet. Blue and yellow make green, blue and red make violet or purple, and yellow and red make orange.

If primary and secondary hues are mixed, an **intermediate** or **tertiary** hue is created. On the standard twelve-step color wheel there are six intermediates: yellow-orange, yellow-green, blue-green, blue-violet, red-violet, and red-orange. On larger color wheels, intermediate hues can be mixed with primary or secondary hues to create **quaternary** colors.

Color Temperature

The color wheel can be divided into two basic areas, or groups, of warm and cool hues. The warm range is comprised of yellow, orange, red, and some hues of green. The cool hues normally include everything from blue-green to the various forms of blues and violets. However, there are few absolutes when dealing with color. Color is relative and will change depending upon the other hues placed next to them or in close proximity, as seen in Figure 4-13. For example, yellow may be warm in relation to blue-green, but blue-green may be warm in relation to violet. Green may be cool in relation to another warm hue such as yellow-orange, but considered warm when it is placed next to blue-violet.

Color temperature can also be used to create spatial effects. Visually, warm hues appear to advance on the picture plane. They seem to move toward us and give the feeling of the color coming out toward the viewer. Cool hues have the opposite effect. They appear to recede into space on the picture plane. These are very important concepts for artists and designers to remember when working with color.

Franz Marc used this spatial phenomenon in *Siberian Dogs in the Snow* (Figure 4-14). He worked with a limited color palette comprised almost exclusively of white, blue, and yellow. The warmer yellow hues are used as highlights and appear to advance

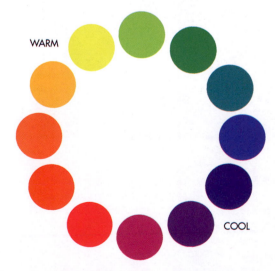

Figure 4-12.
An example of a twelve-step color wheel. Each hue is spaced at equal distances from each other.
© Steven Bleicher

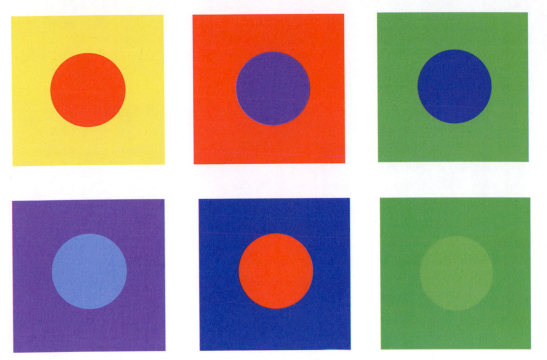

Figure 4-13.
An example of the relationship between warm and cool hues. In the top row the base color or squares are warm and the circles are cool. In the second row the base colors are cool and the circles are warm in relation to the color of the square. So that a hue such as green can be warm in relation to blue, but cool when compared to yellow-green.
© Steven Bleicher

Figure 4-14.
Franz Marc. *Siberian Dogs in the Snow*. 1909-10.
Marc uses warm hues to bring elements of the painting closer to the viewer. Cool hues are used as shadows to give depth to the painting, since cool hues recede into space. Bright yellow is used to show the lightest highlight, and tints of the same hue are used to create a middle ground, along with the tints of blue. Shades of blue are used to create deep shadows.
Image courtesy of National Gallery of Art, Washington. Gift of Mr. and Mrs. Stephen M. Kellen.

on the picture plane. The white becomes a base, or ground, while the blues are used in the shadows. The cool hues recede into the background, which allows the white dogs to stand out against the snow.

More Spatial Effects

Atmospheric perspective is another method of using color to create spatial effects. As objects move farther away from the viewer (or foreground), they lose color. In fact, not only do they become desaturated as they recede in space, the farther back the objects are from the foreground, the less texture and detail that will be visible. As shown in Figure 4-15, the less light illuminating the objects, the less color, texture, and detail that can be seen. Colors do not, as most people think, dissolve into black in the background. In actuality, they fade out into a middle gray. Just look out at any scene where

you have a great expanse or can see a far distance, and you will notice that as things recede into space, they lose their color and become blurred.

Transparency and Space

When working with color, we tend to think about working with solid opaque areas of color. Dense applications or sections of color will work the same way that shapes work in creating spatial relationships. If two solid shapes of color overlap one another, the top shape will appear to be in front of the other shape. This is the traditional concept of overlapping elements defining spatial relationships. However, if the sector where the two patches of color overlap is transparent, then it is nearly impossible to tell which is in front of the other. This creates an arbitrary or ambiguous sense of space. For a hue to look transparent, the middle

Figure 4-15.
Atmospheric perspective illustration.
This photograph of the Blue Ridge Mountains is a perfect example of atmospheric perspective. The warmth of the green hues creates the appearance of a foreground. As we look off into the distance, the green color becomes desaturated, gradually moving from deep green to a cool blue gray. The mountaintops dissolve into a neutral as they move farther back in space.
© Steven Bleicher

hue must be a visual mixture and middle ground of the two hues expressed. This can be achieved through a middle mixture of hue or value within the same hue. This is one of the underlying concepts that allows artists to create many optical illusions (Figure 4-16).

The material an artist uses may also create transparent or translucent effects. Watercolors and thin washes of oil paint are transparent. Many other materials can also have diaphanous qualities, creating visual illusions of space. Katharina Grosse used plastics in *Untitled* (Figure 4-17). Here the material gives the work its transparent quality. As layers of acrylic paint are built up more opaque colors will appear. In addition, the see-through nature of material can further be enhanced by the use of lighter hues. The lighter the hue (or tint) of the material used, the more translucent it

will be. Conversely, the darker the material, the more opaque and dense the effect that will be achieved.

Color Harmonies

Color harmonies, color ways, and color schemes are all different terms for the same thing. They are the ways in which artists and designers pick and use a combination of hues, knowing that they will work together in a composition. In a sense,

Figure 4-16.
An example of transparency and how it affects spatial relationships. In the image on the left, the middle ground of the yellow-green allows the illusion of the cylinder to flip back and forth. In the image on the right, the solid areas of yellow and green give us a fixed and constant view of the cylinder.
© Steven Bleicher

Figure 4-17.
Katharina Grosse, Ohne Titel, 2005, acrylic on canvas, 204,5 × 123 cm, private collection, Berlin. Grosse uses the transparent layers of acrylic paint in creating overlapping planes of color. It is virtually impossible to begin to figure out which layer of color is on top of the other. This creates an amorphous sense of space that constantly fluctuates between foreground and middle ground. Only the white background seems somewhat constant. What do you think?
Copyright © VG Bild-Kunst, Bonn, and Katharina Grosse. Photo by Olaf Bergmann, and courtesy of Galerie Conrads, Düsseldorf.

Figure 4-18.
A color wheel showing an analogous color scheme of red-violet, violet, and blue-violet.
© Steven Bleicher

wheel, yellow-green, green, and blue-green are analogous. As the color wheel gets larger, the range within an analogous grouping can become much more limited. In some large wheels with more than twelve steps, the range is sometimes increased to four hues next to each other. The key is that they are always directly next to each other. This color scheme has the least contrast. Because the colors are so close in hue, they almost seem to blend into one another and can make differentiating form more difficult. This is especially true in the cooler range of hues.

We tend to think of these color ways as working only with paint and pigments, but they are also used in other forms of art, from performance to conceptual art. James Turrell used an analogous scheme in *To be Sung* (Figure 4-19). The cool hues add to the emotional aspects of the work.

they take the guesswork out of choosing color. These harmonies can easily be seen in their relationships to each other on the color wheel. These relationships reinforce the importance of why hues are placed in a circular format.

The most closely associated color way or harmony is an **analogous** color scheme. An analogous group is any three hues directly next to each other on the color wheel (Figure 4-18). In the twelve-step color

Vanishing Boundaries

If two hues are very similar to each other in value and saturation, they will have a dramatic visual impact and interaction with

Figure 4-19.
James Turrell, *To be Sung*, 1994.
Still photograph of a live performance.
Turrell uses an analogous color scheme of red-violet, violet, and blue-violet. These hues create a cool, dark mood in his performance piece, adding to its evocative nature.
© James Turrell Studio
Photo courtesy of Almine Rech Gallery, Paris-Brusselles.

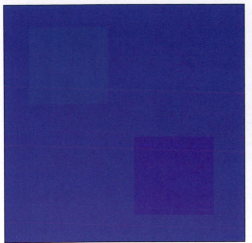

Figure 4-20.
An illustration of the principle of vanishing boundaries. Notice that the two squares in the larger blue box are barely visible. They are close in value and saturation to the larger square and seem to blend into the background.
© Steven Bleicher

Figure 4-21.
Mark Rothko, *Maroon on Blue,* 1957-60.
The edge where the deep blue meets the black seems to dissolve and disappear. This is due in part to the inherent value of the blue, which is very dark and nearly black in value. The vibrant red appears to be luminous because it is the lightest and brightest part of the canvas, and it creates a counterpoint to the dark blue and back areas.
© 2010 Kate Rothko Prizel & Christopher Rothko/ Artists Rights Society (ARS), New York.
Photo courtesy of Galerie Beyeler.

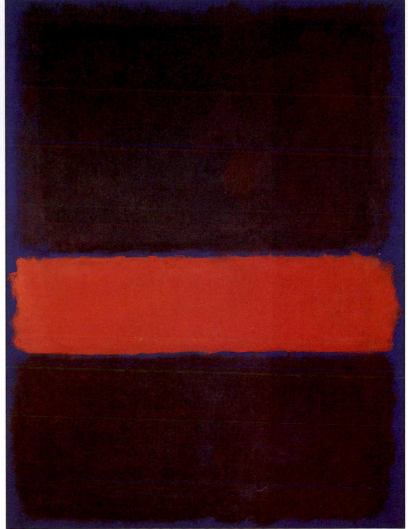

each other. Where the two hues meet, the line or boundary between them appears to vanish (Figure 4-20). This effect is common when working with analogous schemes or with colors that are very close in value or saturation. This visual result can be achieved with both bright and dull hues alike; all that matters is that the hues must be close in value and intensity.

To eliminate this visual blending, simply change one of the colors, and make it either darker or lighter than the other hue or adjust the saturation. In either case, the object is to create a higher level of contrast, thereby eliminating the effect. Mark Rothko purposely created paintings that used the concept of vanishing boundaries as a key element in some of his work (Figure 4-21). At first glance, the painting looks as if it is two-toned—red and black. The areas of deep, intense dark blue are not noticeable. Upon closer examination, the viewer can pick out the thin blue area surrounding the red rectangle. The influence of Albers's color studies is clearly evident in Rothko's work and use of color.

Figure 4-22.
A color-wheel showing
a complementary color
scheme of green and red.
It is no wonder they are
used as Christmas colors.
As complementary
hues they intensify each
other, increasing their
brightness, and are
an eye-catching color
combination.
© Steven Bleicher

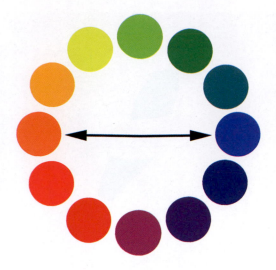

Complements

Two colors that are exactly opposite from each other on the color wheel are known as **complements** (Figure 4-22). They represent the highest form of contrast within the color wheel. If the hues picked are equal in value and saturation and are placed next to each other in a design, the colors will appear to vibrate. They will also appear to be brighter and more intense. This is also known as **complementary contrast**. Complementary contrast is a reaction in the viewer's eye and not with the actual pigments. The cones within the eye are not at rest and the visual color vibration is the result. They could also be thought of as a balance between warm and cool colors.

In any complementary pair, one hue will be warm and the other cool. The Impressionists and Postimpressionists were masters of the use of complementary pairs in their works. This is one of the reasons why the colors in their canvases are so bright and vivid and have an atmospheric luminescent quality. A more modern example of this can be seen in Figure 4-23, *Blue Ridge in the Distance* by Wolf Kahn. Here the orange and blue contrast, intensify, and heighten each other. This intensity makes the blue patch in the upper right portion of the painting appear to float on the picture plane.

As we have seen in the previous chapter, another phenomenon caused by viewing one half of a complementary pair is that it causes the cones in the eye to be overstimulated. If the person then looks at a white or neutral color, the other half of the complement pair will appear or will show up as

Figure 4-23.
Wolf Kahn, *Blue Ridge in the Distance*, 2005. Kahn uses the complementary pair of orange and blue. The use of complements intensifies the two hues and creates the effect of the figure floating on the background. They are so bold in their visual effect that we almost fail to notice the pale tint of yellow-orange in the picture. The use of cool hues also moves those elements to the background of the composition.
Art © Wolf Kahn/Licensed by VAGA, New York, NY.

Figure 4-24.
Jasper Johns, *Flag*, 1965.
Johns's painting illustrates the concept of successive contrast or afterimage. Stare at the white dot on the flag for 40 seconds and then look at the black dot on the bottom rectangle. You should see the flag in its correct colors.
Art © Jasper Johns/ Licensed by VAGA, New York, NY.

an afterimage (Figure 4-24). This action is also known as **successive contrast**. Jasper Johns used this phenomenon in his painting, *Flag*. If you stare intensely at the green and black flag for about 40 seconds, and then look below it at the black point, you will see an afterimage of the flag in red, white, and blue.

Two hues directly opposite each other on the color wheel are the most simple and fundamental use of complementary colors. But there are more intricate and

Figure 4-25.
A color wheel showing a split complement color scheme of blue, yellow-orange and red-orange the same hues used in the photograph of the installation.
© Steven Bleicher

the center leg. The additional color gives the artist more material to work with and allows for more complexity in design. Sandy Skoglund used these colors in her *Revenge of the Goldfish* (Figure 4-26) to heighten the brilliance of the hues and create a more dynamic composition.

In a **double split complementary** color scheme, two colors next to each other and their two corresponding complements are selected (Figure 4-27). This allows for an even greater variation and complexity in design.

elaborate variations. In a **split complement** (Figure 4-25) instead of selecting both opposites, one end is selected and at the other end the two colors adjacent are picked. They form an upside down "Y" shape or one that resembles a peace symbol without

Neutrals

If two complements are mixed together, they form a **neutral** (Figure 4-28). When white is added to a neutral, it becomes almost gray in color. The Impressionists used this technique to make grays and tone down or desaturate hues. Unlike the flat

Figure 4-26.
Sandy Skoglund,
Revenge of the Goldfish,
1981.
Skoglund uses the split complementary hues at equal intensity to produce a visual color vibration, which adds to the surreal dream-like quality of the imagery.
Photo © 1981 Sandy Skoglund.

Figure 4-27.
A color wheel showing a double split complement scheme of yellow and violet paired up with its neighbor of yellow-green and red-violet.
© Steven Bleicher

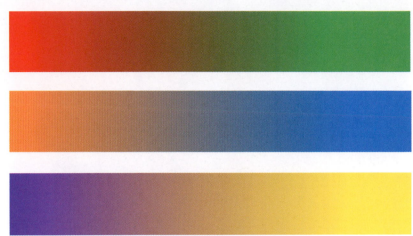

Figure 4-28.
The illustration shows three sets of complements—red/green, orange/blue, and violet/yellow—blending into one another to create their respective neutrals.
© Steven Bleicher

gray produced by adding white to black, the artist can use this process to develop either warm-based grays or cool-based grays. Romare Bearden (Figure 4-29) uses a neutral mixture of blue and orange as well as shades of orange to create a full range of browns in his composition *Early Morning*. The picture tells a narrative story of young man prepar-ing to start a long day of work on the farm. Much of Bearden's work is autobiographical and as in this piece evokes memories of the artist's early childhood. His collage work also has a cubist influence, which is especially recognizable in the patterning of the boy's shirt and shifting planes or views of the table.

Figure 4-29:
Romare Bearden (1911–1988), *Early Morning*, 1964. Collage on board, 9 ½× 10 ⅞ in. (15 ⅝ × 17 × 1 in. framed). Bearden uses neutralizations of blue and orange as the dominant color scheme in his mixed media creation using both collaged elements and paint. The brighter orange hues are used as highlights and visually advance on the picture plane to create a warm foreground.
Art © Romare Bearden Foundation/Licensed by VAGA, New York, NY. Photo courtesy of the New Britain Museum of American Art, Friends Purchase Fund, 1985.1.

Figure 4-30.
A color wheel showing a triad. Here yellow, red, and blue (which are also the primary hues) make up the simplest grouping of three hues equally spaced apart from one another.
© Steven Bleicher

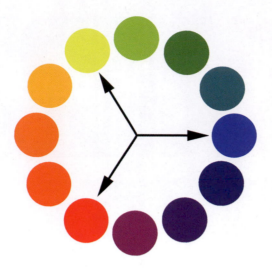

Figure 4-31:
Roy Lichtenstein, *As I Opened Fire*, 1964. Lichtenstein used a limited color palette of flat simple hues in most of his work. In *As I Opened Fire*, he uses a triadic color scheme of primary hues to create harmony between the images. The use of this color scheme acts as a unifying element and brings the three canvases that make up the composition (or triptych) together as a whole. Within the triad, tints and shades of the hues may be used, as long as the color remains visually within the tricolor schema. In this piece, Lichtenstein uses a tone of red in all three panels. This allows the artist a wider range of color choices within this limited hue grouping.
© Estate of Roy Lichtenstein.
Photo courtesy of DeA Picture Library/Art Resource, NY.

Triads

Like the name implies, a **triad** is composed of three hues. Each of these hues must be of equal distance from the other on the color wheel (Figure 4-30). Another way for us to remember the makeup of a triad is to think of it as an equilateral triangle placed inside of the wheel or the shape of a Mercedes-Benz hood ornament. Each color or location touched by a point of the triangle would represent a hue. The most common and simplest form of this color scheme would be the three primary hues or the three secondary hues. But intermediate hues can also make up a triad. Roy Lichtenstein used a triad in *As I Opened Fire* (Figure 4-31). The intensely saturated primary hues add to the graphic nature of the piece and are reminiscent of action hero comic books. The simple bold use of unmodulated color and elements from popular culture were thematic of Pop art. The secondary hues can also make up a triadic group. You could pick three intermediate colors to form a triad, as long as they are spaced an equal distance from one another. The real variable factor is how many steps or hues comprise the color wheel you are using as reference, and that

the hues selected are spaced the same distance from each other.

Tetrads

If a square were placed inside the color wheel, each of the corners of the box would touch upon a hue. The hues touched on create or form a **tetrad** (Figure 4-32). Like a triad, each hue must be an equal distance from one another. A tetrad will always consist of one set of complements made up of a primary and a secondary hue, as well as two intermediate hues for the second pair of complements. Of all of the color ways, the tetrad offers the artist the greatest range of hues and contrast to work with.

The Bezold Effect

Wilhem von Bezold was a scientist involved in textile production. In his work with weavers, he noticed that if one color was changed in a design, it could have a radical effect on the overall composition and feeling of the design. By changing the dominant hue in a pattern, the entire composition could be modified, as illustrated in Figure 4-33. While this effect is most easily recognizable in a pattern, the concept will work in any composition where you have multiple or repeated images of the same subject. By

Figure 4-32.
A color wheel showing a tetrad color scheme. This tetrad consists of yellow-green, orange, blue, and red-violet.
© Steven Bleicher

changing a dominant color, the appearance of shapes and their relationships to each other can alter the overall composition. This is the power and strength of color.

Simultaneous Contrast

Our perception of color is affected by the environment in which we see that hue. Because a color is rarely seen by itself, the surrounding colors will influence and, in many cases, alter the color perceived. This visual phenomenon is known as **simultaneous contrast** and occurs when one color is seen on differing backgrounds. It is commonly associated with complements,

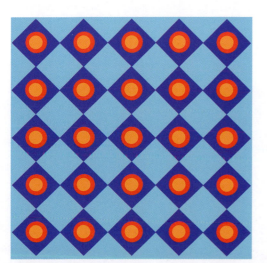

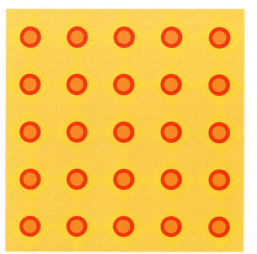

Figure 4-33.
An illustration of the Bezold effect. By changing the dominant hue in a design or artwork, the artist can completely change its look and feel. In this example, the design is the same; only the blue diamonds have been changed to yellow, producing a dramatically different effect.
© Steven Bleicher

but it can also occur in any situation when two or more hues are placed next to each other. This is because the appearance of color is relative and is always affected by the surrounding hues. For example, when a hue of yellow is placed next to a neutral gray, as seen in Figure 4-34, the gray will appear to have a cool or violet cast to it. If that same gray is then placed on a violet ground, it will have a warm or yellowish cast to it. A similar color transformation will occur if we place the same midvalue red hue on contrasting backgrounds, as seen in the lower half of Figure 4-34. The hue in the square literally seems to change color. On the darker background, the midvalue color will appear lighter than it really is, and on the light background, the opposite will occur. In addition, when two hues of equal value and intensity are placed next to each other, they tend to cause a visual vibration at the edges where they meet. This intensifies each hue.

There is an illustrious story of an interior designer working for a famous movie star (who we will leave nameless). The movie star hated yellow or any hue with any type of a yellow tinge to it. She wanted her new home decorated in various hues, shades, and tints of violet, the color of royalty. The interior designer went to work creating the new furnishings. Months later the actor toured her new home and then angrily called the designer, upset by the yellow-toned carpet selected. The interior designer was stunned; he had ordered a light, neutral gray carpet and even checked his invoices to make sure the correct flooring was delivered. So what went wrong? The designer forgot the law of simultaneous contrast. The light gray carpet appeared to have a hint of yellow when it was surrounded by all of the various hues of violet. The viewer's eye automatically placed the complement hue in the neutral (gray carpet) and visually turned it into a yellow tone. This is the same concept shown in the previous example. It really was nothing more than a trick of the eye.

Figure 4-34.
An illustration of two forms of simultaneous contrast. In the top example, a neutral gray is placed on two complementary backgrounds. The gray square seems to be completely different, depending upon the hue of the background. In the bottom example, the same red hue as seen in the stripe below it is placed on contrasting red backgrounds. Although they are the same color, the red square appears to be very different in each. This is an important concept to keep in mind when working with color.
© Steven Bleicher

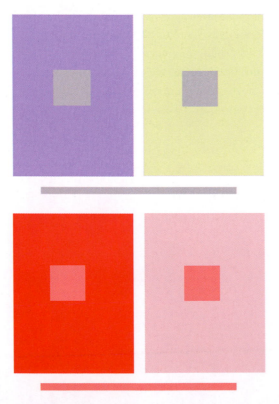

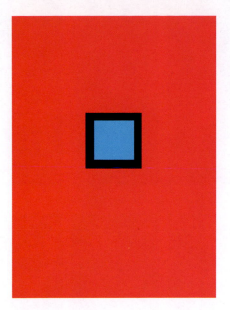 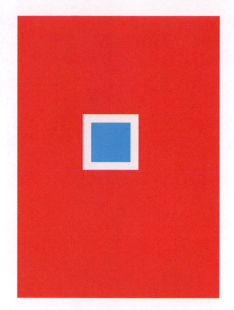

Figure 4-35.
In this illustration, when the blue square is surrounded by the black outline it condenses the color and form, making it look smaller than the square surrounded by the white. The blue square with the white boarder seems to be larger, visually encroaching into the white area.
© Steven Bleicher

Interactions of Black and White

Most of the color studies and interactions we have observed so far deal with one color placed next to or on top of another. For these reactions to occur, the hues in question must be placed directly next to or on top of each other. This is because colors react quite differently when surrounded by either black or white, as demonstrated in Figure 4-35. If a color is seen against a black outline, it frames the hue and constrains its visual presence. It is as if the black frame is holding the hue in and compressing it. But if the color is viewed against a white outline, the hue seems to visually expand into the white area. Even though the white boundary isolates the hue from the background, it allows the color to visually swell into its space.

Value Contrast

Closely related to simultaneous contrast is the concept of **value contrast**. One of the easiest ways to change the look of a color is to place it on a contrasting background. Colors may appear very different, depending upon the background they are placed on or next to, as illustrated in Figure 4-36. Placing a hue on a dark background isolates it and makes it appear lighter, and it also makes the lighter hue

appear larger. Conversely, placing the same colored hue on a light background makes it look darker and smaller. However, there is no reaction if the background and foreground colors are of equal value. There must be a contrast between the hues to achieve this effect.

Luminosity and Luminescence

Another element in the appearance of light and color is **luminosity**. Luminosity is the perceived light given off by an object and goes hand in hand with value. In artistic terms, it most often refers to the lightest part of an image and can be created through the use of high contrast lighting such as chiaroscuro. Contrasting a bright, intense hue off a darker, less saturated cooler hue will also produce a similar effect.

As seen previously in Figure 4-21, Mark Rothko's work was renowned for its luminous quality. In *Maroon on Blue*, the loosely constructed red rectangle seems to glow. By placing the form on a very dark, warm background and outlining it with a very thin, intense cool blue, the red area becomes a focal point. Because it is the lightest and most saturated color, it appears to advance on the picture plane and exhibits a shimmering quality.

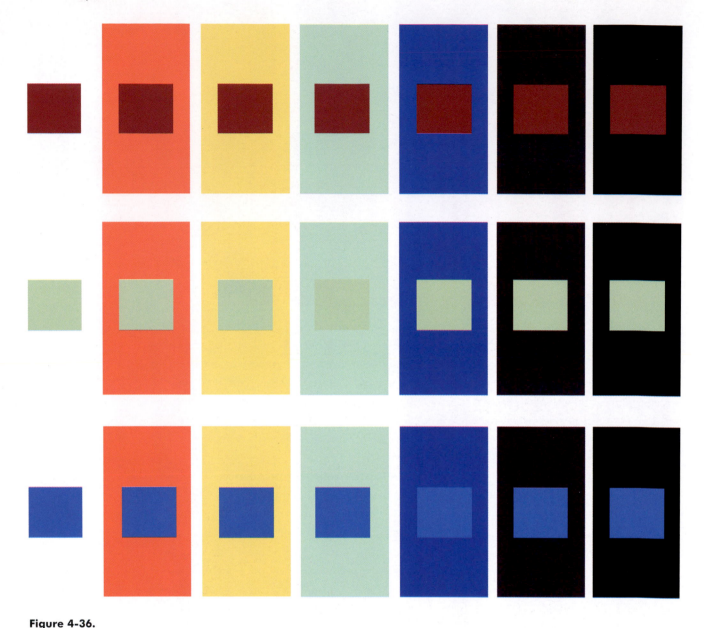

Figure 4-36.
An example of value contrast. Notice how the color changes depending upon the value and temperature of the background hue.
© Steven Bleicher

The more light that appears to be emitted by the colors or object, the closer it will seem to the viewer and the brighter the effect will be. The brightness decreases as its source moves back on the picture plane and is farther away from the viewer.

Luminosity can also be created through the use of actual lighting (or use of lamps) within the work of art, as seen in Figure 4-37. The light given off by the object can be measured in candles or **candelas**; however, in artistic terms it is not thought of as a measurable or quantifiable element. It is the objective measurement of the brightness of a surface that is reflecting or transmitting light. In more technical terms, luminescence is the emanation of light from a source that is not hot enough or does not produce enough heat to be incandescent like a light bulb. Bioluminescence refers to the light emitted by a living organism, most normally insects or fish. If you think of the firefly, the light produced in its tail section is an excellent example of bioluminescence.

Figure 4-37.
Hiromi Takizawa, *Crossing the Pacific Ocean*, 2007.
In Takizawa's work, the luminous quality of the work is created by the use of neon light. The lamps give off a soft glow that expands out onto the picture plane. Unlike the visual luminescence in Rothko's work, here Takizawa works with actual light.
Photo courtesy of Hiromi Takizawa.

Summary

Color harmonies afford the artist and the designer set rules for choosing colors. They take the guesswork out of hue selection and give the artist some guidelines for their use. The color wheel is central to understanding these relationships. Color harmonies are established based on the relationship of one hue to another and the corresponding position of the hues on the wheel. The wheel can also be divided into warm and cool hues, but the visual temperature of any given color is relative and may change depending on the hue selected for comparison.

Color can also create spatial relationships. The proper use of a color can make things look bigger or smaller, lighter or heavier. If the hues are close in value or intensity, it can blur the boundary between the two color areas. Colors can be made to appear transparent by selecting or mixing a visual middle or mixture of the two main hues.

Due to the complex interaction of colors to one another, you must take great care in selecting them. Your specific choices can make or break the design or desired effect. By understanding the interplay of color mixtures and combinations, you will be able to create more complex, evocative, and effective artworks and designs.

Pigments, Colorants, and Paints: Chapter 5

5

Art-making began as the first prehistoric humans took charred sticks from the fire and began to scratch markings onto a rock or cave wall (Figure 5-1). Through trial and error, or maybe purely by accident, these individuals found that the grease from their hands or the liquid from their saliva made the charcoal adhere better to the rough surface. Not only did it bond to the surface more easily, but it flowed in a smoother, more graceful manner. This could be one explanation of how the first mediums or binders were created to aid in the application of color.

As these early humans looked around at their environment, they soon realized that other things—such as plants, earth, and clay—could be ground up and mixed with these liquids to add color to the black outlines. This mixture of simple coloring agents formed the most rudimentary pigments. Through imagination and experimentation, they found new minerals, plants, and animal products to produce an even wider range of hues. Ever since that day, artists, designers, chemists, and dyers have been on a quest to find new pigments to create a wider array of colors.

Today we have many choices of materials and mediums to work with, including oils, acrylics, and watercolors. Artists can choose to work with color in a stick form with pastels, colored pencils, and markers. The computer has opened up a whole new range of color media possibilities with a wide variety of inks available to use in the printing process. There are dyes for cloth and fabrics. And there are even more nontraditional coloring agents used for body decoration

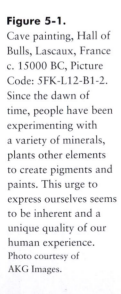

Figure 5-1.
Cave painting, Hall of Bulls, Lascaux, France c. 15000 BC, Picture Code: 5FK-L12-B1-2. Since the dawn of time, people have been experimenting with a variety of minerals, plants other elements to create pigments and paints. This urge to express ourselves seems to be inherent and a unique quality of our human experience. Photo courtesy of AKG Images.

Figure 5-2.
The history of the paint tube from the early 1800s to 1905. Before the advent of the metal tube in 1840, paints were sold in pig bladders. They had a tendency to dry out easily and were very delicate to work with. The metal paint tube also allowed artists to leave the confines of the studio and paint on location.
Photo courtesy of Winsor & Newton.

and tattooing. Artists should experiment with a variety of media to find the ones they are most comfortable with and that can best express their unique vision.

A Short History

Dating back to the earliest recorded artworks such as the cave paintings found in southern Europe, the images created show a limited range of hues. Reds, yellows, earth tones, and black dominated the prehistoric palette. These colors were derived from clay, minerals, and burnt or charred animal bones. Animal fats, saliva, and even urine were used as vehicles to aid in the application and adhesion of the colorants.

James Rand invented the first paint tubes (as we know them today) in 1840. Prior to this, artists' paints were sold or stored in pig bladders, which are similar to the natural casings used in making sausage (Figure 5-2). They were bulky and hard to work with. Imagine having to carry your paints around in something as fragile and awkward as a sausage. Two years later, Winsor & Newton began marketing and selling its paint in these new tubes. This was the time of the industrial revolution, which also brought other new innovations to the art world. New hues were developed and mass produced, includ-

ing cerulean blue in 1860 and alizarin a few years later in 1868. These new hues had a profound impact on the Impressionists who were quick to pick up on and use these new colors. Artists have always been interested in new technology as it relates to making art, and the Impressionists were no different. Some of the variety and intensity of the colors found in their work can be directly attributed to the new paints being developed and produced during this time.

Pigments

Paints are made up of two basic parts: a pigment and a vehicle. **Pigments** (Figure 5-3) are the powdered agents or elements that make up the colored part or hue of the paint. They can be made from a wide range

Figure 5-3.
Dry powder pigments. Pigments are the agents that give paints, pastels, and ink their color.
Photo courtesy of Winsor & Newton.

of natural materials, including flowers, plants, and minerals such as oxides. Today many companies use synthetic or artificial colorants. Whatever the pigment is, it must be ground up as finely as possible so that each particle can be completely coated with the vehicle. The finer the pigment can be ground, the better the vehicle can surround and coat each tiny particle.

Vehicles

The **vehicle** is a liquid or gel that combines with the pigment and suspends it in solution for application. It should completely coat each molecule of pigment and allow it to move and flow freely and evenly. During the Middle Ages, egg yoke and water were used as transporting agents for tempera. Each medium has it own vehicle. Oil paint, as the name suggests, uses oil as a vehicle—normally linseed, walnut, or safflower oil. Acrylics use plastic polymers, and watercolor uses gum arabic. This means that you cannot mix one type of paint with another because their vehicles are different; for example, you can't mix watercolors with oil paints. Since oil and water don't mix, there is no common transportation agent.

Professional Grade Versus Student Grade

If you go into any art supply store, you will find a vast selection of brands of paints by several different manufacturers. Golden, Winsor & Newton, Liquitex, Grumbacher, and many more companies fill the shelves with their products. Even within one manufacturer there can be several categories or grades of paint, each with their own subbrand name. Some grades are more expensive than others. Artist or professional series paints cost more than student grades, and there can even be lesser grades for hobbyists and children.

So why are there so many different grades of paint? One of the first considerations is the paint archival or the number of years it will stay true to its color. As a professional artist or designer, you want to be sure that for years to come the hue will remain constant and true without fading, yellowing, cracking, or decomposing with age. The student or hobbyist may not really care if fifty years from now the painting degenerates with the passing of time.

Along with archivability is the amount and quality of the actual pigments used. The higher the quality and greater amount of pigment, the more expensive it will be. Many low-cost paints use synthetic colorants. The genuine cadmiums of professional grade paints may be replaced by less costly "hues," which are created by using a mixture of several pigments to approximate the color of the pure cadmium.

Another reason paints can vary in price is the manufacturing process itself. The finer the pigment is milled or ground, the more expensive it will be (Figure 5-4).

Figure 5-4.
An example of paint being milled. The more times the paint goes through the milling process, the finer the pigment is ground. Milling also informally surrounds and bonds the pigment to the vehicle. Photo courtesy of Winsor & Newton.

In the highest quality paints, the mixture may have been milled three or more times to ensure that the pigment takes on the maximum amount of vehicle possible. In poorly milled oil paint, for instance, the oil may separate out and float to the top of the tube while the pigment settles to the bottom. If you have ever opened a tube of paint and instead of it having a nice thick toothpaste-like consistency the paint runs out of the tube as soon as the cap is removed, you have experienced a poorly milled product.

The question then becomes: Is one paint really better than another? The answer varies. First, what is the intention of the artist? If you are a professional artist, you will want to spend the additional money to ensure the lasting quality of your creation, as well as the ease of application. As a student, the more reasonably priced paints will suffice and give good quality results. If it's a matter of being able to afford the lesser grade paint or not being able to paint at all, then the answer is to buy what you can afford. Artists such as Van Gogh and Picasso (when he was young) were more concerned with having paint and being able to express themselves than worrying about having the most expensive of materials to work with.

Reading a Tube of Paint

There is a great deal of useful information on your tube or jar of paint if you take the time to read it. All tubes or jars of paint should list the type of vehicle used, and the pigment and lightfastness rating (Figures 5-5a and 5b). These are key elements the artist or designer must understand. The pigment listing should be specific and show the chemical class and color index number. The color index is an international system for identifying colorants. The lightfastness rating will tell you the color's resistance to fading or changing color

Figure 5-5a and 5-5b.
A tube of Winsor & Newton cadmium red paint. Reading the tube of paint can give you important information, including the name of the hue and series or quality level of the paint. The flattened label of a tube of Winsor & Newton cadmium red paint. The label also provides information on the exact pigments and vehicles used, as well as information on the permanence and lightfastness of the paint. Both photos courtesy of Winsor & Newton.

when it is exposed to daylight. Colors that are not colorfast and are affected by exposure to sunlight are known as **fugitive colors**. All tubes and jars of paint should also have the weight or size clearly marked. This will usually be in both ounces and the metric equivalent. The last item that virtually

Figure 5-6a.
An example of the variety of different brush sizes within one brush tip shape. The number on the brush corresponds to its size; the larger the number, the bigger the brush.
Photo courtesy of Winsor & Newton.

Figure 5-6b.
A person attaching the hairs of a brush to the ferrule. The best brushes are handmade and hand trimmed.
Photo courtesy of Winsor & Newton.

all paints sold today have is a seal by the Art and Creative Materials Institute certifying that they meet all standard health requirements.

Other items may also be indicated on a tube or jar of paint. These depend upon the manufacturer and type of paint. They can include the type of finish ranging from gloss, satin, or matte and are most normally found on acrylic or water-based media. Permanence, which is different from lightfastness, may also be indicated. This relates to the archivability of the paint or how long it will actually last. Professional series paints have a longer life than student or hobbyist paints. Some acrylic will also have the viscosity of the paint listed. This tells the user how thick the paint will be when it comes directly out of the tube or jar. Naturally, jar paints tend to be more viscous than tube paint.

Brushes

There are three parts to any brush: the hair, ferrule, and handle (Figures 5-6a and 5-6b). Probably the least important is the handle. As long as it's made out of a good strong wood, there is very little difference among them. Some companies are now producing ergonomic handles that conform to the shape of the hand. One thing to check is if the handle is drying out or has any thin hairline cracks. This may mean that it is old and drying out and my not hold up well or last very long.

The ferrule is the metal barrel of the brush. The best ones are seamless and made from brass or copper, which will not rust. The hair is the key element. The type of hair used will make a great difference in your work. The finest hairs are Kolinsky red sable from Russia. They hold a sharp pointed tip and are very resilient. Weasel is a good and less expensive alternative.

Squirrel is another alternative, but it has much less "snap" to it. It is considered a good choice for working with very liquid paints, inks, or dyes. Camel hair is a manufacturers' trade name for squirrel, horse, or even goat hair. No, there's no actual camel hair—it's too coarse. The name merely refers to the color of the bristles or hairs. Synthetic brushes are getting better and better every year as new artificial materials are developed and may be a reasonable choice for the beginning student painter who may be cost conscious.

More about Paints and Pigments

There are other factors or characteristics to consider with selecting colors. The masstone is how that specific hue of paint looks in a thick layer (Figure 5-7). When applied thickly the color is very solid, dense, and opaque. The undertone is how that same hue of paint would look in a very thin layer. When the paint is applied in a thin layer the true characteristics of the color emerge and become visible. The same color can look quite different when applied in a heavy impasto or in a very thin layer or wash.

The transparency of a particular paint is usually not a matter of how much pigment there is, but is actually a physical characteristic of the colorant itself. Some pigments are more opaque or transparent than others.

There are three major types of paint: oils, acrylics, and watercolors. They are the most widely used mediums. That is not to say that there aren't a number of other possibilities, including tempera, encaustic, and interference colors. Each of them has its own unique properties, chemistry, and uses. In addition, each requires a different type of brush to aid in the application of the paint to paper, board, or canvas.

Figure 5-7.
An example of the masstone and undertone of Permanent Alizarin Crimson. The masstone is the way the paint looks when it's applied in a heavy thick manner. The undertone is when the paint is applied as thinly as possible showing it at its most transparent point.
© Steven Bleicher

Water-Based Paints

Water-based paints can be divided into two major groups: gouache and watercolors. While they are both water-based mediums (meaning they can be thinned with water), there are a few basic differences. As for their similarities, they both use the same vehicle—gum arabic, the best of which comes from the acacia tree. The most highly prized comes from one source of trees in Senegal. What makes gum arabic special is its ability to mix easily with water and be totally transparent. This clarity of the vehicle allows all of the true color of the pigment of the paint to show through.

One disadvantage to watercolors and gouache is the way they bond with paper. The vehicle and pigment actually seep into and bond with the paper surface, or tooth. Because of this, they cannot be scraped or wiped off if you make a mistake the same way oils or acrylics can.

Figure 5-8.
Elyse "Lee" Weiss, *Escarpment*, 2000. Weiss' large-scale watercolors may look abstract, but are really close-ups, a detailed look at nature and natural elements. In this recent series she has become interested in rock surfaces. She finds their warmth in opposition from the cool hues of nature; water, leaves, and snow.
Photo courtesy of Lee Weiss.

Watercolors are transparent and work extremely well by building up layers of color using thin washes of paint (Figure 5-8). They come in both tube and cake form, and as their name implies, they take very well to water and can be thinned more than any other type of paint.

Gouache is opaque and gives the artist nice solid, dense areas of color. They are super loaded with pigments, which also helps to give them their rich full color. They also contain either chalk or calcium carbonate that gives the paint a dull matte surface with absolutely no surface sheen. Most often used by designers and illustrators, gouache was preferred over all other mediums because

of its matte finish. In the past (only about twenty-five years ago in precomputer times), artworks had to be photographed with a stat camera to be used in any type of production such as posters, magazines, or book covers. The dull matte finish made lighting easier because the artist and photographers no longer had to worry about any glossy reflection from the surface of the media. Other mediums, such as oils or acrylics, have a glossy shiny surface, which creates reflections of the studio lights on the surface of the artwork. Another major factor in gouache is that it is self-leveling, which means that as it dries and sets, it flattens itself out to create a smooth even surface. This also makes it ideal for reproduction, because the artist does not have to worry about correctly lighting an uneven surface.

There are three types of paper you can use when you work with watercolors. Hot-pressed papers are actually run through heated rollers in the manufacturing process, which seals the pores of the paper. This creates a fine smooth finish, but adds to the overall cost of the paper. Cold-pressed paper has a rougher surface and does not have a smooth feel, which allows it to absorb more of the liquid medium. Rough paper is the most textured and is excellent for creating dramatic effects.

Oils

As stated previously, oil paints use linseed and other natural oils as their vehicle. Kehinde Wiley uses thin applications of oils to build up the surface and give his work a richly hued quality (Figure 5-9). This is also known as glazing. To thin oils, turpentine or mineral spirits are used. Nowadays more people opt for a product called turpinoid that has the same thinning properties, but doesn't have the noxious smell of turpentine. In either case, both should be used in a well-ventilated space since they are highly flammable.

However, there is a new product on the market, introduced a few years ago—water-soluble oil paints. This may sound like a misnomer, but they are true oils colors that have been specially developed to be thinned with water or mediums. They clean up very easily with just soap and water. They can even be mixed with traditional oil paint on a 2:1 ratio: two parts water-based oil to one part traditional oil paint.

Figure 5-9.
Kehinde Wiley, *Napoleon Leading the Army over the Alps,* 2005. Oil on Canvas 108" × 108" (9' × 9') The title echoes a painting by Jacques-Louis David. Wiley reinvents the historical equestrian portrait substituting a young African American man dressed in urban street wear for the traditional uniform clad heroic figure. He elevates the status of the sitter and in doing so asserts black cultural identity while confronting the traditions of Western painting.
© Kehinde Wiley.
Used by permission

Figure 5-10.
Chris Vasell, *Implosion Commission (To The People That Know That This is Nowhere)*, 2009. Acrylic on canvas Two Panels, 107 × 90 inches each. This diptych use uses soft pastel hues in a manner reminiscent of the psychedelic or Op art movements. These large-scale paintings overwhelm and envelop the audience in what the artist sees as an almost mystical viewing experience.
Photo courtesy of the Artist and Blum & Poe., Los Angeles Photo Credit: Joshua White.

Acrylics

Acrylic paints were developed in the 1940s and really came into their own as true artists' materials in the 1950s and 1960s. They use an acrylic polymer resin as their vehicle and can be thinned with water or mediums, depending upon the desired effect. With acrylics, as the water evaporates, the resin molecules line up in a string formation and chemically bond to each other, creating a hard permanent durable surface. One nice thing about acrylics is that they are very forgiving to the novice painter. If you make a mistake, simply let the paint dry and reapply the new color over it. Because the paint dries hard and permanent, there is no fear that the undercoat will interact or bleed into the next application of paint. Acrylics have a very shiny glossy surface, but this can be changed with the addition of a matte medium. Chris Vasell uses a matte medium in his soft pastel tinted organic abstract paintings (Figure 5-10). Placing the paintings in a corner of the gallery space they appear at first glance to be mirror images. It's only upon closer inspection that the viewer realizes they are really very different, created using approximate symmetry.

Encaustics

Encaustic painting, also known as "hot wax" painting, saw a resurgence in the 1990s. The practice dates back to fifth century B.C. Greece. Its use may have developed out of the Grecian practice of coating their

Figure 5-11.
Jane Nodine, *la camicia del graffiti.01*, 2006. Nodine is very interested in works that incorporate naturally occurring marks and patterns made from iron oxidation (rust) and burn marks. She produces marks that are applied to panels between layers of paper, wax, and encaustic medium. As the layers develop, some elements become obscured in the hazy surface of the wax as others become more evident
Photo courtesy of Jane Nodine.

ships with wax for waterproofing. These war ships were then elaborately decorated as mentioned by Homer in his account of the battle of Troy. One of the most famous uses of encaustic was in the Fayum mummy portraits dating back to about 100–300 A.D.

In encaustic painting wax is melted and mixed with pigments and then applied to a surface such as wood or canvas. The painting can be reheated and worked back into as needed (Figure 5-11). Additional colors can be layered and combined with collage materials. The surface can be textured or polished to a high gloss. Encaustic recipes can include damar resin, linseed oil, or even paraffin. The durability of encaustic is due to the fact that beeswax is impervious to moisture and will not deteriorate. Encaustic paintings do not have to be varnished or protected by glass.

Inks and Printer Inks

Inks come in several different types including permanent inks used for drawing and special inks used for printing computer-generated images. In the 1890s, Winsor & Newton was among the first to start mass-producing inks. Inks are made from dyes mixed with a shellac binder that give inks their permanent water-resistant characteristics. Artists should take care when using inks since they are made from dyes and do not have the lightfast qualities of pigment-based products. White, black, silver, and gold inks are the exception, since they are made from pigments or metallics.

Printer inks for laser and inkjet printers come in four standard colors: yellow, cyan, magenta, and black. They can come preloaded in cartridges, each one especially designed for the make and model of the

Figure 5-12.
Trina Renee Nicklas, *Green Hull*, 2009. Nicklas is able to build up a high degree of intense color in her digitally created works. In the past, the colors an artist could achieve through the standard printing process were limited. Today artists are able to work with a wide range of color as evidenced in Nicklas' work.
Photo courtesy of Trina Renee Nicklas.

Figure 5-13.
Martha Alf, *Two Pears*, 1986. Derwint pencil on Bristol paper/ 14 × 17 inches. Alf uses cool hues of blue and violet in here elegant colored pencil drawing of two pears. She is able to develop layers of color as she uses the cool hues complements of yellow and orange in the under drawing and as highlights.
Collection Paula Kane, Beverly Hills, California/ Photo courtesy of NEWSPACE Resales, Los Angeles.

printer or in a bottle used to refill your printer's cartridge. Artists can achieve a dynamic range of color with these new inks as seen in Trina Nicklas's work (Figure 5-12). The biggest issue with these inks is their archivability. Most tend to be fugitive in nature and do not do well if exposed to direct sunlight for any length of time. Magenta is especially prone to fading. Most ink currently on the market has only a twenty-four- to twenty-six-year life span. This is very short in fine art terms where permanence is highly valued but adequate for most design projects, which don't have the same life span. Still, the artist should be very careful not to unnecessarily expose the printed piece to sunlight and therefore increase the chance of the colors fading. Another important element in insuring the archival life of computer-generated work is to use acid-free paper. Taking these steps will help prolong the life of your printed digital work.

Colored Pencils and Pastels

Colored pencils combine pigment, wax, fats, oils, and other things that are shaped into thin tubes and then dried. The dried media is inserted into a wooden shield or frame for durability and ease of use (Figure 5-13). The wax binding used helps to resist and prevent the color from fading. Unfortunately, the wax can cause a problem called **wax bloom** in which a white hazy film develops over all or parts of the art-work. This problem can develop over time and is a result of the wax base rising to the surface and creating a snowy or milky look. One method to remove it is to take a soft tissue or cloth and very gently wipe it away. The bloom, which looks just like a flower, may return again in time. The only way to stop this is to apply a spray fixative to the work when you are finished. It may take several applications of fixative to seal the work completely.

Pastels as we know them today have been around for about the last 250 years, although artists have been using colored chalks for thousands of years. Since they are made from almost pure pigment with just enough binder to hold them together, they may be the purest form of colored media. The vast range of bright colors that an artist could achieve is what attracted many of the Impressionists to work with pastels. Edgar Degas popularized the use of this medium in his drawings of ballet dancers. Other Impressionists, including Mary Cassatt, also were drawn to the media for its intense vivid color. In the drawing seen in Figure 5-14, Cassatt used the intense color of the media to add a sense of atmosphere to the work. In addition, pastels allowed her to work quickly, capturing the moment at a public event.

There are two kinds of pastels: oil-based and chalk pastels. The pigments employed to make pastels are the same that are used to manufacture oil paints. Chalk pastels can range from very soft to very hard, depending upon how much binder is used. The harder the pastel, the more binder and filler are used in its production. Today the most commonly used binder is methyl cellulose, which will not yellow or become susceptible to mold and mildew. The filler is usually clay or precipitated chalk, although many companies are using a mixture of aluminum, kaolin, and plaster.

Pastels got their name because when the pigment, binder, and filler are mixed together they form a paste. A stick of pastel is more correctly called a *pastellist*. Soft pastels with very little binder have much more brilliant colors, but they tend to crumble and wear away very rapidly. Brightness is determined by the amount of chalk employed, which will also make the media more or less opaque depending upon the amount used. To achieve a full range of shades, black may be added to the pigment mixture.

Figure 5-14.
Mary Cassatt, American (active in France, 1844–1926). *At the Theater*, ca. 1879. Pastel on paper, 21 13/16 × 18 1/8 inches (55.4 × 46cm). The Impressionist's elevated pastels to an accepted art medium. Prior to this time, they were only used as a sketching material. Notice the juxtaposition of the use of complementary hues, which add to the atmospheric quality of light produced in the drawing.
Photo © The Nelson-Atkins Museum of Art, Kansas City, Missouri. Purchase: acquired through the generosity of an anonymous donor, F77-33. Photo by Jamison Miller.

Hard pastels and pastel pencils are much more durable, but they are less vibrant in color. The choice is between intense color or long-lasting durability, though many artists use a combination of both types in their work.

Oil pastels are also known as non-dusting or dust-free pastels. They are not the same thing as oil sticks, which are oil paints combined with a very tiny amount of binder, or just enough to hold the media together in a stick form. They also tend to be much larger in diameter than pastels. However, they use the same pigments as oil paint, as well as a small amount of inert oil and wax as binding agents. Because of this unique type of binder, they never really dry the same way oil paints do. While they may harden somewhat, they can stay workable for years and years. This is one reason all paintings and drawings created with oil pastels should be framed and covered with either Plexiglas or glass.

Figure 5-15.
Robert Yarber, *The Slots are Hot*, 2009.
Yaber is able to develop a very bright, intense palette with his use of crayons. They have an immediacy, which works well with the playfulness of his imagery. The use of the media invokes a childhood innocence juxtaposed to an adult subject matter.
Photo courtesy of Robert Yarber and Sonnabend Gallery.

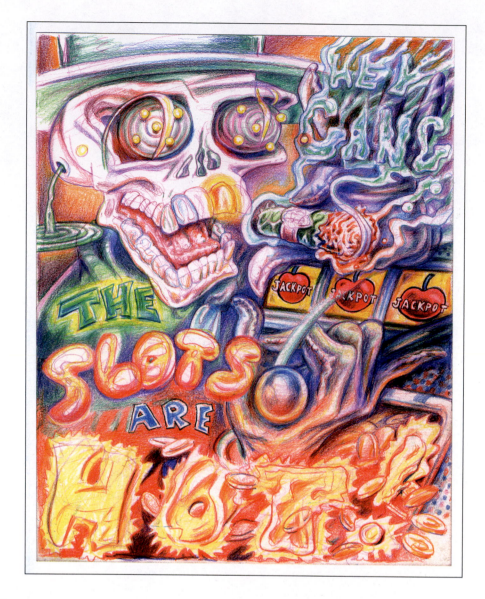

Crayons

The history of the crayon as we know it today dates back to 1903 with the product invented by Edwin Binney and Harold Smith. Crayons were initially packaged in boxes of eight colors that sold for a nickel. The name Crayola, which has become synonymous with the crayon, is a combination of the French words for chalk (craie) and oily (oleaginous).

The first crayons were a mixture of charcoal and oil. Later, powdered pigments of various hues replaced the charcoal. It was later discovered that substituting wax for the oil in the mixture made the resulting sticks sturdier and easier to handle. While they were initially developed as an inexpensive medium for children, today many artists have rediscovered crayons as an art media (Figure 5-15).

Other Media

Contemporary artists and designers are exploring a wide range of colored media to use in their work. These can include but are not limited to oils, vegetable matter, blood, and numerous other liquids and materials. Experimentation is the key motivating factor in exploring alternative media. These new

Figure 5-16.
David Hammons, *Untitled (Kool-Aid)*, 2006. Kool-Aid on paper with silk curtain and terry-cloth frame. 43 ½ × 29 ½ inches (110.5 × 74.9 cm). Hammons uses a staining technique to create large-scale drawings. The soft drink has a very pale color and blends much the same as any water based media.
© David Hammons
Photo courtesy of L&M Arts.

materials add new color choices that may not be possible to obtain with more traditional media. David Hammons used the children's soft drink Kool-Aid as an art media (Figure 5-16). Hammonds has long been interested in nontraditional art media and alternative application methods.

Color Film

Color film consists of three light-sensitive layers of emulsion held on to a film base. Each layer responds to one-third of the colors in the spectrum. One layer is sensitive to blue, another to green, and the other to red using the additive color system to achieve a full spectrum or range of hues.

There are a wide variety of color films on the market. They fall into two basics groups: color print film and reversal or slide film. Reversal films usually have the word "chrome" as part of their product name, such as Ektachrome or Fujichrome. After it is decided whether to shoot slides or negatives, the next categories or groupings

Figure 5-17.
An example of the color cast created by different light sources. All three were photographed using daylight film. The top image was photographed under fluorescent light. The center image was photographed using natural sunlight, and the final grouping was photographed using tungsten light. There is a dramatic color shift when the correct film and light source are not used together.
© Steven Bleicher

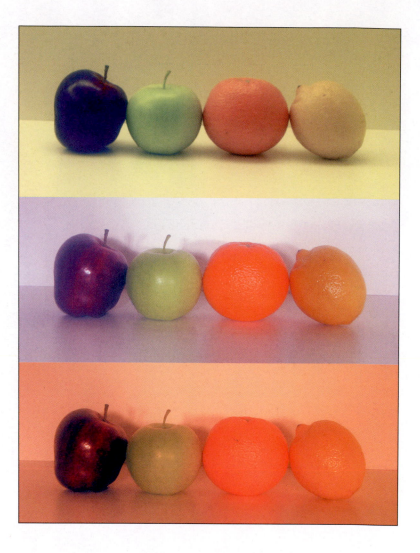

of film are daylight and tungsten. Film is color-balanced to work in either daylight (sunlight) or under tungsten (regular incandescent lamps), according to their exact temperature based on the Kelvin (K) scale. Sunlight on a clear bright day would measure about 12,000 K or higher, while on the other hand, tungsten light measures in at only about 3,200 K.

Sunlight is much bluer than the light given off by standard light bulbs, which tends to have a warmer reddish cast. Most people tend to ignore the color shift and don't even notice the differences. Daylight films are color-balanced to obtain the most natural-looking hues when shot during the day with

sunlight as the main source of illumination. They will also work well with most blue-based or cooler light sources. Color negative film is more tolerant of differing light sources than slide or reversal film. This color balance is less critical with new print films such as Kodak's Ultra Max series. They are formulated to work in a much wider temperature range to allow the photographer a greater number of lighting options. Unfortunately, fluorescent light will not match either type of film and will give off a greenish cast (Figure 5-17). This can be compensated for by using a special fluorescent filter and by opening up the lens one full f-stop. Daylight films are better suited for this purpose than tungsten because they are color-balanced to accept the bluer, cooler color range.

Tattoos

One of the oldest forms of color application is tattooing, which is practiced on nearly every continent, with the possible exception of Antarctica. Many tribal groups from New Zealand to Africa to the Americas and Asia have all practiced this ancient art, including this form of body decoration as an integral part of their culture. In most cultures, tattooing marks a rite of passage usually associated with initiation into manhood or womanhood at puberty. It marks the individual's changing status within the group and moving on from being a child to an adult member of the tribe or group. It is a permanent application of color meant to mark the wearer for life. Psychologically speaking, in today's culture, it represents a person taking control and ownership over his or her own body, making a personal visual statement (Figure 5-18). Tattooing has become more popular in recent years. In a study in the late 1980s, only about 10 percent of people had tattoos, while a recent study by the University of Connecticut of adults age 18 to 29 found that 35 percent of women and 30 percent of men now sported body art.

Tattooing is quite literally art by puncture. Ink or dye is placed (or injected) into the dermis layer of the skin by means of a hollow needle filled with pigment. Ancient tribal groups used bones and thorns by tapping them into the skin to place the color in a desired location. Today, a mechanical device rapidly vibrates a hollow needle that injects the pigment to the proper depth into the skin. In fact, most tattoo inks are not inks in the traditional sense, but can best be described as a pigment suspended in a carrier solution. The carrier has two functions: to place the pigment in a free-flowing aqueous concentration for ease of application and to act as a disinfectant. The first pigments were

Figure 5-18. Tattoos are a way for a person to take control of their own body by making a visual statement about themselves and their ideas for all to see. Photo courtesy of Tomiko Klein.

carbon black and other ground minerals. Today most pigments used are metal salts and the occasional vegetable dye.

Sand Painting

Cultures as diverse as the Navajo and Nepalese Tibetan monks use colored sand as an art medium. One of the chief elements of all sand painting is its impermanence. It is temporal in nature and not meant to last for a great period of time. Their creators purposely destroy them as part of the ritual religious art-making and healing process. Finally, the sand is returned to the earth from which it came and the cycle is completed.

In Tibet, the art is called *du-ltson-kyil-khor,* meaning mandala of colored powers. The mandala, also know as a cosmogram, has a multitude of meanings on many different levels and has both an inner and outer meaning. The inner level represents a map where the human mind may be transformed into an

Figure 5-19.
Navajo Man Sand Painting, circa 1990-2002, Arizona, USA. Sand paintings are created as part of healing ceremonies. After the ritual is completed, the sand painting is destroyed. The sand is applied by hand-spreading the colored grains between the thumb and forefinger. Photo © Danny Lehman/ CORBIS.

enlightened one, and the outer level represents the world in its divine state. The sand painting is a vehicle for reconsecrating the earth and all of its inhabitants. Normal iconography can include geometric shapes as well as spiritual symbols. A single painting may take days, weeks, or even months to complete. Early mandalas used ground rubies for red and lapis lazuli for blue and so on, while today they are commonly made out of dyed sand. When complete, the sand is swept up and taken to a nearby river or waterway to return the sand to its natural environment and spread the healing energies throughout the world.

Navajo sand painting is used and created as part of healing ceremonies, also called Sings or Ways (Figure 5-19). These rites include prayers, sweat lodges, and medical herbology, as well as the construction of a sand painting. For the Navajo, the world must always be in balance or "hozho," and if this delicate equilibrium is upset, illness or some other disaster will result. To return the world to harmony

and beauty, a Singer (medicine man) leads a ceremony in which the sand painting is constructed. These events can last from one to nine days. *Iikaah*, the Navajo word for sand painting, means "a place where Holy People come and go," because they believe that figures created and represented are actually present during the ceremony.

Since these paintings are so powerful, they cannot be created for any other purpose than that for which they were intended. Any painting seen at a gallery or museum is a re-creation with several important elements left out or removed. Only in this way can they be viewed by a secular audience because for many Native American tribes, there is no separation between life, art, and religion. They are one and the same thing.

There are approximately 500 different sand paintings derived from some 50 different chants or ways. For instance, there may be almost 100 different sand paintings within the Shooting Way or Shooting Chant. Each color has its own special meaning. For example, red represents sunlight. Only the sacred colors are used: black, white, yellow, red, and blue. They are linked to the four sacred mountains, as well as the directions of north, south, east, west, up, and down. These colored sands may be made from pollen or ground minerals.

A sand painting can be very small or quite large, measuring up to 20 feet. The Singer creates the images in the painting following a very strict prescribed format. There is no artistic license taken when creating a sand painting. If the images are not made correctly, it will not have any healing power. At the end of the ceremony, the patient literally sits in the middle of the creation while the Singer touches parts of the painting to the patient. Finally the painting is smeared out and obliterated. The sand is collected, placed in a blanket, and then taken away to ensure the health of the person treated.

In contemporary sand paintings, a board is sanded and smeared with a thin layer of glue. The sand or crushed stones are placed by hand and worked in, small areas at a time. The application of the glue must be precise. If it is too thick, the painting will be lumpy and messy, while if it is spread too thin, the sand may not adhere. These paintings are specifically created for a secular audience and are not imbued with the power of a healing work.

Glazes

Glazes are used as a permanent coloring and sealant for ceramic ware. The glaze actually fuses into the clay during the firing process. A glaze is composed of three parts: refractories that aid in viscosity, glass formers or silica, and a fluxing agent. Silicate, the substance that actually forms the glasslike surface, is also a component

of clay and has a very high melting point of over 3,000 degrees Fahrenheit. This melting point can be greatly lowered with the addition of a flux agent such as lead, sodium, or potassium. Lead used to be a major component of most glazes, but has fallen out of use because of the fear of poisoning. It can leach out of a fired piece such as a mug or plate and be absorbed into the system of anyone who might use the ceramic piece.

At first glance, whether in dry powder form or mixed into a liquid, glazes look dull and drab and nowhere near the color they will be after firing. The high heat of firing is the key that unlocks the color. This is one reason why ceramists create test tiles of glaze to see what the final product will look like. A glaze can be matte, glossy, transparent, or opaque depending upon the minerals and pigments used, and they can be applied in several ways including brushing, dipping, pouring, and spraying. In Figure 5-20, Rick Foris uses both glossy and matte glazes in his Raku fired vessels. He is interested in the spontaneity of the process and the range of color he is able to achieve. Working with the oxidization

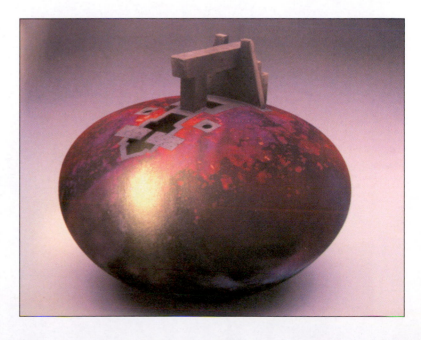

Figure 5-20.

Rick Foris, *Architectural Raku Vessel*, 1989. Foris uses a combination of wheel throwing and slab construction in his work. The metallic luster in his work comes from the sprayed copper matt glazes used. Raku glazes use oxidation to bring out their unique colors. Copyright © Rick Foris/ Photo by William Lemke.

technique involved with Raku is very spontaneous and results can vary considerably. That element of chance and serendipity are a fundamental part of the process and the "Zen of Raku."

Hobbyists and students usually learn by using commercially prepared glazes, which allow for ease of application and constancy in color and finish. The limiting factor is that the range of color available in commercially produced glazes is restricted. For these and other reasons, experienced ceramic artists often prefer to formulate their own glazes. Personalized glaze formulations are known as recipes. Each formula is measured out to very specific and rigid standards. A slight variation in the amount of any ingredient used could result in a drastically different finish.

The temperature during firing is another factor that can change the final look of a piece. Therefore, glazes could be considered color created by using extreme heat to cause a thermal reaction. Just as with paint, ceramic artists use glazes to show their unique, personal color voice and vision.

Summary

As we have seen, color can be worked within a variety of wet and dry media, each having its own specific use. In this chapter, we have reviewed most of the standard materials and the pigments that artists and designers use. We have even explored artworks, such as tattooing and sand painting, which are important because of their cultural or religious meaning. Pigments are the elements in the medium that give it its hue and color. The same type of pigment can be used with different vehicles to create a variety of different mediums.

Understanding which pigments and other elements are in the medium being used and how they have been processed enables the artist and designer to make appropriate choices when selecting a media for a project. The right media can make the piece. It is critical to know what the medium you are using is composed of to facilitate its use and archivability. The latter tends to be more important to fine artists whose original works should last for years to come. Designers are not usually as concerned with this because all of their work will end up in a digital format for commercial production.

All of the colorants and media reviewed in this chapter are part of what is known as the subtractive color mixing process. All pigments, paints, and inks are included in this general grouping. In the next chapter, we will discuss the additive process, or working with light, which is the basis for digital color.

6

If color is the most elusive and complex of all of the elements of design, then digital color is the most ephemeral of all of the aspects of color. In one sense, it doesn't exist as a solid material entity. While you can touch pigment—the dry powders that make up color within paint—a digital color element is pure light and has no tangible physical manifestation. Digital colors can only be seen through a monitor or as a printed piece. The actual digital creation is nothing more than a string of computer code, existing only within a software program such as Photoshop or Illustrator. It has no physical being except for maybe the space the code takes up on a CD, disk, or hard drive.

So when working with digital color we are really dealing with a few things:

- the computer code that creates the color,
- the output devices, such as the monitor or printer and projector, and
- the picture element of pure light.

Digital color has seeped into all aspects of our lives. From the personal computer to every magazine or newspaper we read, from CDs and DVDs to the digital camera we bring with us on vacation, all are inexorably tied to digital color. Less than twenty years ago, few businesses and virtually no households had computers. Digital art was an interesting oddity that few people, including artists, took seriously. Now the digital revolution has come and gone, and computers are an intrinsic part of our daily lives.

There are many variables when working with digital color. Your monitor, scanner, printer, and the individual software program used can all affect the color perceived and produced. It is learning to control these

Figure 6-1.
An illustration showing each individual pixel that makes up an image. Notice that the pixels are actually squares of color similar to a mosaic.
© Steven Bleicher

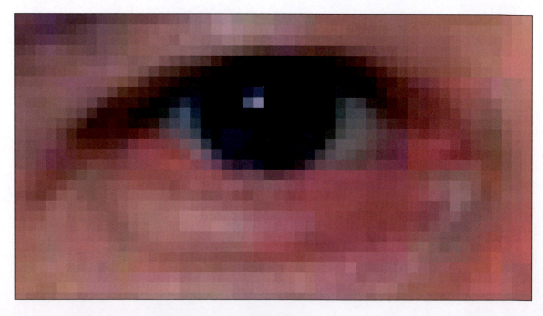

elements in much the same way artists and designers have learned to control traditional color that makes all the difference in creating good digital creations. In my view, one is not inherently better or worse than another. Each has its place in the artists' repertoire. It is really a matter of intention, selecting the right tool for the right job, that will most easily let you express what you want to communicate.

Pixels

The most basic component of digital color is the **pixel**, a combination of the words *picture* and *element*. Composed only of light, pixels are two-dimensional and have only height and width but no depth. They are flat square-shaped bits of light having no specific size (Figure 6-1). Their size is determined by their function and use.

Pixels are lined up in rows called **rasters**. Rows and rows of rasters make up the actual image. The amount of these elements in a one-inch space is known as the **resolution**. You may also hear it referred to as either ppi or dpi, pixels per inch or dots per inch. These terms are interchangeable. The more pixels per inch, the finer the detail that can be displayed in an image and the larger the file size. For example, an 8 × 10-inch image at 72 dpi will be a little more than one megabyte. A 300 dpi image of the same size would be more than 24 megabytes. In the digital world of color, size matters.

Different size resolutions are used for different things. A Web page is displayed at 72 dpi. The smaller file size allows for data to be sent quickly and more efficiently. A standard printed page from your favorite magazine is created at 300 dpi. This has to do with the way things are printed and will

be discussed in more detail later on in this chapter. Line art such as contour line drawings or plans can be as high as 600 dpi. Here the more dots per inch, the finer and more fluid the line will be. If you have ever noticed that when looking at an image you see the stair-step effect on some lines or images, it's as if you are actually seeing the edges of the individual pixels themselves. These are known as jaggies or **aliasing**. Any time you see an anti-aliasing feature in a pixel- or raster-based program such as Photoshop, check the box to turn it on. This will help to alleviate the situation and create a cleaner, more fluid line with no jagged or rough edges.

Color and Pixel Depth

To understand color depth, it is important to understand how the hardware and software operate. The smallest unit of information is a bit. It can be designated as on or off or a 0 or 1. Bits are the basis for binary code or information systems, which are at the heart of all computer applications. Very early monitors used a one-bit system, which means that they are either on and illuminated, or off. These were the primitive one-color monitors of early computing, used primarily for data entry.

Eight-bit color can display up to 256 different colors (Figure 6-2). This is the standard Internet color space. While it is limited in its color range, it provides for fast upload and download time, which is critical

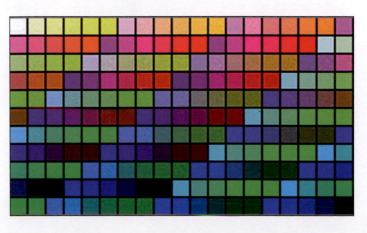

Figure 6-2.
Color swatches showing the 256 Web-safe colors.
Courtesy of
Adobe Systems, Inc.

Figure 6-3.
Clifford Alejandro, *You Must Remember This, Illustration for UCLA Magazine*, 2006. The layering of images allows artists and designers to develop complex photo collages. Alejandro uses an intense analogous palette of yellows and oranges in this editorial cover illustration for UCLA Magazine.
Photo courtesy of Clifford Alejandro.

in Internet applications. No one wants to wait for a page to load. The longer a page takes to come up on screen, the more likely the viewer is to quit out and move on to another site.

Twenty-four-bit color will allow the viewer 16 million different colors. This is the color range of your monitor, which explains why your monitor can display a wider range of color than you can print or use on the Internet. Many modern "video" games are now using this color space with its wider range of hues to create more realistic imagery and game elements.

Figure 6-4.
Nancy Stahl, *Self Promotional Item*. The clean lines and discrete areas of color are characteristic features of vector-based programs. Stahl uses the stamp motif in her self promo as a recognizable element since she has designed several nature-related stamps for the U.S. Postal Service.
Photo courtesy of Nancy Stahl.

Raster Versus Vector

Not every computer program uses rasters. There are two major types of computer programs, raster and vector. Raster-based programs such as Photoshop are made up of pixels, and the image quality can vary with the amount of pixels or dpi in an image. They are also known as resolution-dependent programs, which means that image quality is based on the amount of dots per inch in a given image. Again, the higher the resolution, the better the quality and more detail contained in the picture. The images created can be made smaller, but they cannot be resized and made larger. This is because the computer program algorithm would have to add pixels to create the new information and the picture would become fuzzy or blurry. Raster-based programs are used for photographs, photo collages, and other continuous-tone images (Figure 6-3).

Vector-based programs such as Illustrator, FreeHand, and Flash are not made up of pixels but are created using a mathematical algorithm or formula. Every time you drag the mouse and make an image larger or smaller, the computer recalculates the algorithm and creates the new image. Because they are not composed of pixels, the designs created can be resized at will without any loss of image quality, which makes them ideal for use in working with type, logo design, and many types of illustrations (Figure 6-4).

Additive Color

Previously, we were primarily concerned with subtractive color, which means that as light hits an object of varying or different hues, the wavelengths are subtracted or removed and what we see is what remains—the reflected color. When working with digital color, we are dealing with

Figure 6-5.
Red, green, and blue are the primary hues in an additive color wheel. These hues are composed of light and not pigment, as in the standard primaries of blue, yellow, and red. Notice that in this system, blue and red make magenta, red and green make yellow, green and blue make cyan, and mixing all three primaries produces white.
© Steven Bleicher

additive color or light itself. The primaries change from red, yellow, and blue (RYB) to red, green, and blue (RGB), as seen in Figure 6-5. Only when we print a picture will we again deal with subtractive color and even then the primary system will change from RYB to cyan, magenta, yellow, and black (CMYK).

Color Pickers

There are several ways to pick color digitally. Just as in the traditional world, where there are watercolors, acrylics, and oils with their own unique properties, the digital world also has several color choices, or color spaces, to choose from. And again, just as with traditional colors, it is a matter of picking the right color space for the right job.

Color picking can be divided into two parts: the actual mechanical method for selecting a particular hue, and the overall color space. Each manufacturer has developed its own color selection devices. Adobe, Apple, and Macromedia all have their own proprietary color-picking apparatus (Figure 6-6). The one thing they all have in common is that they are based on a color solid or a three-dimensional color model.

Figure 6-6.
An example of the
Adobe color picker from
Photoshop. The large
square is a slice of the
solid color space. The
spectrum at the right side
of the cube is where the
user selects the desired
hue. On the right side of
the dialog box are the
various color spaces that
can be selected. They
include RGB, HSB, and
LAB. Notice that CMYK
cannot be selected—the
values are only displayed
for informational
purposes.
Courtesy of
Adobe Systems, Inc.

When we select a hue, we are taking a slice through that color space, selecting a specific point containing the hue, value, and saturation.

So whether they are arranged in a circle, sphere, or cube, the end result is the same. The four most standard color spaces or **color modes** to choose from are RGB, LAB, HSB (also occasionally referred to as HSV), and CMYK. Additional color modes also include grayscale, duotone, and a few others that are less frequently used. Choosing a mode is determined by the end use of the digital file or image. Most often artists and designers work in RGB and then convert the file over to one of the other modes when their work is completed. One reason for this is that you are working in the same color space as your monitor and many of the filters and other elements within programs such as Photoshop have only been designed to work in that mode.

RGB may be the most versatile of the color modes. It is for Web page design, as well as the initial creations for video and print work. After the design or artwork is complete, the piece can be easily converted to another color space for final printing or rendering.

HSB stands for hue, saturation, and brightness, or value. In this color space the artist can pick out each element as they define a color to be used in a digital work.

LAB is primarily a device-oriented color space. L stands for luminance, while A and B represent the two color areas within the mode.

CMYK stands for the four primary colors used in printing digital designs and artworks. Those primary hues are cyan (a medium blue), magenta, yellow, and black. Black is used to give depth and body to the images that are created with the other three colors.

The human eye sees a wide array of colors, giving it a very large color space. Computers cannot match the scope and breadth of the eye for the range of color it can reproduce. Color spaces are the defined areas or amounts of color that can be seen and reproduced accurately by a computer. Many of these spaces are created and set up for specific software or hardware. Figure 6-7 shows the differences in several color spaces, including the human eye, LAB color, and Adobe RGB 1998. The largest color space by far is the human eye, which can discern the widest range of color. Just slightly behind the eye would be LAB color, and the Adobe color space is even smaller. Finally, the smallest color space is that of the Internet.

Types of Computer-Imaging Programs

There are several different types of computer-imaging programs, each designed for a specific use. There are vector-based drawing programs, which excel at line art and more graphic uses such as logo and package design. Raster-based programs are designed to work with continuous-tone images such as photographs or painted images. Going hand in hand with these programs are the digital layout programs including QuarkXPress and InDesign. These are prepress programs developed to replace the traditional page layout.

Monitors

Your monitor can have a dramatic affect on color. Such variables as the type, age, and condition of the equipment can radically alter the color displayed. A monitor works in much the same way as your color television set does with the main difference being that your TV has a receiver, channel selector, and antenna or cable hookup. But the picture screen works in exactly the same manner. Today LCD and plasma monitors have taken over and replaced the traditional cathode-ray tube screen. Over the years improvements in technology and reduced costs have made these affordable to all.

Gamma and the Monitor

Monitors use an additive color mixing system (RGB) to produce color. It emits red, green, and blue light in the varying proportions required to show a specific hue. As an example, yellow is made up by combining red and green. Since there is no blue present, the computer assigns it a value of zero. A bright yellow might be assigned the following values: red–241, green–244, and blue–0. To see for yourself, open a computer program such as Photoshop or Illustrator, go to the color picker, and plug in these values to see the actual nature of yellow hue that is displayed.

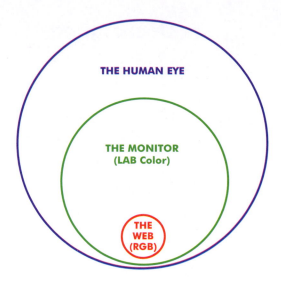

Figure 6-7.
An illustration of the various color spaces. The size of the space determines how many hues can be distinguished. The larger the color space, the wider the range of hues that can be expressed.
© Steven Bleicher

LCD

Most new monitors are **LCD** or **liquid-crystal displays**. They offer the advantages of saving space, a flat screen, and providing a high-quality color display. There is greater color acuity from unit to unit and they need far less calibrating that the old cathode-ray tube monitors. These monitors still operate by exciting the phosphors to produce color. Additionally, LCD televisions are much thinner and lighter than traditional cathode-ray tube sets.

The LCD monitor is backlit using a series of color cathode-ray fluorescent lamps at the rear of the screen (Figure 6-8). These lamps are always on. They produce darker hues and blacks by twisting, which blocks the light. They untwist for whites and bright colors. There are two disadvantages with this backlight design. First, since the light is always lit, they use more electricity, and second, some light leaks through so they do not produce the richest, darkest black when compared with other technologies such as plasma.

LED

Many new models use **LED** or **light emitting diode** technology. They offer brighter color and use far less electricity. Additionally they offer more contrast and richer, darker

Figure 6-8.
LCD illustration.
When unenergized
(left), the crystals line
up with the front and
rear polarizers, and
light travels down their
spiral staircase and
back up to the viewer.
When energized (right),
the "crossed" polarizers
(front and rear at
90 degrees to each
other) cause the center
segment to appear dark.
This example is quite
simple compared to a
n LCD TV set, where
more than six million
subpixel cells are
constantly straightening
and twisting hundreds
of times per second
to achieve the
required color.
Reproduced with permission
from Computer Desktop
Encyclopedia.
(www.computerlanguage.
com)

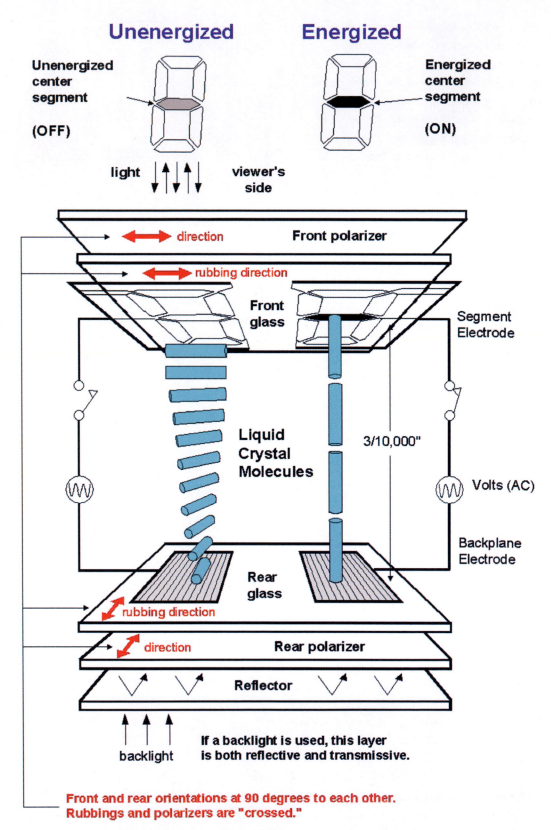

Unenergized

Energized

Unenergized
center
segment

(OFF)

Energized
center
segment

(ON)

light   viewer's
                side

direction   Front polarizer

rubbing direction

Front
glass

Segment
Electrode

Liquid
Crystal
Molecules

3/10,000"

Volts (AC)

Backplane
Electrode

Rear
glass

rubbing direction

direction   Rear polarizer

Reflector

backlight

If a backlight is used, this layer
is both reflective and transmissive.

Front and rear orientations at 90 degrees to each other.
Rubbings and polarizers are "crossed."

blacks than LCD sets. There are two type of LED technology: backlit, where the LEDs are placed across the entire back of the screen, and edge-lit, where the diodes are located along perimeter. Each has their advantages. Edge-lit models are cheaper. Backlit sets offer darker blacks using "local dimming" technology where an area can be shut off completely, so no light leaks through. These new sets are comparable with plasma in the quality of saturated color produced.

A new advance in HD display is **QuadPixel** technology. This proprietary technology pioneered by Sharp Electronics adds a yellow channel or filter to the standard three-hued light primary range. The resulting RGBY system produces a wider color gamut of more than a trillion colors over the standard technology, which produces a gamut in the millions. The color is said to be even more vivid and lifelike. This and other new technologies will keep LCD monitors competitive with plasma displays.

Plasma Displays

Another popular display system is the **PDP** or **plasma display panel**. It is the type of flat panel display now commonly used for large televisions, typically above 37 inches or 940 mm. This technology can produce very large screens, up to 103 inches (measured diagonally). The tiny cells, which are located between two panels of glass, hold an inert mixture of noble gases (neon and xenon). The gases in the cells are electrically turned into plasma, which then excites phosphors to emit light (Figure 6-9). Plasma displays have very good contrast ratio and a wide color gamut, displaying up to 16,777,216 hues. Some find their low-luminance "dark-room" black level generates a darker black, which is more desirable for watching movies. Plasma monitors also have a much wider viewing angle. Their drawbacks include using more electricity as well as being susceptible to screen reflection glare in bright rooms.

Gamma is the measurement and mathematical formula of the relationship of voltage input to the relative brightness of the image seen on the screen. It is measured on a scale, or range, of 1.0 to 3.0. If the gamma is not set correctly or if your computer's operating software doesn't automatically correct for it, the colors and their related values seen on screen will be dramatically affected. Personal computers (PCs) and Unix systems usually run a 2.5 gamma and usually require gamma correction. Macintosh and Silicon Graphics

ONE PLASMA PIXEL

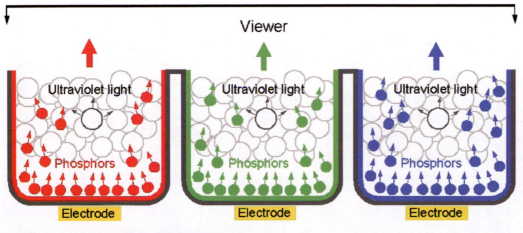

Figure 6-9.
Plasma display illustration. This is an example of one plasma pixel. LCD and plasma screens display colors differently. LCD uses liquid crystals and color filters while plasma uses gas and phosphors. Reproduced with permission from Computer Desktop Encyclopedia. (www.computerlanguage.com)

platforms operate at a normal gamma of 1.8. They do not have to be corrected because the graphics card in the Mac automatically corrects the gamma, and the hardware of the SG machine performs the same function.

Describing Color: Gamut

Each hardware component used to create color images or pages reproduces a varying range of color, or gamut. **Gamut** is the actual range of color each device can display or reproduce. Monitors, scanners, printers, and presses each have their own gamut. Within each manufacturer, the gamut for a product can vary. If one manufacturer makes several different monitors, as most do, each one may have a different color gamut. Also, gamut ranges change from device to device. For example, you can see a wider range of colors on screen than you may be able to print with your printer. Your monitor and scanner use different color models and describe their colors differently than your desktop printer or a commercial press. You may have already noticed that the colors you see on your monitor and the colors of the final printed image can greatly vary. This is why one should calibrate a monitor to the exact make and model of the printer and even the paper that will be used.

Color Management Modules

The gamut of all color output devices from monitors to printers is far less than the range that can be seen by the human eye. To try to correct this situation as much as possible, each piece of hardware uses a **color management profile**. This profile is tagged or assigned to each file as you save it. Have you ever noticed that sometimes when you open a file, you get a warning dialog box that tells you there is a profile mismatch between the manner in which the file was created and the setting on your machine? It then asks you what you want to do about it. Your choices

are usually to correct it in one of two ways or to discard the color profile completely.

You never want to discard the profile and throw it out. Your two choices are to either assign it a profile that matches the machine you are working on, or to use the imbedded profile in which the document was created. If you know how the file was created, you may decide to keep the imbedded profile and if you're not sure, then you may want to go with the working profile of the computer on which you are working. If you are on your home computer, you probably have set up your computer with the correct profiles. However, if you are working in a lab situation, either at school or at a commercial printer like Kinko's or any other commercial printing house, check the settings on the computer before you actually change your file. You never know who was sitting at the computer before you and what their level of knowledge was. Never assume anything. Remember, it's your artwork at stake.

ICC Profiles

Part of the color management model is an ICC profile, which is a standardized formula or format developed by the International Color Consortium (see Chapter 2, Color Theory: Making Sense of Color). These formats describe and explain the attributes and behaviors of color devices such as printers, scanners, and monitors (Figure 6-10). They were developed to be used by all manufacturers as a way of standardizing color. Each device has its own profile and is based upon a table of key reference colors. This table of colors is standardized by device to ensure uniformity between all related hardware platforms. For example, a monitor will have a reference table of the red, green, and blue phosphors that are used in that monitor. Since different manufacturers use different phosphors, individual tables need to be developed for each monitor.

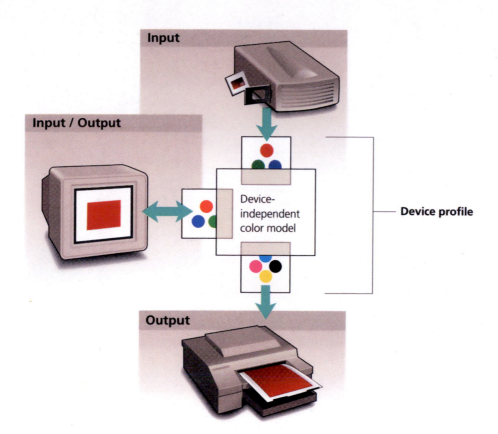

Input

Input / Output

Device-independent color model

Device profile

Output

Figure 6-10.
An illustration of how the color management models and device profiles work together to translate the color space from one device to another.
Courtesy of Adobe Systems, Inc.

Therefore, the most accurate means of color management is to have each file created with the tag of that device that includes its ICC profile. This in turn allows every other device to read the tag, interpret the data, and display the most accurate rendition of the colors used in creating the document.

Color Calibration

The only way to ensure that what you see on your monitor and what your printer will produce are similar is to calibrate the monitor. Calibrating sets up the ICC profile so that other devices, such as your printer, can read it and deliver accurate color. Depending upon the age and type of monitor, you will have to determine how often this function must be performed. The older the monitor,

the more frequently this procedure may have to be performed.

Input Devices

There are several types of input devices or ways to bring an image or artwork into your computer. Scanners, digital cameras, and storage devices of varying shapes, sizes, and styles will all allow you to bring in an image or design. You can even create one from scratch using a painting or drawing program. Keyboards can also be considered input devices since they can add and change data, but they do not bring in or import visual data, which is what we as artists and designers are primarily concerned with. Understanding how your input devices work is equally as important as understanding your

Figure 6-11.
CD–DVD–Blu-ray
illustration.
Blu-ray technology will
allow for the greater
information storage,
which is necessary for
HD technology.
© Steven Bleicher

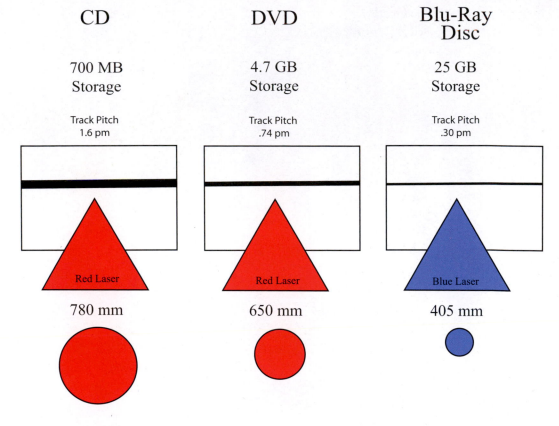

CD	DVD	Blu-Ray Disc
700 MB Storage	4.7 GB Storage	25 GB Storage
Track Pitch 1.6 pm	Track Pitch .74 pm	Track Pitch .30 pm
Red Laser	Red Laser	Blue Laser
780 mm	650 mm	405 mm

output devices. They are both key in creating digital artworks; otherwise, what we would be left with is a series of unreadable ones and zeros locked away within the computer itself.

Blu-ray

A recent innovation in optical disc formatting is known as **Blu-ray**, which is short for *Blu-ray Disc*. The Blu-ray Disc Association (BDA) developed this process. The BDA is a union of the world's foremost consumer electronics, personal computing, and media manufacturers. The list of the companies participating in BDA reads like a Who's Who of modern electronics including Apple, Dell, Hitachi, HP, JVC, LG, Mitsubishi, Panasonic, Pioneer, Philips, Samsung, Sharp, and Sony. This new format was developed for playing and recording in high-definition also known as HD. These discs can store more than five times the data of a traditional DVD. A traditional DVD

can hold up to 4.7GB while the new Blu-ray disc holds 25GB.

The laser is the key to Blu-ray technology. Traditional optical disc technology uses a red laser to read and write data. Blu-ray technology uses a blue-violet laser, giving the product its name (Figure 6-11). This new equipment is compatible with the older technology and can read regular CDs and DVDs. The shorter wavelength of this new laser allows the beam emitted to be focused with greater precision. The end result is that data can be more tightly compressed, storing more information in a smaller space. This has fast become the industry standard for HD.

Scanning

By far, scanning is the most widely used way of bringing in or importing an image into the computer. Flatbed, film, and drum scanners are most frequently used in image creation. As with everything else in the digital world, each has its own specific function and use. By far the most widely used are flatbed scanners. The top lid lifts open much like a Xerox or copier, and a document or image is placed face down on the glass top. It works by shining a bright beam of light that moves down across the entire length of the image. The light is calibrated to the brightness of sunlight for true and accurate color reproduction.

Perhaps you have noticed that when using a scanner, there are two steps the machine goes through before it begins scanning your original. The first step is to calibrate the equipment and the second step is to warm the lamp. Warming the lamp is important for several reasons. First, if the lamp stayed on constantly, it would burn out on a regular basis. It would also become so hot that it would either melt the plastic casing or it would have to be made out of metal to stand the heat produced by the bulb. Users would be forced to wear asbestos gloves to prevent skin burns. In the warming process, the lamp heats up to the correct temperature (measured at about 55,000 degrees on the Kelvin scale) and brightness for accurate color reproduction.

The second step in the scanning process, following the light source, is the CCD chip or charge-coupled device (Figure 6-12). This is what actually scans in your image. It reads the light energy given off by the light reflecting off the original on the platen glass. These readings are translated into a digital format by the scanning TWAIN program and either processed into an image in the native scanning program or translated into a software package, such as Photoshop. TWAIN, which actually stands for "technology without an interesting name," or **twain acquire**, is the technology used in the scanning process. The programmers who developed the scanning protocol inside Photoshop could not come up with a suitable name for this new feature and left it with its working moniker of TWAIN.

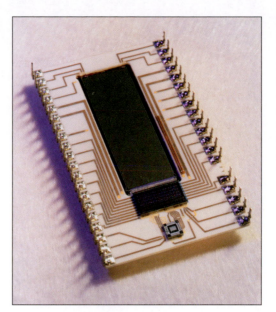

Figure 6-12.
A scientific CCD chip with broadband spectral response manufactured at MPI Halbleiterlabor. A CCD chip reads light energy. It is the heart of your scanner or digital camera.
Photo courtesy of MPI-HLL/Filser.

Megapixels

Most digital cameras also use a CCD chip to capture an image and then store it on a reusable card such as a compact flash or SD (Secure Digital) card. These cards can either be reused or a new card can be installed as the working card becomes full with images. Cellular telephones and digital cameras measure image size in **megapixels** (**MP**). A megapixel is equal to one million pixels. The higher the megapixel, the greater the resolution and therefore print quality that can be obtained. However, anything smaller than 2 MP will not print very well and was designed only to use in low resolution on the small monitor of a cell phone, PDA, or other handheld device. The following chart shows the relation of MP to the resolution and size of a high-quality print that can be produced from a given camera.

MP Size	Resolution	Print Size
2 megapixels	1600 × 1200	4" × 6"
3 megapixels	2048 × 1536	5" × 7"
5 megapixels	2560 × 1920	8" × 10"
6 megapixels	2816 × 2112	11" × 14"
8 megapixels	3264 × 2468	16" × 20"

Web Color

By far the smallest color range is Web color. With only 256 distinct hues, the artist and designer are limited in creative color use. Speed in downloading a Web page is one of the primary concerns of most Web designers. If a page takes too long to come up on screen, a viewer may get bored and move on long before the image can be displayed. So file sizes must be kept small to speed up the launching time. In this mix, something has to give and one thing is color. New software packages have made it easier to work with Web color by creating special color-picking devices that only display Web-safe hues. These eliminate the guesswork regarding whether a color can be displayed properly. In addition, there are special file formats used in Web page design. The JPG/JPEG (Joint Photographer Expert Group) format was developed to work with continuous-tone images and creates smooth photographic Web images. CompuServe GIF (graphic interchange format, the full formal name) is more commonly shorted to GIF and is a good file format for solid color and very simple gradient elements such as backgrounds, banners, and buttons. Another advantage is that GIF files are very small and download quickly.

An alternative to the GIF file format is PNG (Portable Network Graphics). Developed as a patent free format, they provide greater color depth. Closely related to PNG are MNG (Multiple-image Network Graphics). These are used for animation and offer better compression than the GIF files. Both are fast becoming industry standards.

Online Versus Printing

One of the newest file formats is SVG, or scalable vector graphics. They allow the designer to download a graphic from the Web and then directly use it in a vector-based drawing program. As yet there is no such equivalent in the continuous-tone or raster-based world. These types of images cannot be downloaded and printed with any real image quality. Again, resolution is the key factor: a Web image is at 72 dpi and a true professional-quality image for the print world is created at 300 dpi. An image downloaded from the Web and printed will look **pixilated**, which means that you can actually see each individual pixel that makes up the image. These images look grainy and have a very poor quality. So as yet, these two separate worlds (the Web and the printer or printing press) are never to be as one. Even if you were going to reduce the resolution as far as you could at 150 dpi and still print an image off a home printer, the difference in resolution may still be great enough to be visible to the naked eye.

Printing

When printing an image from a computer, you are going from the additive process of the monitor to a subtractive process of printing using inks. Most printers use a four-color ink printing process or CMYK, which stands for cyan, magenta, yellow, and black. Black, which is represented by the letter K, actually stands for the term *key* and is used to add richness and depth or value to the print. As stated previously, you cannot print the full range of colors seen on your monitor. One of the other differences between the monitor and your printed output is that the printed work will appear darker than the screen version. You have to remember that the image on screen is very bright and backlit and is more similar to a transparency than a print or photograph. Its color is more saturated and brighter on screen than your print will be. In addition, things print darker in value than when they are displayed on a monitor. The artist or designer must learn to compensate for these elements when preparing to print a document or image.

Another key factor to remember when printing is that each printer and brand of ink used will produce slightly different colors in your image. When an artist or designer needs to match a color exactly as in the packaging of a product or in a logo, they use what is known as a spot color. The most commonly used spot color system is the **PANTONE** brand color-matching system. PANTONE offers a wide variety of color and paper stocks to choose from.

Most color-picking devices have a separate selection screen or pop-up menu for these colors, as well as a few other color-matching systems (Figure 6-13).

Exact color matching is important because consumers reach for an item based on its color. We have been trained and conditioned to unconsciously react and respond to a specific product's color. But if you're skeptical, just think of the following: What color is the label on a Campbell's soup can? What color is a can of Sprite? What color is the McDonald's logo?

Inkjet, Laser, Giclée Printers

There are many different types of printers on the market today. The vast majority of home printers are inkjet. They offer the widest range of use at the cheapest price. This doesn't mean that they are inferior in quality. Like anything else, you get what

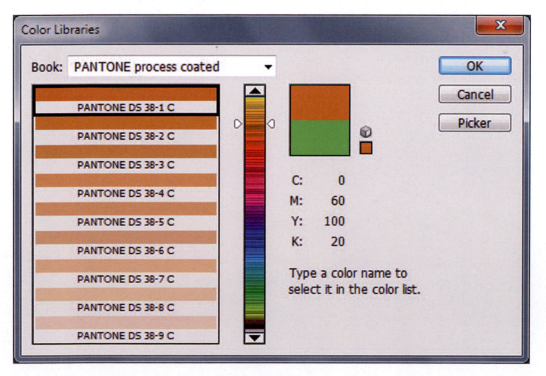

Figure 6-13.
The Adobe color picker using the custom color setting for PANTONE colors. There are several different types of PANTONE colors to choose from, including coated to uncoated and metallic finishes.
Courtesy of Adobe Systems Inc.

you pay for. However, there is a wide range of excellent inkjet printers on the market made by Epson, as well as a number of other companies. Many design professionals use these in their studios for proofing, making comps for clients, and creating fine art prints.

Inkjet printers usually use liquid ink, while laser printers use a dry powder toner. Another interesting note is that for many printing jobs, users do not have to change their images from RGB to CMYK to print out a single copy of an image. The CMYK format is normally used only when printing a large production run, and the file is converted to CMYK only after all of the work is complete and it is ready to go to the printer.

The high end of inkjet printing is the **giclée** print (pronounced Geéclay), also known as Iris prints. The name is derived from the French verb *gicler* meaning to squirt, or more accurately in this case, an extremely fine spray of many different sized droplets. This application of overlapping dots of ink mixes, forming additional color combinations. The application of the inks in this printing process is so fine that there are no discernible dots or droplets on the final print. Many fine

Figure 6-14.
John Campbell
Finnegan, *Temporal
Distortion*, 2002.
The giclée process allows
images to be printed on
canvas, silk, and a wide
variety of fine art papers.
Finnegan combines
photography, painting,
and scanned images in
his fluid abstractions.
Photo courtesy of
John Campbell Finnegan.

artists use this process to produce a limited edition set of prints and high-quality reproductions (Figure 6-14). The specialized inks used in this process are archival, unlike those used in the standard inkjet print, which fade and discolor over time.

Laser printers are ultra high-resolution printers. A heat process melts toner powders onto the paper. These printers are used for single image printing, limited runs, or editions of a print. But for high-volume printing such as magazines, books, and posters, a press is always used.

PostScript

PostScript is a page description language developed by Adobe initially for the Macintosh. It tells the printer specifically how to create and print an image on a page. Over the years it has become the gold standard for desktop publishing and printing. At the time PostScript was developed, Microsoft's software developers were busy concentrating on business-based applications and let the graphics market fall by the wayside. This is one of the reasons why most graphic designers or people who are concerned with the printed image tend to be Mac enthusiasts.

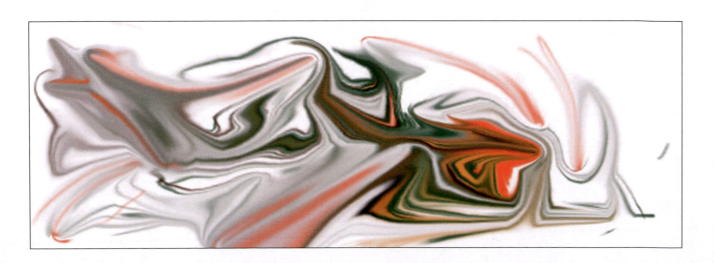

Raster Image Processor (RIP)

A **RIP** or **raster image processor** works hand in hand with the PostScript language and actually interprets the data or code, translating the instructions. A RIP is built into most desktop printers, but it is a separate module for imagesetters.

Dot Gain

One of the many variables in printing is the porosity of the paper and the spread of the ink. These variables are known as dot gain. The rougher the paper's surface or tooth, the more the ink will bleed or spread as it is applied to the paper's surface. On the other hand, if the surface of the paper is smooth, the ink may bead up and only spread out a tiny amount. This flow of the ink onto a particular paper can be compensated for and set up in the application or printing programs. For example, in a

program such as Photoshop, the flow of ink is adjusted or set up in the Color Settings menu application.

Production Printing

Production or commercial printing is normally done for large runs of prints, from several hundred to several thousand. Most presses also use a standard four-color printing process (CMYK), but they can also be loaded with special inks for a wider range of color and exact matching of color that is not normally available in other printing processes. These special colored inks are called spot colors. They can be PANTONE, Trumatch, or Focoltone inks. The newest form of production printing is high-fidelity color printing. Instead of four inks, additional colors—including orange, violet, and green—are added. This allows for a larger color space, as seen in Figure 6-15.

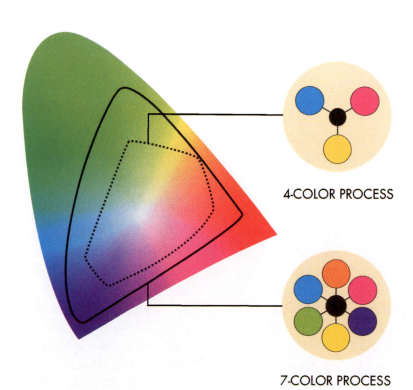

4-COLOR PROCESS

7-COLOR PROCESS

Figure 6-15.
A diagram of the ICC color profile showing the traditional four-color space and the new seven-color space. Notice how much larger the new space is. This means a greater variety of color can be produced and printed without the addition of spot colors. Courtesy of Adobe Systems, Inc.

Figure 6-16.
An example of the CMYK separations. Each of the four channels will be made into screens for the production printing of the artwork or design. *Separations courtesy of David Bleicher.*

Four-Color Separations: Plates

To print on a commercial press, each image or page of images must be divided into four parts, one for each of the four colors of ink (Figure 6-16). These are called **separations**. In the past, these separations were produced photographically and created by means of colored filters. Today they are created digitally and stored as files. Normally there are only four separations created unless spot colors are also used. In this case, a separation must be made for each spot color as well. A halftone screen or plate is created for each of the separations. Each plate will be loaded with ink and used to print the piece, as seen in Figure 6-17. Computer-to-plate imagesetters are also used to create printed pieces. These are also sometimes referred to as direct-to-plate imagesetters. This process eliminates some of the steps in the printing process and thereby saves printing costs.

Video and Video Cameras

There are many types of video cameras. Traditional analog video cameras use magnetic tape to capture the image. Digital cameras use a CCD chip, the same capture device as a scanner. It captures the light hitting it and converts it into electrical impulses. So why go digital over analog? Digital videos can be copied easily and these copies are as clear and sharp as the original. They have CD-quality audio. But most of all, they use component color sampling, which retains three times as much color information as analog video and gives the user more intense and accurate color reproduction.

Figure 6-17.
This final printed piece, the face of a postcard, was used as an invitation to a gallery opening for a solo exhibition of my work in 1992 in Washington, D.C.
© Steven Bleicher

The newest entrants into the software market are digital video editing programs. They can be as simple as I-Movie, which can be learned in a matter of hours (and comes preloaded in all new Macintosh computers) or as complex as Adobe Premiere or Final Cut Pro, which are professional-level software packages. They enable artists and designers to create, edit, and produce movies, commercials, and even their own music videos. This is revolutionizing the industry because now designers or design teams can create their entire production in-house and not only save money, but also retain complete artistic control over the product.

Animation

Animation used to be a laborious process where individual cells were drawn, inked, and painted by hand. Thousands and thousands of these were then photographed one by one to create an animated movie. This process was expensive and may have in part led to the decline of animated productions in the 1970s and 1980s. In the 1990s as computers began to dominate still art in the design fields, new software programs were developed to create animated or moving images. The 1990s saw a resurgence in cartoon or character animation with such Disney hits as *The Little Mermaid* and *The Lion King*. While most of these movies were produced using traditional animation techniques, the filmmakers began adding elements that were digitally created, as in the stampede scene in *The Lion King*. Today, digital animation has gained a strong foothold and has overtaken conventional cell animation.

Most digital animation software programs are vector based. They allow the user to set

Figure 6-18.
Scene from *The Game Room*, Exodus Entertainment. Notice the detail and fullness of the figure. The animators are able to achieve a great variety of textures through careful lighting and attention to the effects of light on color.
Photo courtesy of Exodus Entertainment.

up a virtual two- or three-dimensional space depending upon the program's capabilities. This fabricated space is where the action will take place. Programs such as Flash are 2-D programs that are used in all aspects of design. Flash is also one of the primary programs for creating animation on the Web. Three-dimensional animation programs including Maya, SOFTIMAGE/XSI, and 3DS MAX allow filmmakers to create convincing dimensional characters and environments, as seen in a scene from *The Game Room* (Figure 6-18).

Most 3-D programs use a **wireframe** model that is covered with a **texture map**. Figure 6-19 shows a wireframe, which is like a digital armature. It is a structure on which the animator can apply a skin that consists of texture and color information. The texture map contains information on the simulated textures and their corresponding colors (Figure 6-20).

The other basic element in these programs is the lighting component. The 3-D programs use light and light direction or camera angles to integrate their relationship to color. It is important for animators to understand the effect of light (and lighting) on color. Poor color and lighting management creates flat characters. On television, if you watch many of the digitally animated shows that cater to very young audiences, you will find that the color tends to be overly bright and that the images appear a bit flat with a very shallow sense of space. This occurs when the lighting on the character or object is off. In many television productions, color form management is sacrificed in favor of economics. Time and money are key factors in producing these shows. Spending the necessary time to get the lighting correct is a luxury only permitted to the makers of feature-length animated films.

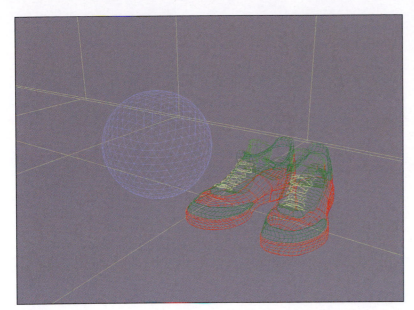

Figure 6-19.
Brett Baker, 3-D Studio Max.
An example of a wireframe model. Notice how not only the ball and shoes each have their own wireframe armatures, but the space they exist in also has its own wireframe structure.
Photo courtesy of Brett Baker.

Figure 6-20.
Brett Baker, 3-D Studio Max.
The same scene as in Figure 6-19, but with the color and texture map laid over the wireframe model. Baker uses image-based lighting to create the naturalistic illumination and color for the elements.
Photo courtesy of Brett Baker.

At the other extreme, companies such as Pixar invest heavily into developing accurate and correct lighting and color management. Companies today develop their own hardware and software to produce the desired visual effects. One of the first totally digitally animated features was *Toy Story.* Later releases such as *Finding Nemo* and *Shrek 2* have raised the bar on digital animation. In fact, *Shrek 2* has become the highest-grossing animated movie of all time. This could soon be surpassed by several new films scheduled for release. Digital animation is here to stay. In fact, it may not be long before actors in live-action films could be replaced entirely by virtual counterparts, as was alluded to in the movie *S1m0ne*, in which Al Pacino plays a director who creates a virtual leading

Figure 6-21.

James Cameron, *Avatar*, 2009.

Cameron blends live action with computer-generated images to produce the virtual world of Pandora and its Na'vi inhabitants.

© Twentieth Century-Fox Film Corporation/The Kobal Collection.

Photo courtesy of The Picture Desk, Inc.

Figure 6-22.

An example of a scene colored and lit using a High Dynamic Range Image.

HDR and radiance map images courtesy of Christian Bauer.

Figure 6-23.

The same scene as in Figure 6-22, now showing what it would look like at night. The advantage of this type of lighting is that the scene can be changed from day to night (and everything in between) without reshooting or additional editing.

HDR and radiance map images courtesy of Christian Bauer.

lady. This has effectively become a reality with the release of *Avatar*. James Cameron's unique mix of live action and computer graphics has made it the model for the future. Approximately a quarter of the film uses tradition live-action; the rest takes place in an entirely computer-generated world, which combines performance motion capture with virtual environments (Figure 6-21).

Another method used in digital animation to develop correct color and lighting is **image-based lighting**. The process emulates how light reflects off an object and scatters over surfaces. This process is accomplished by taking several digital photographs of an object, ranging from extremely overexposed all the way through completely black and underexposed. These lighting samples are combined through a special algorithm into a High Dynamic Range Image, or HDRI. The HDR images are then used as the actual light source for the image or scene. They are also used to predict the reaction of light falling on an object by creating the proper color relationship to the quality of light on a given surface. The information is then modified using the hue, saturation, and value adjustment. The images in Figure 6-22 and Figure 6-23 show the same scene reflected on a highly polished sphere. The sphere acts to distort the light and take in more of the image or scene, similar to using a wide-angle lens. Even under these complex conditions, the color and lighting in the cityscape scene are convincingly re-created. Using this new technique, digital animators can create more realistic color and lighting. After all of the sequences are shot and mapped, they must be compiled to produce the video or film.

Safe Color Rendering

To produce the final output, the digital files must be **rendered**. This is the process by which the computer collects all of the data from the digital animation program, the lighting, effects, and specified camera angles, and compiles all of the information to videotape or film. When transferring a digital production to film or video, intensely saturated hues such as bright oranges and reds can get blown out. This means that they appear to expand or flash over the object. It may look as if the color is bleeding or being smeared off the image. The actual color of an object can also be changed in this transfer process, as seen in Figure 6-24. This can be avoided by picking less saturated colors.

Figure 6-24.
An example of the difference between RGB and NTSC color spaces. The image on top uses RGB color, which has a much larger range of color than NTSC. In the bottom image, the color space was changed from RGB to NTSC and therefore simulates what would happen in the rendering process. Notice that the bright yellow in the upper-right corner of the top image is lost in the bottom one, and the color displayed is now a light yellow-green. In addition, in the center of the flower, the bright red-orange is too intense for the NTSC color space and is broken down into a few darker colors. What other differences can you find between the two images?
Courtesy of
Adobe Systems, Inc.

Figure 6-25.
An example of a gamut warning found in Premiere, a digital video program. The triangle with the exclamation point warns the user that the color selected is not an NTSC-safe color. If the user clicks on the little box below the warning symbol, the computer will select the next closest hue that can be reproduced properly. Courtesy of Adobe Systems, Inc.

Another method for avoiding this type of color shift is to use only the National Television System Committee (NTSC) safe colors in the initial production. In 1953, the NTSC set the pre-digital standard for video broadcast in North America. Since many television stations have not moved to HD, this standard is still being widely used. As more television stations move to the wider gamut of HD broadcasting, this standard is being replaced by Advanced Television Systems Committee (ATSC). Even with this upgrade there can still be some rendering issues with saturated hues, especially bright reds.

Many animation software programs have an NTSC-safe color filter built into the program. Users should make sure the filter is enabled and turned on. When choosing colors for graphics such as titles or logos, the color picker of most digital video programs has a gamut warning (Figure 6-25). This is similar to the warning device found in print programs such as Photoshop or Illustrator. The difference is that in a digital video program, the warning is that the color picked is not an NTSC-safe color. Newer software program updates may also include an ATSC-safe color filter. The final method of testing for this type of color jitter is to view the production on a standard television monitor and not a computer monitor, which has a higher range of visible color.

Summary

Digital color is here to stay. Understanding it is as important to the fine artist as it is to the designer. Light is at the heart of digital technology. The artist or designer is now manipulating and mixing light to create color. The final product may stay on the screen or may be printed or transferred to film or video. Understanding how the transfer process takes place enables the artist greater control over the final product.

Today, there is no longer one primary color system. With digital color, the new primary systems of RGB and CMYK are added to the repertoire of artists and designers. Some people say that working with this new technology is more cerebral and less intuitive, but to the people who know how their hardware and software create and work with color, this method can be equally supple and expressive.

Digital technology never stands still. It's always continually moving forward and reinventing itself. Artists and designers must keep up with technologic advancements, keeping pace with an ever-changing marketplace.

Up to this point, we have looked at color with an emphasis on two-dimensional art and design. The addition of the third dimension—depth—adds new complexities for working with color. No longer are we concerned about creating an illusion of space on a flat picture plane. We are now dealing with tangible space. There is a front, back, sides, bottom, and top to the object. It is real and exists in actual space.

All of the theories discussed previously still apply when creating art in the third dimension. Color harmonies are as important to the sculptor as they are to the painter, animator, or graphic designer. Every product purchased has been designed and great thought has been given to the color of that product. Toaster ovens, refrigerators, cars, and even toys are all three-dimensional objects designed to fulfill a need or desire. In many cases for the design of a product, extensive market research has been done to select the color of the item. Nothing is left to chance.

For the artist or sculptor, the choice of color may be more personal. Artists may choose a color to allow the piece to blend in or stand out. Sculptors understand that color can work like a magnet by drawing the viewer's eye to the piece. For all its importance in sculpture, color is normally ancillary to form. The overriding primary concern of the sculptor is the

Figure 7-1.
Barbara Hepworth, *Mother and Child*, 1934.
As light falls on the sculpture it creates highlights and shadows showing off the organic forms and adding to the rhythmic nature of the work.
© Tate, London, 2010/ Barbara Hempworth Estate.

shape and articulation of the forms, with color being used as the chief supporting element.

There are special considerations when working in the third dimension with color. There are several choices that the artist must make before the piece is begun. Color can be derived from many different materials and applications. The material itself can have an intrinsic color, such as using stone, wood, or even metals. Color can be applied after the fact—the piece can be painted, stained, or patinaed. The color can be mixed into the medium when casting an object in plaster, plastics, or other material. But color is never an afterthought; it is an intrinsic element, and it can be a unifying element that brings the entire piece together.

Value and Light

Since sculptures are three-dimensional objects, light plays an important role. The light falling on the object can create shadows in the crevices or undercuts by accentuating a specific part of the form. Value is also created on the body of the object by developing highlights in the parts closest to the light and shades of the original color in the portions farthest from the light source. Sculptors use these shadows as in Barbara Hepworth's *Mother and Child* (Figure 7-1) to bring out important aspects of the volumes as they move in space. The carved stone form of an abstracted female figure and child with its highly polished surface not only shows off the veining and color of the alabaster, but also creates a surface for the play of light. The void (the hole that penetrates the sculpture) produces shadows and dark values. It also allows light into the form and illuminates the planes of the figure, which can be easily seen in the highlighted areas at the side of the shoulder, torso, and child, bringing out their form and mass. Hepworth is credited as one of the first sculptors to pierce the form in this manner, foreshadowing the use of this device by Henry Moore. The conceptual value of the void suggests that the figure of the child developed from and outgrew the unoccupied space.

Innate Color

Innate or natural color is the color of the object itself. It could also be considered the local color of the object. Many artists who work in wood or stone choose a specific material because of its natural color and grain. Wood can range in color from birch, which is almost pure white, to ebony, which is a very dark brown, nearly black in color. Stone, especially marble, can vary in color from white to green to pink and more, as seen in the examples in Figure 7-2. An artist will choose a specific type of stone or wood because of the color, as well as its ease of ability to carve and its permanence.

Looking at the gleaming white marbles of ancient Greek statuary, it is hard for us to believe they were once highly colored and decorated. Today, we see the unadulterated white stone as the purest and highest state of the art.

Figure 7-2.
These four examples begin to show the great variety of colors of stone that are available to sculptors and architects. Many artists choose a particular stone for its color. The lines running through the stone are called veins and are similar to the grain of wood.
© Steven Bleicher

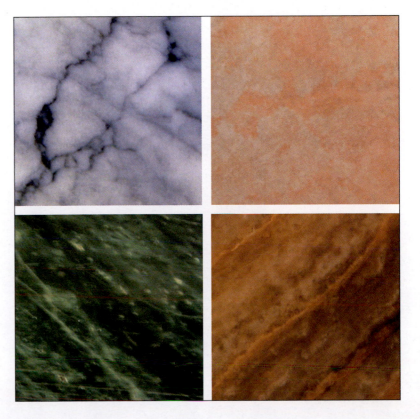

For us, the white represents a classic beauty and purity. If someone were to paint these objects, there would be a loud cry that they were being desecrated. But in reality, they were painted with flesh tones to resemble skin, and their garments were also highly decorated and painted to add to their majesty and opulence. It is only by today's standards that we believe this concept is unthinkable.

Part of what led us to this belief is the pure white marble statues of the Renaissance. The sculptures of Michelangelo, with their highly finished surfaces, have become our measuring stick for sculptures from antiquity. What we must remember is that by the time Michelangelo saw these earlier works, the paint had worn away and he was laboring under the same misconceptions and misinformation as we often do. So he thought he was emulating the past in the way he finished his sculptures.

Truth in Materials

The concept of allowing the actual nature and look of the materials to show through was at the heart of Constantin Brancusi's work. He espoused the philosophy of **truth in materials.** He felt that sculptures should show the natural beauty of the material with which they are created. Stone should look like stone, wood like wood, and so on. Wood should not be painted, and clay or plaster should not be patinaed (painted) to make it look like another material. The surfaces should be finished off in such a way as to bring out the natural and innate qualities of the material. He believed that artists should give great thought to what material they were going to use before starting a piece. The material and the conceptual essence of the work must go together and be thought of as one.

In *The Seal (stone)* (Figure 7-3), Brancusi's streamlined forms and highly polished surfaces became a hallmark of modern sculpture. His concept was to find the essence of the form and then to sand and polish the materials to bring out their natural beauty. He influenced the next generation of sculptors, including Henry Moore and Barbara Hepworth. Brancusi's influence can still be seen today in the work of Ursula von Rydingsvard, David Nash, and many others.

Figure 7-3.
Constantin Brancusi, *The Seal (stone)*, 1936. Brancusi's concept of truth in materials led him to create sculptures with highly polished surfaces to bring out the natural elegance of the materials. He took great care in selecting the material for each piece so that the color would go hand in hand with the forms he created.
Photo © 2010 Artists Rights Society (ARS), New York / ADAGP, Paris.
Photo courtesy of CNAC/MNAM/Dist. Réunion des Musées Nationaux / Art Resource, NY.

Figure 7-4.
Examples of the treatment of a wood finish. In the example on the left, the bare wood has been sanded smooth to bring out the natural grain of the basswood. The center image shows the same type of wood, to which a clear coat of polyurethane has been applied. Notice that it changes the color of the wood and creates a yellow cast. In the image on the right, a walnut polyurethane stain has been applied. The wood now has a deep rich color that still allows the grain to show through.
© Steven Bleicher

Stains

Artists will often search for a specific piece of wood and try to find one with just the right color and grain. Sanding and polishing the final sculpture brings out the inherent natural beauty of the material. Artists often use the grain of wood or stone as linear elements within a sculpture. Stains can be applied to the wood after it is sanded to add additional color while still allowing the grain of the wood to show through (Figure 7-4). They may have a very distinct hue or be applied in a more natural, neutral shade to resemble the color of another wood, such as maple, oak, or walnut. They are painted on, rubbed in, and then wiped off to leave a thin coating that seeps into the wood. Varnish, shellac, or polyurethane is then applied to seal and protect the finish.

Applied Color

An artist has several choices when working with a particular media—either sand and finish the material, exposing the natural beauty of the material, or paint it. This leads us to another major philosophical outlook, which is to deny the intrinsic look of the media. In essence, the materials used—whether they are clay, wood, plastic, or metal—are nothing more than a structural entity used to create the artist's idea or concept. The material plays no importance in and of itself other than defining the form or forms of the sculpture. A material may be selected for ease of creation, weight, structural quality, or permanence. It can be painted or colored in any manner the artist desires to simulate a particular material, or it can be painted without any special concern to the original media.

One of the chief practitioners of this type of color usage was Duane Hanson. He painted his plastic resin cast figures to look as lifelike as possible. This method of working could be considered a form of *trompe l'oeil*. He worked from body casts of real people and then painted and dressed his figures to accurately resemble living beings. Hanson was part of the photorealist movement and his figures are so lifelike that people will actually stop and try to talk to them. Years ago when visiting the Milwaukee Museum of Art, I saw someone actually go up to Hanson's *Janitor* (Figure 7-5) and try to ask directions.

To Paint or Not

Whether an artist decides to work with the natural color of the material or change it, it is purely an individual artistic choice. It is not a matter of right or wrong. Both are equally valid concepts when you are dealing with materials, whether you are building sculptures or anything else. These are some of the basic concepts that define the artist or designer and lie at the philosophical heart of the work.

Paints, Colorants, and Patinas

Artists can use a variety of paints and colorants when creating a three-dimensional work. For coloring plaster, any water-based media, such as acrylics, and dry powder

Figure 7-5.
Duane Hanson
(American, 1925–1996),
Janitor, 1973. Polyester,
fiberglass, and mixed
media. 65 ½ × 28 × 22 in.
(166.37 × 71.12 × 55.88 cm).
Hanson's figures have
such a high degree
of verisimilitude that
people will come up
and try to talk to the
sculpture. Most of the
people portrayed are
the artist's friends and
studio assistants. It was
considered a great honor
to be asked to be cast for
one of Hanson's pieces.
Art © Estate of Duane
Hanson/Licensed by VAGA,
New York, NY.
Photo courtesy of
Milwaukee Art Museum,
Gift of Friends of Art
M1973.91/ Photo credit
John Nienhuis.

pigments can be mixed into the wet plaster. This is not a new technique—fresco paintings were created by mixing pigments into the wet plaster before applying it to a wall. Dyes can also be mixed into plastics before casting or direct fabrication.

Wood and metal are normally painted after the completion of the sculpture. Here the determining choice of paint may be made based on where the artwork will be shown or exhibited. If it is to be displayed indoors, a wider range of paints and colorants may be employed. If, on the other hand, the piece is to be exhibited outdoors, then acrylics or enamels must be used because they are impervious to the changing weather conditions.

Patinas are referred to when speaking about any coloring that is used to resemble and create the look of a weathered metal surface and are most often associated with plaster or ceramic sculpture. But true patinas are chemical agents used to color cast bronze and aluminum. These chemical solutions are most often used to oxidize copper, brass, and bronze, as well as ferrous metals,

nickel, silver, zinc, and aluminum. Other chemical treatments include cupric nitrate, cobalt nitrate, and potash sulfurated (also known as liver of sulfur), which are primarily used on brass and bronze. Phoebe Adams takes advantage of the myriad of available patina hues in *The Waste That is Our Own* (Figure 7-6) using two different patinas. She allows the natural metallic coloring of the bronze to shine through the finish. This underlying color helps to unify the sculpture.

Figure 7-6.
Phoebe Adams, *The Waste That is Our Own*, 1987.
Bronze is used and highly valued for its durability and permanence. Adams creates a cast bronze sculpture that employs both two different patinas as well as bringing out the natural color of the metal in the pitcher.
Photo © Phoebe Adams.

Clays and Glazes

We normally think of clay as ranging in color from red to brown. But the clay body itself can vary widely in color, due either to its natural color or by having minerals and oxides mixed in with it. This is most easily done while the clay is still in the dry powder form. White clay bodies can be mixed with cobalt to make blue, chromium for green, and carbon for black. The advantage to working in this manner is that the color is not just on the surface, but homogeneously mixed within the clay itself.

Between adding a colored clay body before modeling and applying a glaze after modeling, a stain can be used. Stains can allow for a wider range of hues and be more color stable than the oxides used in creating colored clay bodies. Another benefit to using stains is that their color tends to be brighter and more iridescent. As with creating colored clays, truer hues can be achieved when using a white clay body rather than using one containing iron oxides. Beth

Ravitz paints and stains her clay sculptures (Figure 7-7), creating a blended surface. The look she achieves is more akin to the glazing method used in oil painting. She feels she is able to obtain a richer and more dynamic range of color using this method. She uses color to accentuate the modeled forms and to reinforce the underlying rhythmic structure of the sculpture.

Glazes are not only used in functional ceramics, but can also be used in ceramic sculpture. They are used in much the same manner as in creating utilitarian pieces. The added benefit to glazing a ceramic sculpture is that the glaze literally bonds with the clay in the firing process. This also seals the work and can make it invulnerable to the elements. One disadvantage of glazing is that a very large kiln may be required to fire a massive sculpture.

Color and Dimensionality

Color can be used to enhance the three-dimensionality of an object and make the shapes appear more deeply cut into the form,

Figure 7-7.
Beth *Ravitz, Tetrial,* 2002.
Ravitz uses paints and stains on her stoneware sculptures. She uses color to bring out and enhance the forms she creates and further the organic feel of the work. Ravitz uses cooler colors on the body of the piece and warmer hues to bring out the details on the surface.
Photo courtesy of Beth Ravitz.

or it can be used to deny the dimensionality of the form and flatten it down.

The proper use of color can make the object or sculpture appear even more round and full of form than it actually may be. The Native American tribes of the Northwest Pacific coast were experts in their use of color to enhance the dimensionality of their sculptures. Totem poles or, as they are more correctly known, memorial poles are an archetypal art form of the tribes of the Pacific Northwest. These works are normally carved from large cedar poles with animal and other totemic figures stacked one on top of another. They are created and carved as one long, continuous piece and never constructed of separate sections. These forms may tell the story of an important event or tribal legend. Memorial poles (Figure 7-8) are carved in a very shallow fashion, almost in a low relief or three-quarter fashion since the backs of the poles are rarely carved or detailed. They are meant to be seen from the front or side. What gives them their sense of form and dimensionality is the application of color. Color is used to outline and define each individual form and make them more pronounced. The hues used may vary between tribal groups and usually have specific meaning that relates to tribal lore and mythology.

Western artists have also used this concept to create contemporary sculptures. Jean Dubuffet created large sculptures out of cement and other materials. His childlike creations, which he dubbed "Art Brut," were meant to have a raw uncivilized feel as if they were untouched by traditional culture. Due to his use of color, they look more highly rounded than they really are. Each plane of the form either has its own color or is painted with lines going in different

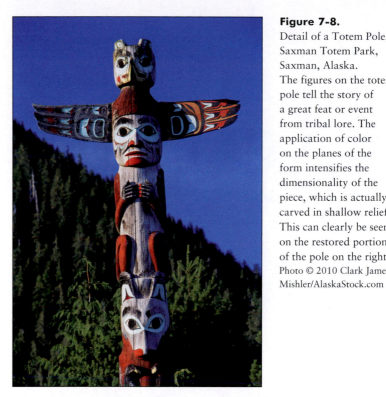

Figure 7-8.
Detail of a Totem Pole, Saxman Totem Park, Saxman, Alaska. The figures on the totem pole tell the story of a great feat or event from tribal lore. The application of color on the planes of the form intensifies the dimensionality of the piece, which is actually carved in shallow relief. This can clearly be seen on the restored portion of the pole on the right. Photo © 2010 Clark James Mishler/AlaskaStock.com

directions. By defining and showing off each plane, he gives a three-dimensional look to his sculptures, which were actually fairly flat with few if any undercuts. In this way, color creates form.

While using light to create value or painting each plane can bring out the dimensional look of the sculpture, color can also be used to flatten or negate the feeling of volume and mass. By painting or coloring an entire piece using very dark colors, the light falling on the sculpture cannot create visible shadows in the undercuts. This tends to flatten out the work and give it the appearance of a silhouette. The darker the hues used (including black), the flatter the forms will appear.

Another means of denying the dimensionality of the form is to paint the piece using vivid patterns and designs. Frank Stella used this method in creating

Figure 7-9.
Frank Stella, *Jarama II,* 1982.
The multicolored, highly patterned surface of this relief confuses the eye and visually appears to flatten out the piece. This method of color application is used to deny the dimensionality of the form. This begs the question, at what point does a painting become a sculpture and vice versa?
© 2010 Frank Stella / Artists Rights Society (ARS), New York.
Photo courtesy of the National Gallery of Art, Washington.

Jarama II (Figure 7-9). The wild patterns create a visually confusing surface. Since the viewer cannot make out or discern the edge and contour of the form, it flattens out the mass, giving it an even look.

Over the years, three-dimensional form has come to include more than just traditional sculpture. It now has become the catchall for diverse things such as conceptual art, installations, performance art, and environmental works. In essence, anything that isn't two-dimensional or computer generated has been lumped into this category. Just as with traditional types of art, these newer forms also use color and each may have their own special considerations and color concerns.

Glass

The newest entrant to the arena of sculpture is glass. Artists such as Dale Chihuly (Figures 7-10 and 7-11) have rediscovered the beauty of working and shaping molten glass. Colored glass surfaces can range from transparent to completely opaque. Chihuly has a painterly approach to color and treats it in a fluid fashion. He is interested in the effect of light passing through the various layers of colored glass, which creates multilevels of transparency. Colorants usually in the form of metals or oxides are introduced into the glass in the molten state to create the wide array of hues used in glass objects and sculpture. In earlier times, gold was used as one of the metals used to create red, making it one of the highly prized and most expensive hues. Coloring glass in its liquid state can be tricky due to the high heat required and because it must cool very slowly to avoid cracking and shattering. Today, commercially prepared stains can be purchased to color glass. One of the drawbacks to using these colorants is that they are just painted on the surface and do not fuse with the material. This makes them susceptible to scratches and damage.

Interiors

Interiors are also three-dimensional spaces. Artist and designers must understand the impact of color on both intimate and over-sized interiors. Color can affect the way we feel about a space and can impact its habitability. Warm-hued walls tend to advance visually, making the space feel larger and more expansive. The warm feeling of the color tends to make the space feel cozier and more intimate. People will actually feel warmer in a room with light or warm-hued colors as the hues can actually raise their adrenaline levels.

Cool colors tend to visually recede in space, which can make the room look smaller. The use of dark cool hues can actually make the person feel depressed and blue. In a very warm climate the color can actually

Figure 7-10.
Dale Chihuly, *Flori di Como*, 1998.
The Bellagio Resort, Las Vegas, Nevada
In this piece, the ceiling of the lobby of the Bellagio Resort, Chihuly is able to capture a variety of vivid hues while working with the transparency of the glass. His work is very theatrical in that it uses swirling lines and layers of color to move the viewer's eye throughout the ceiling. Working with glass in this manner is very labor intensive. It takes several assistants working closely with Chihuly to create a glass sculpture or an installation of this magnitude. The image on the cover is a detail of the same ceiling.
Photo courtesy of Dale Chihuly.

absorb the sun's rays, heating up the space and making air-conditioning more expensive.

Lighting design has become an important aspect of interior design not only for the home but also for industry and public areas. Dark spaces can be dangerous and foreboding. The dull cast from fluorescent lighting can sap the warmth from a space. This is often the case with large expansive public spaces such as airports. To combat this situation, designers of the McNamara Terminal/Northwest World Gateway at Detroit's Metro Airport have created a mood-enhancing sound and light environment in one of the

Figure 7-11.
Dale Chihuly, Detail of *Flori di Como*, 1998.
The Bellagio Resort, Las Vegas, Nevada
In this detail of the ceiling, the transparent nature of the glass becomes more evident. The shapes of the glass forms Chihuly uses are reminiscent of flowers, shells and other organic forms.
Photo courtesy of Dale Chihuly.

Figure 7-12.
Detroit Metro Airport Tunnel.
The music and colored lighting envelops passengers as they make their way through the expansive tunnel making their experience more pleasant and enjoyable. Passengers have given the new terminal upgrade rave reviews.
Photo courtesy of Kenneth Rice.

sprawling terminal walkways (Figure 7-12). The space is illuminated by an intelligent LED-based system with sculpted glass panels. The choreographed lighting system constantly changes, captivating passengers as they pass through the terminal. The LED lights require minimal maintenance.

Architecture

Not only are new materials and their use of color impacting interiors, but innovative materials such as titanium are also being used to revolutionize architecture. The single most recognizable building of the new millennium is the Guggenheim Museum in Bilbao, Spain. Designed by Architect Frank Gehry, it has an organic feel of something that has sprouted rather than been constructed. The building has completely changed the region, making it a new tourist destination, and is credited with the economic rebirth of the Basque region. Surveys have shown that 80 percent of the visitors to the area are there to see the museum. This type of signature architecture has come to represent the city in the same way the Opera House has come to symbolize Sydney, Australia. These buildings are immediately recognizable and have become icons of their respective cities.

While the museum started as a sketch on paper it was transferred to digital medium and engineered with the help of three-dimensional computer modeling programs. The metal used to fabricate the outside, titanium, works like a skin. Because of the complexity of the curved surfaces the CAD programs insured that each part would fit together and that the half-millimeter metal membrane would fit onto each block. Gehry says that the bottom part of the building is kind of a boat shape while the titanium panels remind visitors of the scales of a fish. The water that surrounds part of the structure further reinforces these aquatic allusions. The metal surface reflects light and seems to change color depending upon the time of day and weather. In Figures 7-13 and 7-14 the color of the water and sky resonate in the polished metal skin of the building. It changes color depending upon the weather, time of day, and time of year. The ever-changing façade is as much a draw as the artworks inside the museum.

New Issues of Dimensionality

Contemporary artworks have transcended the physicality of objecthood. Artists became increasing interested in the underly-

Figure 7-13.
Frank Gehry,
Guggenheim Museum,
Bilbao, Spain.
A view of the museum
as seen at midday. The
bright sunlight creates a
golden cast to the metal
skin of the building. The
blue of the surrounding
water is also reflected in
the shimmering surface.
Guggenheim Museum
Bilbao, Spain. © The
Solomon R. Guggenheim
Foundation, New York.
Photograph by Steven
Bleicher. All rights reserved.
Total or partial reproduction
is prohibited.

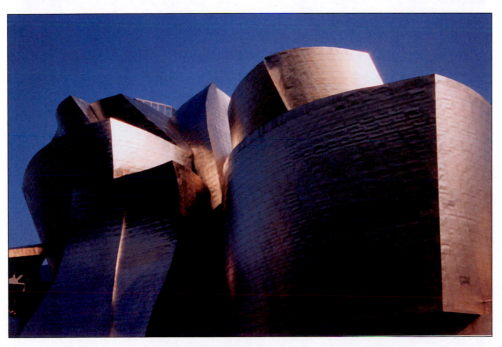

Figure 7-14.
Frank Gehry,
Guggenheim Museum,
Bilbao, Spain.
In the late afternoon sun,
the colors of the building
change to a variety of
deep oranges and reds.
Violet is also reflected
from the surrounding
water. The building
seems to change color
like a chameleon.
Guggenheim Museum
Bilbao, Spain. © The
Solomon R. Guggenheim
Foundation, New York.
Photograph by Steven
Bleicher. All rights reserved.
Total or partial reproduction
is prohibited.

ing concept and conceptualization of their creations. These new works explored the new territories of concept, exhibition space, the body, and technology. Many of these new entities somehow became included in the area of new forms, which became allied with sculpture and 3-D. This may be in part due to their use or inclusion of physical objects or elements within their work. These new areas included site-specific installations, earthworks, and body art. One element these new works had in common was an interest in the underlying conceptualization of the work

Conceptual Art

Conceptual art is a rather large area to cover and can encompass a wide range of art activities. It can take the form of written instructions or be comprised of photographs that document a previous activity, creation, or event. It may be the most elusive of all the art styles to define or categorize. In conceptual art, the idea or concept is more important than producing a tangible lasting object. The act is the primal element, and it may be recorded in photographs or not, as desired by the artist.

But even conceptual art with its denial of the object and form uses color as an integral element. Most conceptual artists favor white as a noncolor and thereby severely limit any cultural or psychological associations. In Yoko Ono's *Play it by Trust,* all of the pieces on a chessboard are painted white. After a few moves, it would become impossible for one player to tell his or her pieces from the other player.

In the late 1990s, blue bikes (Figure 7-15) began popping up all over Broward County in south Florida. Blue bikes were chained wherever one could conceivably lock a bicycle—from bike racks, to sign poles, and so on, blue bikes of all shapes and sizes magically appeared, one after another. Steve Sticht, the artist who created these **guerilla artworks,** came up with the color blue when he was working on construction, painting lines or stripes for handicapped parking spaces. Sticht said the commercially prepared blue paint reminded him of the Day-Glo posters he had as a teenager. In the dark, the bright blue paint shined with an iridescent quality and allowed the bikes to be seen at night. Several years ago, the company changed the paint formula and altered its look, so Sticht had to bring in a sample and have the color matched. Now the bikes are all painted with what has become their own unique "blue bike" hue.

The bikes work on many levels. They are mundane items that would normally go unnoticed and be taken for granted. But the intense color forces the viewer to really look at the bikes and their surroundings and ponder the questions of why they were there, how they got there, and what their meaning was. Sticht believed this phenomenology reawakens a sense of wonder about one's environment. With more than 200 bikes placed within the area, the project is ongoing. However, many of them succumb to life in the city. Recently, one was totaled in a car accident in which a limousine jumped the curb, taking out a street sign with the bike attached to it. Still others have been stolen or dismantled and taken as souvenirs. The most recent additions now come with a sticker with Sticht's e-mail address to allow interested viewers to contact him for more information.

Figure 7-15.
Steve Sticht, *Blue Bike,* 2002.
The blue color of the bikes makes them stand out grabbing the public's attention. The shade of blue is specially mixed for Sticht and has become his own "blue bike" hue.
Photo courtesy of Steve Sticht.

Light Installations

Another kind of art that is hard to classify is the use of light. Whether it is the use of natural light or of lamps, these works tend to fall into the category of installations. This type of artwork can range from Dan Flavin's use of fluorescent lamps set up in a gallery or museum, to Walter de Maria's *Lightning Field*, a series of brightly polished steel poles placed in a grid in the New Mexico desert. The poles attract the discharge from lightning and create great arcs from the bolt to the pole that illuminate the sky.

A pioneer in the use of light and electronics, Nam June Pike created *Magnet TV* in 1965 (Figure 7-16). He was a founding

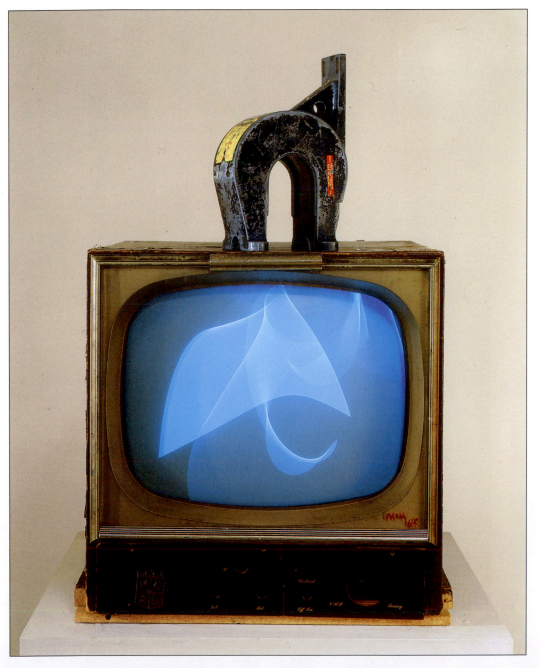

Figure 7-16
Nam June Pike 1932-2006, Magnet TV, 1965.
17" black and white television set with magnet, 28 ⅜ × 19 ¼ × 24 ½ in. (72.07 × 48.9 × 62.23 cm).
Pike uses a magnet to alter the electromagnetic field of the picture tube, which creates the blue arcing lines on the picture tube.
Whitney Museum of American Art, New York; Purchase, with funds from Dieter Rosenkranz. 86.60a-b.
Photo © Nam June Paik Estate.

member of the Fluxus group, a vague association of international artists. Their goal was to intermix art and commerce and create artworks that were both inexpensive and accessible. In this piece, the magnet interrupts the standard television signal and creates a series of vibrant blue dancing lines. The form the lines make constantly changes and moves, producing a form of kinetic sculpture or abstract television program.

Landscape and Environmental Art

A number of artists today work directly in the landscape, both as the place and subject of their work. The landscape becomes both subject and material. One of the most notable landscape artists is Andy Goldsworthy. He creates large sculptures made solely out of elements found in the selected locations and never uses any additional elements such as adhesives, paints, or dyes. The colors in his works are from found leaves, rocks, or moss (Figure 7-17). All of the items used in his works are natural elements and come directly from the site of the piece. These works are also know as **site-specific** works, since they are developed for a specific location and actually become part of the environment. His work is ephemeral and impermanent. A photograph of the piece is the only lasting memento or record of the work.

Performance and Body Art

Performance art is art that is acted out or presented in some manner or form. It may take place on the street, in a gallery or museum, or just about anywhere.

Figure 7-17.
Andy Goldsworthy,
Rowan Leaves & Hole,
1987.
Goldsworthy always works from the objects he finds on location. He gathered leaves from the site in the varying colors seen.
Photo © Andy Goldsworthy.

Figure 7-18.
Ogechi Chieke, *Thee Creation Theory*, 2005. (Photograph of a performance at the Galerie Stadler, Paris) In performance art it is the act that is important. In Chieke's work its not paint but blood and milk that give the work its unique color. The photograph becomes the only record of the event. Photo © Ogechi Chieke.

Photographs or videotape may be made to document the event, but the act itself is the actual artwork. The art is in the doing. Both performance and body art arose, in some sense, in direct opposition to the highly intellectualized work of conceptual art. These works tended to be rawer and engaged the viewer in real time. They evolved from the feminist movement, in which a number of artists focused on issues of female identity and coming to terms with one's own body. Men were also influenced by these concepts of taking control and command over your own body. The art took on a sexual and graphic quality. The dangerous actions turned the viewer into a voyeur in a society where people had become immune to violence and bloodshed on television. These acts confronted the viewer with a harsh reality.

Ogechi Chieke sees her performance piece *Thee Creation Theory* (Figure 7-18) as she is an impression and her own visualization of a time before time. The work is a symbolic depiction of the first or primal birth. The liquid elements represent those primal life components of blood and milk, which mix and then melt away into the creation of the first woman, and the primordial "Eve" is revealed. Chieke uses her own body as the canvas. These are not Hollywood special effects. This is a powerful work because the viewer knows the elements are real, the blood and milk are real; the pained look on her face is real. And because of this, we have an immediate visceral response to the work.

Summary

Color is not just the domain of the two-dimensional artist or designer. It plays an equally important role in sculpture, industrial design, and all other forms of three-dimensional design. Color can also be used to make an object stand out and be noticed. The choice of material can dictate the color of the object. The artist can choose to bring out and enhance the natural color, grain, and texture of the media by sanding and polishing it to follow Brancusi's idea of truth in materials. Or the media can be painted over to form either a polychrome finish or a faux surface that simulates a wide variety of materials from stone to metal.

Color can be used to either enhance or deny the three-dimensionality of sculpture. Painting the various planes of an object with discrete areas of color will make the planes stand out and create a greater illusion of dimensionality, even in a shallow carving or relief.

Using wild patterns or designs can confuse the viewer's eye and flatten down the appearance of the object. The object can also be painted to mimic and blend into its surroundings, which is the basis of camouflage used by the military. With dimensional objects, the artist or designer is also dealing with the concept of value. As light hits the object, areas of highlights, middle tones, and shadows are created.

Whether it's finding new uses for materials as Gehry did in the Guggenheim at Bilbao or exploring the realms of new technology, color never stands still.

Color is an essential aspect of fine art. Whether it is painting, drawing, sculpture, or new forms of art, color is always a defining element. Even today's cutting-edge digital creations are concerned with the application and rendering of color.

There have been many art movements over the last 150 years, but the majority have been more concerned with imagery and subject matter than with color. Color was relegated to a supportive or ancillary role. Only a few of these schools of thought have placed color at the forefront of their philosophy. In this chapter, we will review some of the movements in art in which color played a major or dominant role in the underlying aesthetics of the artworks created.

It is interesting that something as powerful as color was not featured more prominently in more schools of thought. Color is one of the only elements in art that has an immediate unconscious response from the viewer's brain. As we have seen in previous chapters, people respond to color before they form conscious thoughts about what they are viewing. The first group of modern artists to understand the full impact of color was the Impressionists. The impact of light and its effects on color was the major focus of their work.

Impressionism

In some sense, contemporary art started with Impressionism. Our ideas of bohemian artists living in lofts or garrets and suffering for their art evolved from the myths and stories surrounding the artists of this time period. It may be the most overly romanticized time period in all of art history. But like all great stories, much of the tales are true.

Impressionism was a clear and dramatic break from the past and traditional academic painting. In everything from their use of color to the subject matter of their paintings, the Impressionists broke new ground. The effect of light and color was

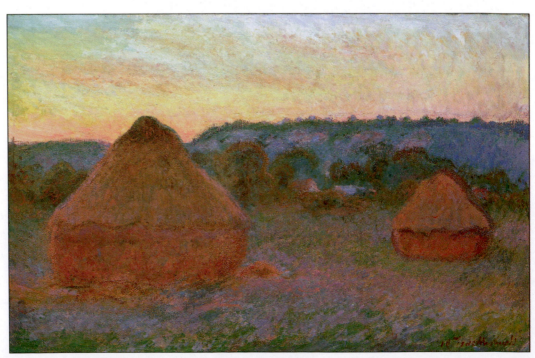

Figure 8-1.
Claude Monet, 1840-1926, *Stacks of Wheat (End of Day, Autumn)*, 1890-91, Oil on canvas, 27 ⅞ × 39 ¾ in. (65.8 × 101 cm), Mr. and Mrs. Lewis Larned Coburn Memorial Collection, 1933.444, The Art Institute of Chicago. Monet used a warm palette of intense hues to create this painting of haystacks in the summer sun. He also placed complementary hues next to one another, which added to the luminous atmospheric quality of the painting. Photography © The Art Institute of Chicago.

the primary focus of the group; however, each member concentrated on his or her own particular area of interest. Claude Monet focused on the great outdoors and even created his own gardens at Giverny. Edgar Degas became interested in the ballet, while Pierre Auguste Renoir had a lifelong fascination with the effects of light on the human figure.

The Impressionist's goal was to bathe the subject in light and paint the atmosphere to capture a moment in time. They were the first to understand and realize that as the time of day changed, so did the light and therefore the color. Monet and Renoir would bring several canvases with them when they painted outdoors. As the time of day and light changed, they would stop working on one canvas and begin another. This was a radical departure from the past when artists would bring one canvas with them and work on that painting all day long. They understood that in the morning the softer light would produce specific tints of color and that at noon when the sun was strongest, the color would be more intense and saturated with fewer shades. As the light of day began to fade in the late afternoon, more shades of a given hue would be used. Not only did the light change throughout the day, but even the time of year would have an effect on the color. As the seasons changed, so did the quality and amount of light and color. Monet did several paintings of the same subject at different times of the year. These studies included the Rouen Cathedral, the Houses of Parliament during his extended stays in London, and the wheat stacks pictured in Figures 8-1 and 8-2.

The Impressionists also limited their use of black. They would only use it if the actual item they were painting was black, such as a man's shoes or a locomotive. But they planned out their pictures and subject

Figure 8-2.
Claude Monet, 1840-1926, *Stack of Wheat (Snow Effect, Overcast Day)*, 1890-91, Oil on canvas, 26 × 36 5/8 in. (66 × 93 cm), Mr. and Mrs. Martin A. Ryerson Collection, 1933.1155, The Art Institute of Chicago. Monet felt the color of the atmosphere (especially in winter) was violet. He used a cool palette composed of blues and violets and added its complement— the toned down orange color of the haystack. There are a few traces of pure hue used as highlights at the top of the haystack to create highlights and give the feeling of the winter sun. Photography © The Art Institute of Chicago.

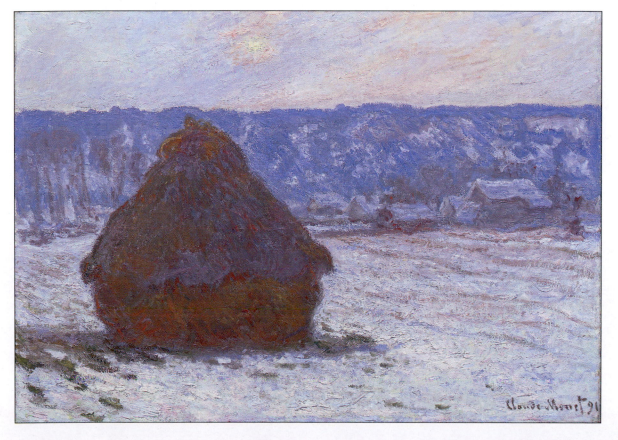

matter to avoid these items. Instead of mixing black with a hue when creating a tone or shade, they would mix the complement of the color to darken and desaturate it. They would also add white to the complementary mixtures, which creates a warm or cool grayish color. This too was a departure from the traditional academic training of a painter.

In addition, they would juxtapose complementary hues to heighten the color in a painting. By placing two complements next to each other, they would cause a sensation in the viewer's eye, making the color appear more intense and vibrant. This added to the luminous atmospheric quality of their paintings.

In the traditional painting of this time period, the paint was laid down and applied in a very smooth manner. The objective was to hide the actual stroke of the brush and create a completely smooth surface. The Impressionists, however, applied their paint in short dabs or strokes, breaking up the surface. This also led to the pronouncement of the critics that their work was unfinished.

In fact, the term *impressionism* was actually an insult hurled at the group by an art critic. The painting that sparked the debate, *Impression, Sunrise* by Claude Monet, was ridiculed saying that it was unfinished and merely a study, not a complete, finished work of art.

The Impressionists also wanted to paint contemporary life. They believed that they were living the ultimate in modernity and embraced the changes brought by the industrial revolution. They painted their friends and the places they frequented—the bars, cafés, and even the brothels. It would be as if today's young artists painted the bars, dance clubs, mosh pits, and even the malls where young people hang out. This concept of one's life being a worthy subject matter to paint was novel. With the rise of a burgeoning middle class, this change in subject matter had an audience, and this made their paintings more accessible to the general public.

During this time period, new artworks were beginning to enter the marketplace. Japanese prints (Figure 8-3) were being

Figure 8-3.
Katsushika Hokusai (1760-1849). The Great Wave at Kanagawa (from a Series of Thirty-six Views of Mount Fuji). CA. 1830-1832. Japan. Edo Period. Polychrome woodblock print; ink and color on paper, 10 ⅛ × 14 ¹⁵⁄₁₆ in. (25.7 × 37.9 cm). Published by Eiudo. H. O. Havemeyer Collection, Bequest of Mrs. H.O. Havemeyer, 1929 (JP1847). Flat areas of unmodulated color were dominant features of Japanese prints. The use of asymmetric compositions was another common element in these prints and greatly influenced the Impressionists' use of space in their compositions. Image copyright © The Metropolitan Museum of Art/ Art Resource, NY.

brought over from Asia, and their flat use of color influenced the group that came to be known as the Postimpressionists. The large off-centered groups of dancers found in Degas paintings and pastels are a spatial device gleaned from Japanese prints. Paul Gauguin and Vincent Van Gogh even painted versions of the prints they saw and collected. They were influenced by the use of broad areas of flat, unmodeled color and the sense of space. Gauguin's flat watered-down planes of color may also have been adapted from the styles seen in these prints.

Pointillism

While Georges Seurat may be the most notable of artists who painted in this style, he was by far not the only one. Pissarro, Siselly, and Bonnard all experimented with pointillism (Figure 8-4). Not only did it continue the themes of modern life, but it also broke new ground in its use of color and application of paint. Painting with small dots or dabs, Seurat took

Rood's color concepts and applied them to painting. In visual color mixing, artists do not premix their colors on a palette and then apply them to the canvas, but instead they paint tiny dots or points of pure unmixed color. These hues, when placed next to each other so that they literally touch one another, blend in the eye or mind of the viewer. While Seurat may receive the most recognition and credit for developing this method of painting, he was not the only one to paint in this manner. French painters Camille Pissarro and Alfred Sisley both took turns working with this method of painting. Even Vincent Van Gogh used a variation on this style in several of his canvases. But instead of tiny dots of paint, Van Gogh used longer brush strokes of color, placing them one next to the other. Since his application of paint was so thick and heavy, where the two colors met they sometimes actually blended, as one brush stroke of wet paint touched the following brushload of wet paint.

Figure 8-4.
Camille Pissarro, 1840-1926, *Haying Time*, 1892, Oil on canvas, 25 ¾ × 32 in. (65.5 × 81.3 cm). Gift of Bruce Borland, 1961.791, The Art Institute of Chicago. Pissarro portrays peasants harvesting ripened grain in the late summer sun. The green tones of the painting are enlivened with dots of red, orange, yellow, purple, blue, and violet. The effect is a shimmering colored textured surface that unifies the composition. Photography © The Art Institute of Chicago.

Figure 8-5.
Chuck Close, *Elizabeth*,
1989.
Close uses photographs
as the basis of his
paintings. He transfers
to the canvas using
an underlying grid
structure. The highly
decorative surface of his
work keeps the viewer's
eye moving between the
colored dots that make
up the patterned surface
and the overall image.
Photograph by Bill
Jacobson, courtesy of The
Pace Gallery.
© Chuck Close, courtesy of
The Pace Gallery.

In the 1980s Chuck Close revived elements of this style in his large-scale portraits (Figure 8-5). While visually they make reference to pointillism, his painting process is more closely related to four-color production printing, with one color placed on top of another in a layered effect. In this way, his work has an immediate relationship to halftone and screenprinting, in which an image is made up of tiny dots. He starts out with a photograph of the sitter, enlarging it to a monumental size. A grid is drawn over the enlargement and a corresponding grid is marked out on the large canvas. Close then goes about painstakingly painting each cell, building up the colors. He was never really part of the photorealist movement; his paintings don't share their same smooth surface. But still, his work has an unemotional surface treatment more closely allied to minimalism.

A more contemporary use of pointillism can be seen in the work of Vik Muniz (Figure 8-6). He does not use paint but torn pieces of magazines as his color medium. These works at once have a historical basis while the use of mass culture materials speaks to our own present-day society and market-driven culture. Muniz's work shares a similar rich surface texture that acts as an additional unifying element. The monument scale of his collage work shares a postmodern sensibility with artists like Chuck Close.

Cézanne

The later part of the nineteenth century saw great advances in the use of color through the medium of painting. Another artist interested in developing a formal structured approach to painting was Paul Cézanne. A contemporary of the Postimpressionists, Cézanne's mission was "to make Impressionism into something solid and enduring." Instead of working with light and value, he developed his canvases in terms of simplifying planes into patches or facets of color. He abandoned traditional perspective in favor of his own interpretations or sensations of nature and used warm and cool hues to develop and model form (Figure 8-7). His approach was more deliberate and constructive than that of his contemporaries. Cézanne did not blend his paint colors but worked in rectangular "open brushstrokes" of color to develop an evenly faceted surface. His work has had a lasting impact on modern art, influencing Braque and Picasso in their development of cubism as well as countless others.

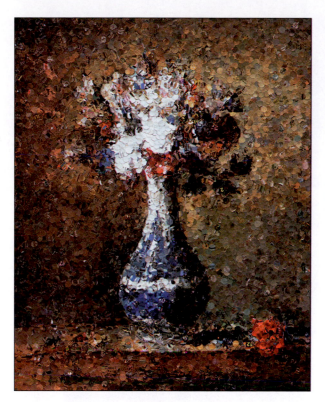

Figure 8-6.
Vik Muniz, *Flowers in a Blue and White Vase,* 2005.
Muniz uses bits of paper to produce his large-scale pointillist works. He uses the same concept of visual color mixing as Seurat to generate his chromatic hues.
Art © Vik Muniz/Licensed by VAGA, New York, NY.

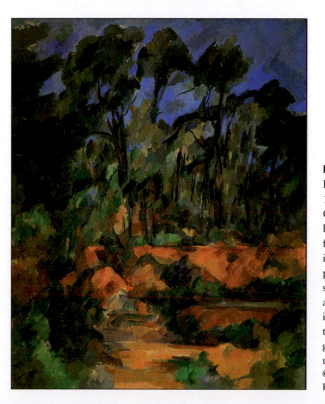

Figure 8-7.
Paul Cezanne, *Forest,* c. 1902-04.
Cezanne's use of open brushstrokes creating faceted areas of color is clearly evident in this painting. He employs the same constructed planar approach to everything in the painting including the sky, trees and grounds creating a unified surface.
© Erich Lessing / Art Resource, NY.

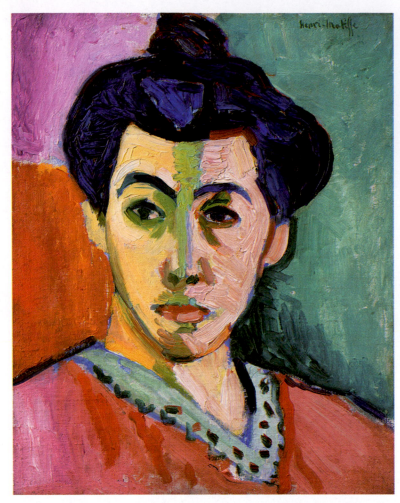

Figure 8-8.
Henri Matisse, *Madame Matisse (the Green Line)*, 1905.
The left side of the face has warmer hues while the right side contains more cool colors. The violet eyebrow on the right side of the face is a complement to the dominant yellow used on the left. Matisse was highly regarded for his use of color and is considered one of the supreme colorists.
© 2010 Succession H. Matisse / Arts Rights Society (ARS), New York. Photo courtesy of Statens Museum for Kunst.

Fauvism

Brilliant color was at the heart of Fauvism. This new movement grew out of the path blazed by the Postimpressionists Paul Gauguin, Vincent Van Gogh, and Pierre Bonnard. Artists in both France and Germany sought to liberate color. No longer were they tied to local color; it could be used purely as a means of expression. Events could take place on the canvas that were not tied to reality. André Derain painted red boats on a yellow river with a violet bridge. He used color for its emotional quality and not as a representational element. Henri Matisse began his career as a Fauve painter. He felt color should be used in an expressive manner. In Figure 8-8, Matisse paints his wife in a free, bold style without reference to natural hues. The subtitle of the painting, "the green line," refers to the light green line running down the center of the woman's face. The line divides the face into two hemispheres: one on the left in harsh yellows and one on the right in a more natural tint of ochre. The background is simply flat planes of color used to fill out the composition. This new freedom of not being bound to the natural world helped pave the way for cubism and the move toward abstraction. The Fauvists broke away from all forms of naturalistic representation.

Abstract Expressionism

Abstract expressionism and its descendant, color-field painting, seemed to be natural outgrowths of the cubist and surrealist movements. In these new styles, the imagery of the past was cast aside completely for pure of color paint. Taking its cues from automatic writing and Jungian philosophy, abstract expressionism sought to release the unconscious mind of artists and allowed them to create raw uncensored works. In the post–World War 2 era, these new movements were now becoming American art forms centered in New York in response to the past, in which Europe and especially Paris were the centers. Artists such as Jackson Pollack stepped away from the tube of paint and turned to the commercially produced can of paint. This is an important change for painting and color. No longer was color to be squeezed out of a tube of paint and mixed on a palette, but used straight from the can. It was felt that new forms of art need new materials—modern materials.

Color-field painting was directly concerned with the application of color to the canvas. In these works, the canvas was removed from the stiff formality of the stretcher and used as a space where the

Figure 8-9.
Janet Gold, *Intimate Space,* 2002.
Gold uses pastels for the richness of their color. You can make out the individual strokes of the pastels as she builds up a complex layering of color. Her color scheme is primarily composed of secondary hues.
Photo courtesy of the Artist.

liquid events could take place. Paint became a vehicle for color—watered down and at times used right out of the can. In both of these forms of painting, but most prominently in color-field painting, the happy accident was promoted and became an elemental part of the work. One of the most renowned painters of the genre is Helen Frankenthaller. She creates richly textured layers of color using stains and washes of color (Figure 8-9). The artist would set up a situation of how the paint might be thinned or poured but the actual results are partially up to chance. The artist's hand and most importantly the brush stroke is removed form the final artwork. In more

contemporary interpretations of color-field painting, the primary interest is still color, but the artist's hand has returned, as seen in the gestural strokes or patterned marks.

Minimalism

Minimalism was in sharp contrast and direct opposition to the more ephemeral and emotional aspects of abstract expressionism and color-field painting. The desire of artists Donald Judd and Carl Andre was to eliminate traditional spatial illusionism in favor of the pure plastic quality of the materials. The artist's hand and any trace of it—such as brush-strokes, imagery, or even the tactile surface quality of the material—was eliminated in

Figure 8-10.
Ellsworth Kelly, Yellow/Orange, 1968. Oil on canvas, two joined panels. 62 × 62 inches (157.5 × 157.5 cm). Kelly uses color for its optical sensation, negating any meaning or symbolism.
Each colored element echoes the square motif. He has a unique aptitude in suggesting solid forms using intense contrasts.
The Museum of Modern Art, New York, The Riklis Collection of McCrory Corporation. Photo courtesy and © Ellsworth Kelly.

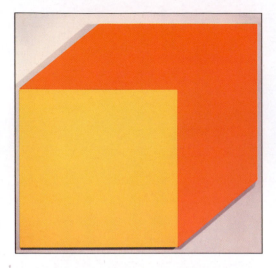

favor of a pure streamlined, almost antiseptic, surface (Figure 8-10). Minimalism, as its name implied, sought to refine and reduce form down to its most basic element, allying it more closely with architecture of the international style. In this style, color was also pared down or even eliminated in favor of the natural color of the materials that echoed Brancusi's truth in materials. When used, color was bright, saturated, and simple so that it would not take away from the form of the work itself or create any illusionist attributes.

Op Art

Op art, or optical art, was a movement that emerged during the same time period as minimalism. Both shared the use of simple flat unmodulated color. They also shared the complete absence of any evidence of the artist's hand to produce slick smooth surfaces. Op art used kinetic effects and optical illusions to create the feeling of movement in still flat surfaces. Victor Vasarely's *Kedzi* (Figure 8-11) appears to

Figure 8-11.
Victor Vasarely, *Kedzi,* undated.
The sculpture, which appears to be fully three-dimensional, is really a flat plane. The 3-D effect is purely an illusion. The creation of illusions were a major factor in op art.
© 2010 Artists Rights Society (ARS), New York/ADAGP, Paris.

be a fully three-dimensional sculpture. It is, however, completely flat and only offers the viewer the illusion of dimension. The colors are shaded as if to suggest that light is hitting a perpendicular surface—a complete illusion.

Art, especially modern art, is constantly working in opposition and in contrast to what preceded it. As each new "–ism" or style emerges, it seems to be in direct contrast to what directly preceded it. The new photo-realists of the 1980s were a direct response to color-field painting, minimalism, and conceptual art. They returned to the human element and the craft of painting. One had to be quite skilled and able to paint in a photo-realistic manner. This style returned realistic local color to the mainstream. Color had to be rendered correctly and accurately to aid in the naturalist look of the work. The high degree of verisimilitude brought back issues of atmospheric perspective and shading as important for the artist. Their paintings also had the glossy look and surface of the photograph. Since these artists grew up with photography and television as seminal influences in their lives, it is only natural that they would be reflected in their artwork.

These artists were intrigued by the commercial landscape of the city, which became their primary subject matter. Unlike earlier movements, the natural pristine landscape is nowhere to be found. It is the city with all of its bright shiny consumerism that attracted the artists. In still-life painting of this period, highly reflective surfaces such as mirrors and crystal dominated. These surfaces were hard to capture realistically and showed the virtuosity of the artist's skill. A prime example is Nancy Hagin's *White Muslim* (Figure 8-12), which contains a range of textures and surfaces from the soft draped cloth fabric to the hard surfaces of the pitcher and the enamel coffee pot. Hagin renders each object with an exacting eye and captures their local color and value accurately.

Neo-Expressionism

Arriving on the New York scene at about the same time as the photorealist movement, neo-Expressionism was primarily a European import most notably from Germany and Italy. This makes sense, since the earlier expressionist movements of the 1900s also had their start in southern Europe and Germany. It was yet another response against the established genres of minimalism and conceptual art. Sandro Chia was one of the leading proponents of this style to arrive on the New York art scene from Italy.

Americanized versions of this movement, led by Basquiat's graffiti style, have been linked to pop culture in the forms of rap and hip-hop. In both of these groups, however, there was a renewed belief in the power and possibility

Figure 8-12.
Nancy Hagin, *White Muslin*, 2009. Hagin presents the viewer with a wide variety of textures and surfaces. She uses a realistic naturalist color palette. The color is slightly heightened. Hagin uses color in a traditional manner with bright whites and warm soft hues used to bring objects to the front of the picture plane while the cool shades recede in space creating a sense of depth.
Photo courtesy of Fischbach Gallery, New York.

Figure 8-13.
Jean-Michel Basquiat, *Untitled (Skull), 1981.* The warm bright hues in the skull create a feeling of frenetic movement pushing the image to the foreground. As the colors move into the background they become less saturated which helps to create some sense of depth. As with earlier expressionist movements color is used for its emotional content without regard for the natural world.
© 2010 The Estate of Jean-Michael Basquiat / ADAGP, Paris/ARS, New York. Photo courtesy of The Eli and Edythe L. Broad Collection, Los Angeles.

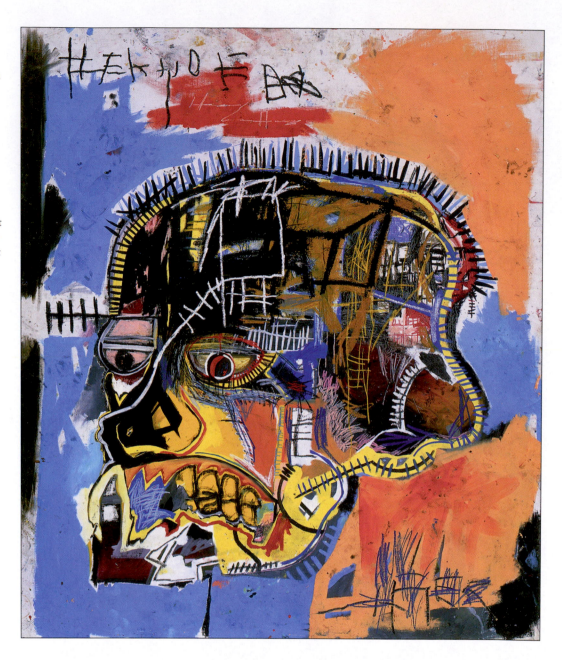

of painting. The neo-Expressionists' paintings were emotionally and physically charged. By using color as an important element, it gave the artists a more visceral component and enabled them to reach the viewer's subconscious by tapping an emotional wellspring.

In *Boy and Dog in a Johnnypump* (Figure 8-13), Basquiat uses very fluid gestural brush strokes to convey the feeling of quick rapid movement. The dripping paint shows the immediacy of application and the hurried strokes have the feel of graffiti. The warm saturated hues reinforce the action, creating a frenetic underlying rhythm to the work. The gaze of the boy and dog are vague and unfixed, adding to the unsettling feel of the work.

Aboriginal and Outsider Art

Issues of feminism, sexual identity, AIDS, and race came to the forefront during this time period. These were dynamic

Figure 8-14.
Darby Jampijinpa *Ross, Water and Emu Dreaming,* 1989. The colors used are reminiscent of the natural earth tones that would have been used in traditional dreamtime paintings. Brighter hues are now incorporated into their palette, including the pinks and reds that come from the use of modern acrylic paints. In paintings such as this that are created by men, the wavy lines usually represent ceremonial journeys.
© 2011 Artists Rights Society (ARS), New York/ Vi$copy, Australia.

times where the art world was constantly in movement and flux. New interest in other forms of art also surfaced. Outsider art, including that of untrained or self-trained artists and the artwork of indigenous peoples, began to gain respect by the traditional art establishment.

In Darby Jampijinpa Ross's *Water and Emu Dreaming* (Figure 8-14), the colors used are reminiscent of the desert where he grew up, with its yellows and ochres. As with Navajo sand paintings, the true nature of the art cannot be presented for secular

viewing. Their art forms are sacred, and over the years versions have been adapted and developed for general audiences. Ross, like many other aboriginal artists, creates paintings like this one for a secular audience. On the most superficial level, the painting tells the story of the rain and the clouds it came from. It shows the path of the floods caused by the downpours. The two circles are their campfires and between them are the digging sticks that are used to find food. The dot patterns, which are typical of aboriginal art, represent the

Figure 8-15.
Eden Garden, 2001.
A scene from *Genesis*.
Photo courtesy of
Entropy8Zuper! – Auriea
Harvey & Michael Samyn.

"dreamtime," which may be described as the relation and balance between the spiritual, natural, and moral components of the world. It is a time prior to living memory or experience—a time when creator ancestors and supernatural beings roamed the earth and sky.

The Yuendumu and Warlpiri use a full range of hues in their work, unlike many of the artists from other regions of Australia who prefer more traditional subdued palettes. They believe that the use of color should be celebrated. If you ask a Warlpiri artist about this, they will tell you that these colors are everywhere and all around them. These are the colors of the world—the blue from the sky and the yellow from the sun. Because of their love of color, they have adopted the use of acrylic paints, which were brought to them by a visiting anthropologist. The new media affords them a wide variety of intense hues with which to work.

The 1990s saw the boom and commercialization of the personal computer. Technology began to take a more dominant role in art and culture, therefore reflecting its importance in daily life. Computers were everywhere—at work, in the home, and as entertainment in the form of video games. It was only natural that artists began to pick up and experiment with it as an art tool. Art and technology have always gone hand in hand, and artists have been interested in the technology of their day.

Auriea Harvey still considers herself a sculptor. She says that all she has done is to trade in her traditional tools for digital ones. In *Entropy8Zuper!* (Figure 8-15), the Web site she created with her partner, Michael Samyn, they exhibit *Genesis, Exodus,* and *Leviticus.* Their work has been influenced by the movies in the widescreen format and video games. In *Exodus,* viewers (or users as they might be called) are offered the chance to blow up airplanes. Their flat, unmodeled images work well within the limited color space of the Web.

The use of the computer and other digital technologies includes both two-dimensional and three-dimensional creations. Some artists have worked in a purely digital world with their art remaining on the computer and viewed only via a monitor or projected onto a screen. Others use the medium as a creative tool and print out the final work on everything from paper and canvas to acetate. Diane Fenster creates her photomontages on the computer and then has them printed on special papers or canvas (Figure 8-16). Using the computer, she can add or change any specific hue to suit her work without regard to its natural color. Fenster's bright saturated palette works to unify the picture plane and intensify the impact of her imagery. In this pictorial reality discordant images of staircases can stand alongside truncated body parts. This is also evidence of cubism's continued influence on contemporary artists. The canvas has been replaced by the monitor and virtual space, but it is still an arena where anything is possible and the artists can interpret their own reality.

Exploration of New Media

Artists and designers will continue to push the bonds of traditional media and find new means of expression. The use of color will be an intrinsic element within that exploration. Artist Joe Chesla is working with biological materials, growing algae in 3,000 plastic bags that lined the windows of the William and Florence Schmidt Art Center (Figures 8-17 and 8-18). The work produced living, developing organisms that changed their color and form as part of the growth cycle. Chesla is concerned with natural evolving sequences, which include a

Figure 8-16.
Diane Fenster, *Canto Six/In the Shadow of the Cathedral*, 1995. Fenster uses an underlying grid pattern in her work. She balances off a predominantly warm color palette with selected areas of cool red-violets and violet hues. The handwritten elements work to unify the composition and act as a ground for her imagery.
Photo courtesy of Diane Fenster.

previous work with the evolution of rust on a metal surface.

Summary

The works of art discussed in this chapter show the schools and movements of the twentieth century that were primarily concerned with the use and application of color.

In modern art, color could be used for color's sake without any thought to its relationship to nature or the natural world. It was a liberating time of experimentation in which the sole subject of a work of art could be its color and use of color. In some instances, even the traditional paintbrush was abandoned in favor of alternative methods of applying paint, including dripping, pouring, or staining into the fabric of the canvas. As the century progressed, some artists returned to more naturalistic applications of color. This resurgence continues to this day with computer-generated works of art. With the advent of the computer, artists were also freed from the limitations of working on canvas. The monitor and the Internet open new realms and avenues for expression, with the only limitations being the limited size of the color space.

Figure 8-17.
Joe Chesla, *Letting Go a Breath I didn't Know I Was Holding,* 2009. Installation view. Depending upon their placement in the installation, the amount and quality of light and heat each bag received influenced the algae's growth. This impacted the color and patterns created within each of the units.
Photo courtesy of Joe Chesla.

Figure 8-18.
Joe Chesla, *Letting Go a Breath I didn't Know I Was Holding,* 2009. This close-up of a single bag shows the color range that was produced. Each unit developed a differing array of analogous hues from blue to green.
Photo courtesy of Joe Chesla.

Color and design are natural partners because color is a common element in good design. It is used to emphasize and accent the features of a design or product, and it can make a product better, more usable, or more pleasing to the eye. Since color has the ability to generate an unconscious response from viewers, it can influence viewers' ideas about products, graphics, or advertising. Therefore, color choices are based upon the person's sex, age, and economic status. Before viewers realize it, they are hooked by the color, and, in fact, more than half of a person's choice in purchasing a product is based solely on its color. So the color selected by a designer can make, or break, a product.

Figure 9-1.
USA Today developed the concept of using full-color images on a daily basis. Notice how your eye moves from the largest color image, which is directly under the masthead, to the medium size color image below it, and then back up to the smaller color images on the left. This creates a circular motion, which keeps the viewer involved and scanning the page.
Copyright 2008, USA TODAY. Reprinted with permission.

As design students, you may make color choices that are more personal rather than making choices with the general public in mind. You may want to please other designers, your classmates, or your professor. This is acceptable because a student's first portfolio of work is aimed at senior artists, art directors, and creative directors. In the real world, however, a focus group, an industrial psychologist, or even a color-forecasting service may determine the color. The personal choice of the designer may have little to do with the color of the final product. Yet designers can have an influence on the color of the final product if they know how color works and how to discuss color with clients and other design professionals.

Color grabs attention. Studies have shown that on the average, a reader will spend a fraction of a second scanning a black-and-white ad on a page. If the same ad is produced in full color, the viewer will spend at least two seconds or more viewing it. Color also captures the eye and holds it. The longer you can keep the viewer's attention, the better chance you have of getting your message across. These studies further showed that the eye is drawn to large color images. The viewer's eye will scan across the page and move in size order from the largest color image to the smallest, and then back to the text. Color also aids recall and retention. A color ad generates four times more memory retention than the same ad in black and white.

How important is color? Just ask *The New York Times*. For years the "old gray lady," as it was known, kept to its traditional format of black-and-white photos on its front page. The *Times* cautiously tested the waters by using color images in their Sunday supplement's travel and arts sections. Some worried that this would signal a change in the paper's serious nature and its reputation for in-depth coverage of the news. The reason for this concern was that previously only the tabloid-style papers such as *USA Today* used color extensively, and they were not known for their critical news coverage or journalistic integrity (Figure 9-1).

But late in 1997, even the *Times* began using full-color photos on its front page. The idea, according to one editor, was to make the paper more accessible and easier to read. The use of color was part of the evolution of the paper, or as another editor explained, the idea was to redesign the paper for a new generation of readers and advertisers. This was important because studies had shown that fewer and fewer young people were reading the *Times*, and readership means money. At the same time, new digital technology made full-color printing cost-effective and easier. The underlying concept was that color could capture the attention of a whole new generation of readers who were used to color from the Internet, television, and video games. Color in newspapers has now become the norm, and even the conservative *Wall Street Journal* now uses color.

Design and the Fine Arts

The fine arts have had a major impact on design. Many designers started out as fine art students before developing an interest in more commercially viable fields. And, in turn, advertising has influenced the fine arts. Andy Warhol's Campbell's soup cans and Brillo boxes are derived directly from package design and consumerism. This exchange of ideas has been in evidence for more than 150 years now and is not likely to stop anytime soon. Artists have even commandeered computers, which were once the sole domain of designers.

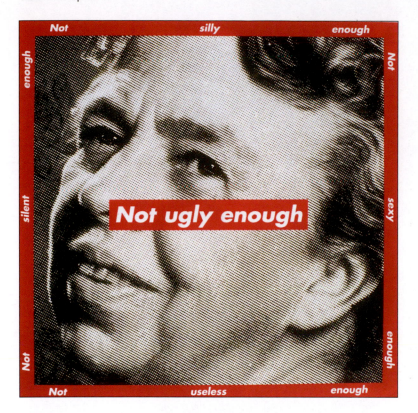

Figure 9-2.
Barbara Kruger, *Untitled (Not Ugly Enough), 1997.*
Framing the image in red helps to focus our attention and isolates the image. The white text on a red banner background creates very readable type and is a signature element in Kruger's work. The use of banner boxes or headlines is directly appropriated from advertising and newspaper graphics.
Photo courtesy of Mary Boone Gallery, New York.

Barbara Kruger

The relationship between design and the fine arts is evident in the work of Barbara Kruger. She uses elements of advertising and type in her large-scale pieces and installations and addresses the issues of power, sexuality, and identity. Trained in art and design, she worked as an art director at *Mademoiselle* magazine and was later promoted to head designer. Using a "vernacular of signage" as she calls it, Kruger creates large works and installations that juxtapose words or slogans and images, creating a visual dichotomy. The strong feminist underpinning of her work is evident in *Untitled (Not Ugly Enough)*, Figure 9-2. Kruger uses her trademark white text on a red banner. This use of text directly relates to mass communication as seen in billboards and advertising.

The Sixties: Psychedelic Color

There was a resurgence of the primacy of color in the late 1960s and early 1970s. The psychedelic colors used for posters and clothing made a bold statement for the times. Color was used not only to grab attention, but also to say "we are different from you." The "you" in this case was the establishment, including parents, teachers, and authority figures from police to politicians. The counterculture of young people used color in everything from tie-dyed clothing to posters to make a statement and to stand out. The statement was "I am different. I'm an individual." Color was an effective part of this philosophy because at that time men tended to dress alike in dull blue or gray business suits with the overriding credo to fit in and go along with the group.

Wes Wilson captured the spirit of the counterculture in his work. He created posters for the Filmore West and Avalon Ballroom run by music legend impresario Bill Graham. His creations were more than just announcements of who was playing on a given evening, but bold visual color statements. Wilson used vibrating complements to create shimmering effects of movement in his work. People avidly collected and displayed his work in their homes. He could be viewed as a modern era oulouse Lautrec with a major difference being that the majority of Wilson's work was created solely with color and type. In Figure 9-3, the complementary hues of red and green work together with the imagery of the fire making up the letters of the names of the bands that would be playing that evening.

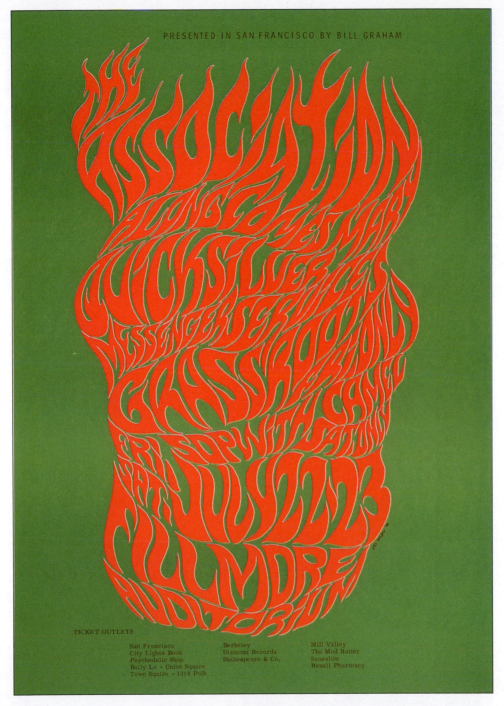

Figure 9-3.
Wes Wilson, *Poster*, 1966.
Bill Graham Archives, LLC
Wilson often designed his own type and used complementary color schemes for their visual vibration. This meant the hues he selected had to be close in value and saturation in order to create the vibrating visual effects.
© 1966 Wes Wilson.

The vibration of the hues (which are caused because the complements are very close in value and saturation) creates the upward movement working in concert with the direction of the type created to look like flames.

April Greiman

As one of the founders of the postmodern movement, along with others such as David Carson, April Greiman changed the face of design. Type no longer had to be sharp and legible, but could be

Figure 9-4.
April Greiman, *Does it Make Sense?* No. 133 issue of *Design Quarterly.*
This piece is interesting because it can be viewed from any orientation. There really is no top or bottom. The use of the monochromatic color scheme unifies the divergent visual elements.
Photo courtesy of April Greiman.

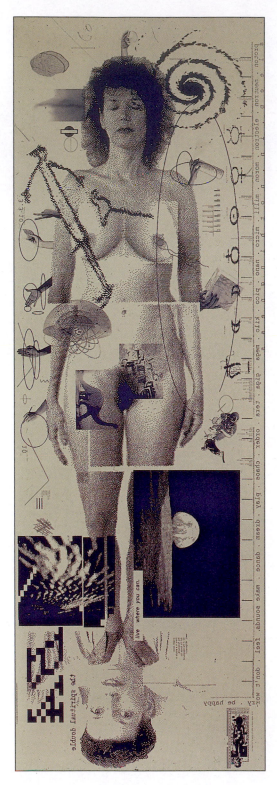

used solely as design elements. It could be roughed up, rotated, and faded out; the same holds true for her use of color. Greiman was one of the leading proponents of the Macintosh computer. She believes that the computer is not merely an instrument but an intelligent tool, which means that it can be a viable part of the design process. And hers is a process-oriented approach. In her poster *Does it Make Sense?* from the No. 133 issue of *Design Quarterly* (Figure 9-4), Greiman created a personal statement with a nude self-portrait. What could be more personal than that? She uses a monochromatic range of blue as a unifying element to the vast array of shapes, textures, and images used in the piece. When Greiman travels, she carries a plastic box to collect a variety of materials to add to her palette of colors and textures. These collected souvenirs then find their way into her work.

Graphics and Brand Identity

As we have seen previously, many of our reactions to color are learned responses. Red for "stop" and green for "go" are things we are taught by our parents to keep us safe and to protect us. Society reinforces these regulations to create rules for an orderly society and to keep people safe. But these are not the only ways that we learn to associate color with an idea or practice. Branding, or brand identity, is also a learned response. Commercials in both print and television condition us to recognize a symbol (a logo) and its color with the name of the company. With the addition of the Internet and pop-up windows that advertise every imaginable product, we are constantly bombarded with images of products and their names and logos. Each company has its own color or color scheme that is burned into our brains. If you don't believe it's true, ask any four-year-old to name several companies, and he or she will be able to tell you the color and shape of the logo for each one. When companies are successful, they no longer need to have their names in their logo—the shape and color are all that are required. How many companies can you name by just seeing their logo?

To preserve this color identity, many companies use the PANTONE MATCHING SYSTEM® (Figure 9-5). Also known as spot colors, these are specially mixed inks that will produce an exact hue, including the specific saturation and value. These inks may cost more, but they ensure the color consistency, which is at the heart of brand identity. If the color of a product varies even slightly, it will break the unconscious psychological connection with the customer or viewer. This brief split second is enough time for the people to reconsider their purchase. For most of our purchases we are on "automatic pilot," grabbing up the product without ever giving it a second thought.

Package Design

The package for a product may be as important as, if not more important than, the product itself. If the package is not alluring and inviting, the product will never be purchased. The color of a product (and its packaging) becomes synonymous with the product itself. PANTONE colors are used in product packaging to ensure that the color identity is maintained across geographic regions.

Color recognition is important because people reach for a product based on its color before they consciously read the name of the item on the package. If the

color was not exactly the same, the visual difference would stop the purchaser for even a fraction of a second. In that time, the buyer would have enough time to think about their selection, possibly changing their mind and selecting another product instead.

What do you think are the most popular colors for packaging in the United States? Red, white, and blue. The underlying theme of patriotism helps to sell the product. The subtle message in the use of these colors is that the product is all-American. Take a walk down the aisle at the grocery store and really look at the colors of the packages. Complementary pairs, especially red and green, are the next choice. Contrary to popular belief, red and green are not just Christmas colors. They are used to sell everything from salad dressing to hair spray. Legibility and contrast are key factors in labeling. While yellow and black are the most visible, they are rarely used because of their connotations to danger, stinging bees, and so on. As illustrated in

Figure 9-5.
The PANTONE® formula guide. There are actually several types of color formulas, including coated, uncoated, metallic, and pastel inks. They are the most commonly used brand of spot color inks and are employed in graphics, packaging, and products.
Photo courtesy of Pantone, Inc. PANTONE® and the PANTONE MATCHING SYSTEM® are the property of Pantone, Inc.

Figure 9-6.
An illustration of the readability of color and type. The greater the contrast, the easier it is to read. As the background color and the color of the type become closer in hue or value, they are more difficult to read. Analogous color schemes do not work well for this reason.
© Steven Bleicher

Some color combinations are easy to read.
Some color combinations are easy to read.
Some color combinations are easy to read.

Some color combinations are harder to read.
Some color combinations are harder to read.
Some color combinations are harder to read.

And some are almost impossible.
And some are almost impossible.
And some are almost impossible.

Figure 9-6, black on white followed by red, green, or blue on white are also easy to read and easy on the eyes. The least legible and hardest color combinations to read include red on blue, black on green, and orange on blue. Strong contrast in large type may be acceptable and stand out smartly, but it is not used on small type, or what is commonly known as body copy. In addition, hues close in value or saturation are also hard to read. This is one reason why analogous groups are rarely used in type and packaging.

Economic conditions also play a major role in product design and color selection. Color clearly reflects the financial condition of an era. Flashy bold colors are signs of great economic prosperity. The 1920s and 1980s are both prime examples, where color is viewed as disposable and used as fashion statements. In a booming economy, high-key colors are used to show the opulence of the owner. In times of economic uncertainty or recession, a more subdued palette is used. Classic colors that people will want to live with for long periods of time have also become popular. The products created have clean lines, and the use of white, blue, and black increase substantially.

A Fragrance is Born

It is rare that a company begins the design process of a product by starting with the selection of its color, but such was the case with a perfume by Christian

Dior. A deep emerald green was the starting point for Poison. The fragrance was developed and geared to a young audience. In fragrances, the color green (usually a very light version of the hue) was normally associated with citrus and lime scents. Christian Dior selected the deep vibrant green hue to go with the shocking new name, as well as to set it apart from all the perfumes on the market. The deep green color was selected to remind the user of emeralds. The bottle and packaging design came next. The two-tone tortoiseshell design on the package created an exclusive look. The fragrance was then developed with a combination of oriental and floral scents. It possesses a blend of amber, honey, berries, and other spices, and because of its strong nature it is recommended for evening use.

In 2003, Dior announced a change to Poison perfume. The traditional deep green was being replaced with a bright intense red (Figure 9-7). The change was to bring the perfume up to date for a new market. In a press release, they used the following: bewitching red, forbidden fruit, enticing serpent. The allusions to the Garden of Eden are quite clear. The new color of the perfume is the color of the apple. The underlying message is that the color and its fragrance are irresistible, and if you use it, you will be as well.

Product Design

Apple revolutionized the computer with its iMac (Figure 9-8).

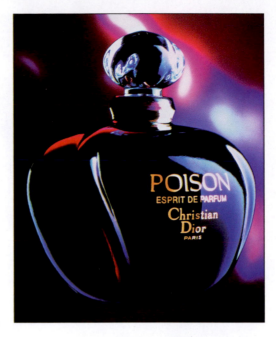

Figure 9-7.
Poison Tendre perfume by Christian Dior, 2003. The new red color gives the perfume a contemporary look. The underlying associations of the apple and Eve are used to convey the idea that this perfume could be a bit dangerous. The underlying message would not be as effective with another color. Red adds to the sensuality and passion that Dior wants to convey. Photo courtesy of Christian Dior Perfumes.

It was the first computer to be sold in colors, since up to this point all computers sold were an institutional gray or putty color. They were a purely utilitarian machine, and aesthetics were never an issue. Apple changed the face of selling computers with its low-cost iMac, and the visionary behind this move was Jonathan Ive and his design team. He felt that this was the meeting of technology and the individual. The idea was to change the very

Figure 9-8.
Jonathan Ive, the iMac, 1998.
Steve Jobs shows off the new iMac line at Mac World Expo. Ive's design team made a bold move in creating the first computer in five different colors or flavors; blueberry, strawberry, lime, tangerine and grape. The bright, saturated hues, contrast nicely with the pure white base. Photo © Alan Dejecacion/ Getty Images.

Figure 9-9.
Jonathan Ive, iMac, 2003.
The shape of the new base was echoed in the form of the twin stereo speakers. All of the corners, from the monitor to the keyboard, have been rounded off as well. The use of an absolute pure white again separated Apple from the rest of the pack.
Photo © Dan Krauss/ Getty Images.

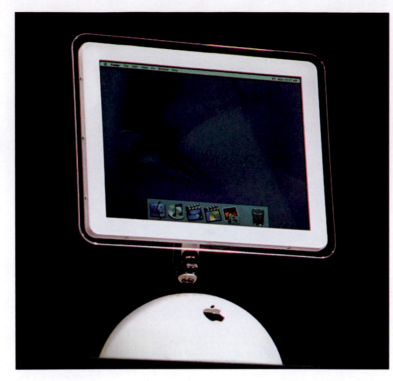

Figure 9-10.
Jonathan Ive, iMac, 2008.
The computer is now a metallic screen floating on a brushed metal sculptural base. Its minimal design continues to influence its competitors as well as dominate the market.
Photo © David Paul Morris/ Getty Images.

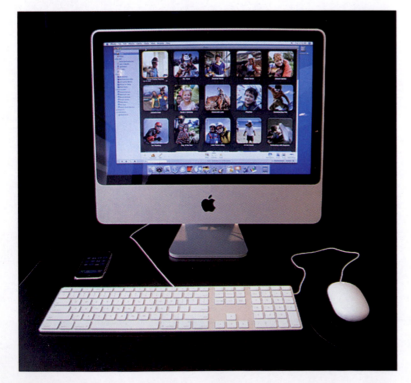

life. The computer could now be seen as furniture not to be hidden away, but as part of the room décor. By offering the computer in five colors, it could be marketed to both sexes and all age groups. This two-tone style was so trend setting and popular that it cropped up in every thing from tabletop cooking grills to microwave ovens. Even the Mini Cooper has a similar two-tone styling.

meaning of the object. By changing its color, Apple moved the personal computer from the industrial to personal. Their concept was to make the computer relevant to daily

As other companies such as Dell jumped on board, Apple continued to experiment with different color combinations. They extended this concept of color to their laptop computer models, and the iBook was born. The higher-end versions of these machines were offered in Graphite, a dark gray. This color appealed to a more business-conscious client who might be embarrassed to be seen owning a bright orange or green computer. As more companies brought their own versions of colored computers to the market, Ive and his design team changed gears and redesigned the iMac with a flat screen and hemisphere base in a matte sanded white finish called snow (Figure 9-9).

Apple continued to push the bounds of both function and design with its newest iMac computers, moving from snow to a brushed metal look known as titanium. The name of the color also had a subliminal message as to the sturdiness and strength of the new computer (Figure 9-10). Its design was further streamlined to house the entire unit with the monitor standing on its angled brushed metal base. The keyboard was also streamlined, barely rising from the surface of the desk or table. These design innovations have helped to keep Apple and its Macintosh brand ahead of its competition.

Not only computers were redesigned, but also mundane items such as vacuums were overhauled and revamped. The vacuum, an item that most people consider purely utilitarian, was redesigned to enhance both its function as well as its look. Richard Dyson changed the function and color of the traditional cleaning device. Replacing the conventional fixed wheels with a single moving ball, the new design allowed the machine to be more maneuverable. It was designed with an ergonomic handle that doubles as the extension wand. He also went with a simple color scheme for the new machines, yellow for the entry-level unit and its complement purple (the royal hue) for the deluxe model. Their concept was to connect the design technology with the brand name, so that the style of the new instrument would become synonymous with the company's name. The Dyson Ball™ Vacuum effectively blends its name and function into one.

Another product that has become synonymous with its color is DeWalt's power tools. The bright yellow high-impact plastic has become recognizable as their color trademark (Figure 9-11). The intense yellow hue was selected for a few reasons. The color was easily recognizable on the construction or job site, which made the tools easy to locate in a hectic environment. The yellow hue has overcome any feminine associations because it has been used so widely for waterproof sports products from radios to underwater cameras. In this way DeWalt made the yellow not only a palatable color for men's tools but has also made it a masculine hue.

Figure 9-11.
DeWalt Tools
Power tools normally come in an array of silver and black colors. DeWalt's use of yellow not only makes their line of tools easily recognizable but has also worked as a branding trademark.
Photo courtesy of DeWalt Power Tools.

Toy Design

Toy designing is not a game, but a serious business. The color used for a particular game or plaything is based both on the function of the toy and the recommended age range. Bright, simple primary hues are used for toddlers. As a rule, toys for girls still employ a soft, warm range of colors and pastel hues. On the other hand, toys for boys are usually made with brighter, more saturated hues, especially blues and bright reds. Sexual stereotyping begins at an early age. Wilder hues and color combinations are used for teens that are trying to assert their independence. Color is another means for teens to assert their control on their environment and self-image. One of the underlying elements is choosing colors that their parents will not particularly like, to reinforce the notion of independence and autonomy. Color combinations become more complex as the age range for the product increases.

Jesse DeStasio, a toy designer and animator, was faced with a design dilemma when his character Rex Ganon was going to make its debut in the established line of Plan B Special Forces figures. His color scheme for the figure was important to ensure that it would fit in with the rest

Figure 9-12.

Jesse DeStasio, Rex Ganon action figure, 2003.

The work starts out as a sketch on a page. It is scanned in, and in this case, he uses Photoshop to add the color, which allows him to pick and choose from several shades in order to get the right one. PANTONE colors are used to ensure accuracy and consistency in reproduction.

Photo courtesy of Jesse DeStasio (www.jessedestasio.com)

of the existing line. Rex's clothing was reminiscent of World War 2 uniforms, so he decided to work with a more subdued color palette. DeStasio decided on the red jacket, which he says added a nice spark to the figure, as well as fitting in with the time period. He used PANTONE shades for his colors, as seen in Figure 9-12, because of the language barriers in dealing with overseas production. As he said, "It's tough for a Chinese worker to understand 'Mulberry,' but PANTONE 492c is universal." The four PANTONE color swatches are noted on the final drawing. By doing so, there can be no confusion regarding the designer's choice of color. Using these spot colors ensures that wherever the figure is produced, the color will remain consistent and true. The photographs of the final figure produced can be seen in the press release for the toy line, in Figure 9-13.

Figure 9-13.

Jesse DeStasio, Rex Ganon action figure, 2003.

The press release for the action figure shows the last step in the design process. The figure can now be marketed and shipped to toy stores.

Photo courtesy of Jesse DeStasio (www.jessedestasio.com)

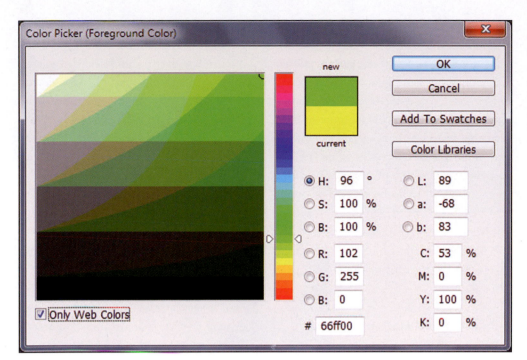

Figure 9-14.
The Adobe color picker
with the Web-safe color
option selected. It makes
selecting colors for the
Web as easy as pointing
and clicking.
Photo courtesy of
Adobe Systems, Inc.

Web Sites

The newest method of distributing information and advertising to a mass audience is the Internet. Formally know as Bitnet, the Net was once a computer network for people in education and the military. Its explosion of popularity began in the 1990s and was spurred on by the accessibility and affordability of personal computers to the general public. The Internet is now a worldwide phenomenon, with Internet cafés in every distant part of the globe. Cyberspace is a universal domain not bound by any culture or country. Since colors have both regional and cultural associations, you must plan out and research your color choice before finalizing the site.

While the Internet has become one of the largest communications mechanisms—literally spanning the world—the color space it uses is quite small. Of the millions of colors the human eye can see or a computer can display, there are only 256 colors available to artists and designers for the Web. Creating Web-safe color is no longer the chore it once was. Most software

programs, such as Adobe's Photoshop and Illustrator, have built-in Web color pickers (Figure 9-14).

Each of the Web's 256 colors has a related numeric value, which stands not only for the actual hue, but also its size and the amount of memory it uses. Black uses the least digital space and has a numeric value of 0. All other colors are larger and take up more space and computer memory. This is an important factor to remember because Web designers must work with files or image sizes that are relatively small. The larger the file size, the longer it will take a Web page to open. By limiting the palette to 256 colors, speed is achieved. Size limitations and opening speed take the place of color complexity on the Web. Users won't wait for your page to open, and even today not everyone has a high-speed digital subscriber line (DSL). Even though most users are still using slower modem hookups, there are a few ways around the issues of speed. Several small images can be used or one large image can be cut up into several pieces and **tiled** together to allow for faster page opening.

Color Complexity

Studies have shown that when the image and site complexity were not sufficient, users lost interest and moved on. But complexity doesn't mean confusion—viewers were also turned off by visual information that was not presented clearly. Confusing sites can interfere with cognitive processing, which means understanding the aim of the site. The use of animation also had positive effects on attention, perceived interest, and users' attitudes toward the brand portrayed. Color complexity also had positive effects on viewers' attention span as well as their intention to purchase the items shown.

Animation and Motion Graphics

The animator is in an interesting position—sometimes considered a designer and at other times an artist. The skill set employed is the same; only the person's intention creates the difference.

One of the most important color relationships for animators is the use of warm and cool colors. Since the computer's range of color or color space is much larger than that of film or videotape, animators are sometimes forced to work within a narrower scope of hues. By understanding the push and pull of color temperature, anima-

tors can select hues that will work off each other. One basic method is to place cool hues in the background and the warmer ones on the foreground or main character. Since cool colors appear to recede in space, they push the background farther back and create a deeper sense of space. The warm colors used for the foreground elements allow them to stand out more from the background and visually appear to push forward on the picture plane or screen. This same concept also applies to other film and video elements, such as motion graphics. Alex Donne Johnson (AKA Vector Meldrew) used a color combination of a cool blues that transition to a gray background and warm reds and oranges for their motion graphic for Pattern.One, a one-off music based event with the aim of "bridging the gap between music and art" (Figure 9-15). Contrast is also a concern for the animator. If the colors selected are too close in hue, value, or saturation, the images will not stand out on screen. For example, analogous color schemes tend to blend into one another and become harder to be seen. Another form of contrast regularly used is desaturated colors for the background and more highly saturated hues for the foreground. This concept is

Figure 9-15.
Alex Donne Johnson (AKA Vector Meldrew), Motion graphic for *Pattern.One.*
The cooler grays of the background appear to visually recede pushing the warm red and orange hues of the circular arcs to the foreground. Within the graphic element the violets and blues visually recede while they red and orange appear to advance give a feeling of depth and space. The well-planned use of color can enhance the visual dynamics.
Photo courtesy of Alex Donne Johnson.

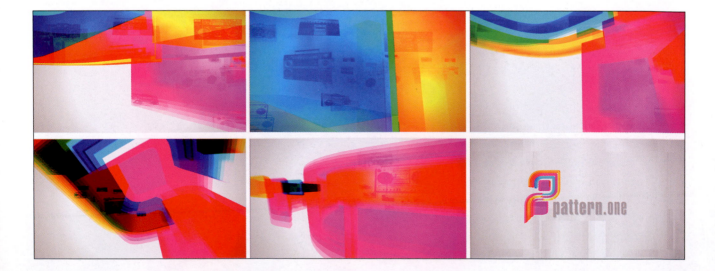

Figure 9-16.
The Game Room,
Exodus Entertainment.
Here reverse contrast is
used. The background
includes lighter, softer tints,
while the main character
in the foreground is
composed of deep blues
and violets. The use of
this color scheme helps
to isolate the figure from
the background, as well as
focusing our attention on
the main character.
Photo courtesy of Exodus
Entertainment.

clearly illustrated in Figure 9-16, a scene from *The Game Room.*

Gaming continues to represent a growth area in design. The number of innovative games and platforms will continue to increase. Many new games and devices use an HD color space, which allows for millions of hues (Figure 9-17). This allows for greater lighting effects, which enhance the believability of these virtual environments. The amount

Figure 9-17.
38 Studios LLC, unveils
the new *"Kingdoms of
Amalur: Reckoning"*
video game during the
Electronic Arts Inc.
annual Studio Showcase.
Game designers still
use many traditional
design principles and
elements. Notice on the
screen the background
is a cool blue; less
saturated and has a
soft focus. This use of
atmospheric perspective
helps to isolate the
monstrous figure from
the background, as well
as focusing the attention
on the main action.
Photo © 2010 Bloomberg/
Getty Images.

of detail that can now be achieved with nearly photographic quality will continue to heighten the gaming experience.

Summary

The choice of color can make or break a design. Studies have shown that it may be the single most important factor when a consumer selects an item for purchase. It acts as a magnet by drawing the eye and can be used to create a focal point. Color trends change with the times and are constantly evolving. The artist and designer must understand that culture and technology affect attitudes regarding color. As technological advances occur, new colors and new forms of color are made available to the designer. The Internet and the mass acceptance of digital technology have opened up new avenues for color expression.

Designers must constantly update their palette to keep pace with market expectations, and all products must be designed with color in mind. The public has become savvy and more sophisticated when it comes to color, and designers must keep pushing the envelope to make their work stand out and be noticed.

There is no one universally accepted practice for how color is used. Throughout the world people view and employ it differently. It is seen and used in relation to one's national origin, religion, cultural upbringing, and more. However, color usage can dramatically change from one part of a continent to another. In addition, socio-economic factors may also play a part in how a person feels about color. This illustrates the complexity of global color utilization and association.

A color and its usage may distinguish a people and can be used for its symbolic nature. It can quickly identify a faction or a single individual. Since color has an instantaneous subliminal human response, it can trigger a whole host of associations without any additional imagery or text. This is, in part, why groups, whether they are religious, political, or cultural, use identifying color markers. They give the group a visual identity and connection.

For example, in the twentieth century the color red became linked with the communist party, especially in Russia and China. The associations to the hue were numerous. There was *Mao's little red book*, a handbook of his philosophy and sayings, the *Red Guard*, and the *Red Brigades*. In the 1950s during the Cold War, communist sympathizers were branded as *pinkos*, another red association. Three hundred years earlier in 1690, orange

Figure 10-1.
William McFarlane Memorial Lodge at Kilmarnock's Orange March. The orange sashes immediately identify the marchers as of Irish Protestant descent. The color has become a symbolic icon for the group and its members.
Photo © John Stewart.

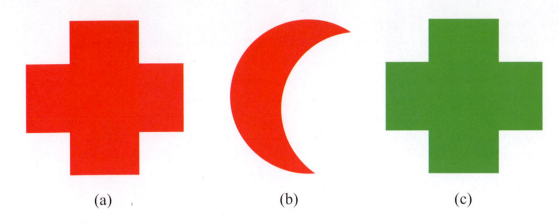

Figure 10-2.
a. Red Cross, b. Red
Crescent, c. Green Cross
© Steven Bleicher

(a)   (b)   (c)

became associated with the Irish Protestant religion. It started when William of Orange, the King of England, Scotland, and Ireland, defeated King James II, a Roman Catholic, in the Battle of the Boyne near Dublin. The victory ensured Protestant military dominance on the island. It has been a source of tension between the two religions ever since. Although the "Orange" in William's name actually referred to a southern French province, the color reference stuck. This is why orange now appears in the Irish flag, reflecting the Protestant Irish minority (Figure 10-1). This use of emblematic color identification is in contrast to the use of green signifying the Catholic majority, which is also widely known as the hue worn on Saint Patrick's Day.

Color and Meaning

Another reason to study global color usage is the underlying psycho-cultural associations. What may work for one geographic location may not work in another, even on the same continent. Inexorably tired in with color are symbols or icons used and their inherent meanings. This can be easily demonstrated when looking at a service organization like the American Red Cross and its related organizations (Figure 10-2a). In America the group uses a red cross. Most of us are familiar with their symbol and its underlying meaning. The red cross has come to signify first aid—medical assistance as well as aid and comfort.

In the Mideast, the red cross holds different underlying meanings and associations. In Islamic nations, the cross may hold negative connotations as a reminder of the past and medieval crusades. In much of the Mideast, Far East, and northern Africa the symbol for aid organizations is the Red Crescent (Figure 10-2b). People in these regions see the pictogram and have much the same associations as above.

However, even these two insignias are not universally accepted. In southern Africa, the color red symbolizes death. You would not want your aid organization to identify itself with a color that many may find distasteful, revolting, and off putting. In these regions, a green cross is used (Figure 10-2c). Green has life-affirming sentiments and qualities. Medical offices and pharmacies throughout these areas also use the green cross icon to denote their services. In fact, throughout much of Europe this same emblem is used for the same medically related services and practices. As people become more globally conscious, there may come a time when the use of the color green as an insignia supersedes the use of red.

From Red to Green

Around the world, color symbolism and usage can be modified, changing with the times, prevailing sentiments, and issues within a country or region. A case in point is the traditional red AIDS ribbon, which has undergone a metamorphosis in Botswana. Believing that red was too closely allied with death, the color of the AIDS ribbon was changed to green to convey a feeling of hope that with new medications there was a more positive prognosis for those who had contracted the disease. The symbol underwent another change, becoming a green- and white-colored ribbon. The addition of white was to symbolize transparency, meaning that no one who had contracted the disease should be ashamed or embarrassed. The emblem now clearly represents the country's progressive stance in dealing with this epidemic.

Wedding Color

It may be easier to examine the difference in color usage and symbolism by looking at a specific life-changing event.

There may be only a handful of these significant events—marriage, the birth of a child, or the death of a loved one. There may be many other important benchmarks throughout one's life, but these three are universally common to all people, no matter their religion or nationality. One of the most traditionally celebrated is a wedding and it can be used as a way of looking at the symbolic use of color.

Traditional White

In the West, white has long been the customary color for the bride's gown (Figure 10-3). The tradition for the use of white relates to the Christian religious events of christening and confirmation. It is also the color worn by women taking religious vows. Historically one of the first women to wear a pure white wedding gown was Mary Queen of Scotts. However,

Figure 10-3.
Robinson, Theodore (1852-1896). *The Wedding March*, 1892. Oil on canvas, 22 ⁵⁄₁₆ × 26 ½ (56.7 × 67.3 cm). Daniel J. Terra Collection, 1999.127. By the end of the nineteenth century the color white had become synonymous with marriage and weddings. Its popularity quickly grew and it was embraced throughout Europe and America.
© Terra Foundation for American Art, Chicago / Art Resource, NY.

the public did not embrace it, as it was still seen at that time as a color for mourning. It did not become popular until the 1840s, after the marriage of Queen Victoria. Prior to this, a woman could wear any color except black (Figure 10-4). During the Victorian era, off-white, cream-colored, and even dark-colored wedding dresses were in

Figure 10-4.
Jan Van Eych, *Giovanni Arnolfini and His Bride*, 1434.
Van Eych uses a number of symbolic elements within this marriage portrait. The green gown represents fertility, the dog: fidelity, a broom: domestic life and on finial of bedpost a stature of St. Margaret, the patron saint of childbirth.
© National Gallery, London / Art Resource, NY.

vogue. This was, in part, because a dress was expensive to produce, so that one made using a cream or dark color could be worn again for other occasions, making it more economical and practical.

Another misnomer about the white wedding gown was that it represented the bride's innocence and purity. Historically blue, not white, was the color associated with virginity. This is in part why within the phrase "something old, something new, something borrowed, and something blue," the blue represents the purity and chastity of the bride. The ideas of the "blue laws" from the 1930s and '40s were to uphold community standards of decency and purity. Again, in this use, the blue represents virtue and wholesomeness.

Until recently, a white wedding gown was also the sign of a woman's first wedding. Normally a woman did not wear white on a subsequent marriage. Nowadays many of these traditions have fallen by the wayside and a bride may wear any color, though white still may be the most popular wedding dress color.

Nonwestern Color

Around the world, color plays a greater role in bridal wear. In Northern India, China, Vietnam, and other parts of the Far East, red is the traditional color for a wedding dress (Figure 10-5). It symbolizes good fortune, prosperity, and wealth and therefore is considered a joyous hue. In Hindu weddings, red is a sign of happiness. It is the color of the bride's dress, the groom's robe and scarf, as well as the holy powder the groom places on the bride's forehead. In addition, the wedding party's hands are decorated with red-hued henna.

In Southern India, the bride wears an off-white or cream-colored sari. A Japanese woman will wear a white kimono on

Figure 10-5.
Red Wedding Sari In the Far East and parts of India, red is considered an extremely festive, joyful hue. This colorful wedding attire signifies good luck and prosperity. Some suggest that the hue may also have underlying associations with fertility.
Photo © photosindia/Getty Images.

the first of the three-day wedding ritual (Figure 10-6). It symbolizes her death from her birth family. In the subsequent days of the ceremony she is allowed to wear more brightly colored garments. Prior to WWII, a Japanese wedding dress for a normal bride was a long-sleeved, mainly black kimono. It wasn't until the 1960s that ornate wedding kimonos with heavily brocaded or embroidered jackets with cranes, flowing water, and flower motifs came into fashion. These colorful garments became a regular characteristic in the average wedding ceremony, worn with a simple white kimono underneath.

On the continent of Africa, there may be more than a thousand different cultures and tribal groups. While many northern Africans are influenced by Muslim traditions, those further south are split between Christianity, Hinduism, and other tribal customs. Because of the diversity and variety of African weddings within particular ancestral groups, more colorful traditions are observable. Much depends upon the specific tribe, locale, and religion. In contemporary African society the traditional colors and dress are being supplanted by western practices. Western-style white wedding gowns have become very popular.

In West Africa, white is the traditional color for weddings. The groom wears a white dashiki and the woman a white kaftan. In Muslim tradition white represents purity and is also the favored color for wedding garments. However, green can also be worn as it represents nature and the Koran. In southern Africa, the Zulu people don't rely as much on ceremonial wedding dress as they do jewelry, including necklaces and bracelets, to show one's marriage status (Figure 10-7). For example, a black-, blue-, and white-banded bracelet

Figure 10-6.
White Wedding Kimono The color white in this instance represents the bride's figurative death from her parents household and invokes her new societal status. Photo © Christian Kober/ JAI/Corbis.

Figure 10-7.
Zulu Beaded Love Necklace White is the only color without any negative associations. Consequently, when white beads are placed next to another hue, the colored beads take on positive meanings. When a necklace has very little white, it sends a negative message. Photo © Roger de la Harpe/ Getty Images.

Figure 10-8.
Australian Aboriginal Body Painting Different colored clays and ochres are applied in a variety of designs according to the person's totem. The dancers flanking the musician in the center are wearing a traditional bee's nest motif. The totems or ancestors depicted are spiritually awakened during the body painting ritual. Photo © Howell Walker/National Geographic Society/Corbis.

made from leather and beads would signify the wearer is married. These become visual symbols to others in the tribe and act much in the same way that a gold wedding band does in the west.

Australia

The Aboriginal people wore limited clothing except in colder weather or climates where animal furs and skins were worn. Their traditional colors were taken from the earth, and included white, natural ochre, red, brown, and charcoal (Figure 10-8). In many rituals, white and a variety of reds taken from clay were painted directly onto the skin. They did not practice marriage in the form of monogamy solemnized with an initial ceremony (though there were the equivalent of marital

relationships). Nowadays, Aboriginal people wear European-style clothes and select from among colors the same as non-Aboriginal Australians. Additionally, a couple may opt to use the colors of the Aboriginal flag, which are yellow, black, and red. They represent the sun, the indigenous people, and the ochre of the earth.

Global Color: Natural Hues

While color symbolism varies from continent to continent and on a smaller scale within a geographic region from tribe to tribe, there are a few generalities that can be made. Most of the hues used by primal ancestral peoples throughout the world have a natural color basis. Their colors are found in the natural elements such

Figure 10-9.
Natural Hue Illustration
Many primal peoples
use a variety of plants
including their flowers,
stems, fruits, berries, and
seeds as natural dyes and
pigments.
Photo © Kim Steele/Getty
Images.

as local plants, clays, minerals, and insects (Figure 10-9). These basic schemes usually include white, gray, black, red, blue, and yellow. These color schemes are similar to other primal societies who predominantly use the earth's natural resources for their colorings and pigments. Green is seen less frequently as it is harder to produce, coming only from a few minerals. But the rarest hue of all may be violet. It's hard to manufacture a deep, vibrant hue with lasting colorfastness. This may be one reason why, for so many primal groups, it was the hue most closely associated with the highest authority and royalty.

For the most part, the use of bright hues, which are normally synthetic, is found only after western contact. However, there were a few indigenous groups producing vibrantly hued pigments or dyes. Bright colors have been especially integrated into contemporary Australian Aboriginal paintings. These traditional artists have developed an affinity for acrylic paint in their contemporary works. This may in part be because of their availability, ease of use, and archivability or colorfastness.

We can start to make some generalizations by looking at a specific continent or region but must always be mindful that they are just that, generalizations. They can provide some insight into a place and its cultures and begin to sensitize an artist or designer to other ways of thinking about color utilization and its power as a visual image or entity.

Global Color Chart

	RED	ORANGE	YELLOW	GREEN
AFRICA	South Africa, Zulu: love or anger, strong emotions. Central Africa: Ndembu warriors paint themselves with red. It is a symbol of life and health. West Africa, Ivory Coast: mourning		Egypt: mourning, Zulu: wealth	Contentment Zulu: nourishment virility, vitality associated with vegetation. In north Africa symbolizes Islam.
ASIA	Good luck and good fortune, the traditional wedding dress color. It also represents happiness, marriage, and prosperity.	China and Japan: happiness, Yang, the earth, strengthens concentration, purpose, and organization Buddhism: humility (brown)	Wisdom, wealth (gold) China: royalty, rebirth, honor Japan: courage	Life growth energy eternity family health prosperity peace China: infidelity Japan: life Indonesia: a forbidden color
AUSTRALIA ABORIGINAL	The land, earth, and ceremonial ochre	The land (brown)	The sun	
INDIA	Purity, joy, fertility, martial status, wedding dress color	Saffron, a sacred color, mourning (brown)	Vishnu, the merchants color, the color space in between sensuality and chastity single girls wear yellow clothing to attract a mate, a happy color symbolizes fertility and sexuality, good luck, ancient times believed to combat illness, merchants color.	Festive color - not for widows to wear.
MIDEAST	Danger, evil Israel: sacrifice and sin		Prosperity Islam: gold butter and honey faith, wisdom Egypt: mourning	Islam perfect faith, paradise, fertility Saudia Arabia: wealth, prestige Israel: new growth, fertility, renewal
SOUTH AMERICA	Brazil: fertility (Kayapo Indians) The Tucano of the Amazon: red ochre shields against evil spirits	Nicaragua: disapproval (brown)	Mexico: mourning	Represents danger and death in countries with dense jungle areas

Table 10-1
© Cengage Learning, 2012

Religion and Color

What may be useful in a dialogue about global color usage and to bring a bit more clarity to the discussion is to look at the five major world religions and their symbolic color use. These are Christianity, Judaism, Islam, Buddhism, and Hinduism. While there are many more faiths and belief systems, these five have the greatest plurality and are often called the dominant religions of the world. However, there are extremely few countries in which everyone shares the same religion. There are certain countries that have a state-sponsored religion. For example, in Israel Judaism is the official religion, in Indonesia it is Islam. But even in these nations there are people practicing other religions, and an artist or designer should always be mindful of this.

Christianity

Christianity encompasses many religious groups, including Catholics, Protestants, Baptists, and Methodists to name a few. One key element in all of these religions is that followers believe Jesus was the son of God, died on the cross, and was resurrected. When we tend to think of western culture it usually refers to this dominant religion of Europe and North America.

In Catholic and Protestant churches liturgical color signify the various feast days and seasons. These colors can be worn on the vestments during religious services. As part of the history of colors in the liturgy, it should be noted that the early church initially favored a pure white. It was Pope Innocence III who, in 1200,

	BLUE	VIOLET	WHITE	BLACK
AFRICA	Zulu: faithfulness Egypt: virtue, wards of evil	royalty Egypt: virtue, faith	Purity, traditionally the color for death and mourning Zulu: purity, Maasai: ceremonial color of passage into adulthood (adornment of white chalk on one's body)	Egypt: death and rebirth (Anubis who watched over the dead as a black jackal) Zulu: marriage, rebirth
ASIA	China: torment foretell death blue use considered ugly - people of bad character. Japan : Villainy, Mongol culture: the color to destroy enemies Korea: mourning	Royalty, wealth Thailand: mourning Tibet: sacred	Death, funerals, mourning, peace, purity, travel	Evil, evil influences, knowledge, penance, mourning, self-cultivation, destruction and disorder China: color for young boys Thailand: suffering, decomposition
AUSTRALIA ABORIGINAL			X-ray style of aboriginal painting, symbolizes the act of creation	Color of the people
INDIA	The lower caste – the Sudra or untouchables, an impure color. Color for Krishna represents change.	Soothing, sorrow	Highest social caste, chastity, purity, spiritual rebirth, mourning, happiness	Death, evil, night, considered unattractive, inferior castes
MIDEAST	Protection, spirituality, heaven, the Nile river Iran: mourning Israel: God's color	Iran: mysticism, the future Israel: redemption or purification	Islam: the absolute uniqueness of god, purity, and mourning Israel: life, purity and innocence	Islam: vengeance sadness and death. Those with a vulgar nature are said to have black heart.
SOUTH AMERICA	Columbia: associate with soap Mexico: trust, tranquility, mourning	Negative associations, despicable Brazil: death, mourning Aztec: royalty Mayan: festive		Wealth (Spanish influence) Aztec: war

introduced a new arrangement of colors, which were regarded as mandatory under Pius V.

Within Christianity white symbolizes purity and innocence and became synonymous with the coloring for angels. Black conversely is most closely associated with death (Figure 10-10). The biblical stories

Figure 10-10.
Ellis Wilson, *Funeral Procession*, c. 1950.
Wilson's work portrays people dressed in the basic funeral colors of black and white. The white clad figures represent the old world (traditional African custom) of wearing white while the figures dressed in black represent the contemporary western dress. The painting shows these two traditions are coexisting.
Photo courtesy of Amistad Research Center.

use black as the color of pestilence, the plague, famine, and disease. It is also the color of sin and judgment. Mary Queen of Scotts popularized it as the color for funerary dress, rejecting the conventional use of white feeling it did not express the depth and gravity of her loss of her husband. Many religious groups, such as the Protestants, adopted its somber color as a color for clothing because it imbued the feeling of solemn piety. Black clothing was not flashy or gaudy, showing one's humility and devoutness.

Green represents life and can be seen in the vestments worn by many clergy on most Sundays. It is the color of grass, leaves, and new growth. The hue is naturally seen as a color of the earth and has been adopted by the ecological movement. Greenpeace and others use the color for its long-standing associations with nature and the earth. The color green is viewed as triumph over death. In nature this can be seen as the color of renewal and new life each spring.

Red is a passionate hue symbolizing blood and fire, and it is also the color of martyrdom. In the Catholic Church it is the color of the Holy Ghost. It symbolically represents blood and can, therefore, represent life. But it is the transient nature of human life that is represented in the color red. This may also have to due with the concept of original sin and may be one of the reasons why people thought blood was red, as a reminder of this transgression and sin and mortality. This is in part why adultery is symbolized with red as evidenced in the book *The Scarlet Letter*.

Mary and her traits of honesty and truthfulness have long been associated with the color blue. Today, these traits along with their mantle of authority are represented by dark navy blue. It is worn by the police, military, and many politicians. It is also the color of the sky and water, which nourish life. Violet, the blending of blue and red, is the symbol of quietness and penitence.

Orange and yellow are mostly seen as gold in the color of the halo or as God's light (Figure 10-11). The halo represents oneness with God. These hues symbolize the divine and enlightenment and are most closely associated with God and Jesus.

Judaism

Judaism is the religion of the Jewish people, based on principles and ethics embodied in the Torah and the Talmud. The Torah, also known as the five books of Moses, could be considered the Hebrew Bible. Judaism began around 2000 BCE,

Figure 10-11.
Anonymous, *El Sagrado Corazon de Jesus, The Sacred Heart of Jesus,* no date.
Retablos are traditional Mexican religious motifs that are normally painted on tin. The yellow rays represent God's light while green seen in the background and cross represent nature and in this case may also be associated with growth of life sustaining crops. In Catholicism red represents both the Holy Ghost and the transient nature of life.
Photo courtesy of the New Mexico State University Art Gallery collection.

making it one of the oldest religions still practiced today. Primal to Judaism is the belief in one god. Jewish history and doctrines have influenced other religions such as Christianity and Islam. Throughout the Torah, there are many references made to color, symbolizing essential principles and ethics.

Blue is one of the two main colors of the flag of Israel. It is considered the color of God's glory, representing the color of sea and sky (Figure 10-12). The Torah says to put fringes, known as *tzitzit*, on the corners of one's garments and weave within those fringes blue thread. It is to be a daily reminder to conform to Jewish law, resist temptation, as well as a symbol of their separation from all other religious groups.

As with Christianity red has a duality. It can represent life's blood, joy, and happiness as well as sin. The red of sin mixed with the blue of God's glorification produces purple, which stands for redemption or purification.

White also has dual meanings; it can stand for life or death. It is also related to salt, which was believed to be one of the intrinsic elements required for survival. White is understood to be the true unadulterated color of light and therefore purity and innocence. Close to this concept of the color of light, the celestial light of God is represented by yellow, which is most often represented as gold.

Islam

Islam is a monotheistic religion based on the teachings of Muhammad, a seventh-century religious and political figure. The term *Islam* means submission,

Figure 10-12.
Shoni Labowitz, *Be the Miracle: A Journey To the Self*, 2007.
In her in installation, Labowitz references the Israeli flag and her Jewish heritage using the stereotypical traditional hues of blue and white. While both Jewish and Islamic law prohibit the portrayal of graven images, which forbids the use of representational human imagery, many contemporary artists have relaxed their adherence to this strict code.
Photo courtesy of Rabbi Shoni Labowitz

or the total surrender of oneself to God, Allah. One who believes in Islam is known as a Muslim, meaning "one who submits to God." There are between 1 and 1.78 billion Muslims, making Islam the second-largest religion in the world.

The color green may be most closely associated with Islam. It is the color of the

Figure 10-13.
Rafa al-Nasiri, *Untitled*, 1967. (Gulbenkian Foundation)
Heavily influenced by Chinese brush painting, al-Nasiri uses Arabic characters as integral part of her imagery and composition.
The Koran and Islamic practice are subtly referenced through this use of letter-forms and text within the painting.
© Rafa al Nasiri.

earth and of nature and life (Figure 10-13). Green is also the color of the covering and bindings of the holy book known as the Koran. This adoption of green may also be in part because it was said to have been worn by Muhammad. Closely related to green, blue is the color of paradise and the afterlife. Because of this it is also a favored color for mosques.

Red is a bit of a paradox. It stands for courage and sacrifice. It is the color of the Red Crescent and is present as a predominate hue on many flags of Islamic nations. However, there are prohibitions against men wearing garments of solid red. Men may only wear red if it is mixed with other hues, and it cannot be the dominant color of the garment.

White symbolizes purity. Men wear white going to the mosque for Friday prayers. It is also the color of garments to be worn on the *Hajj*, or pilgrimage to Mecca, where it symbolizes equality. When everyone is dressed in white, you can't discern someone's social status. It is also worn for its association with death, in that death is the great equalizer. As with western cultures, black can also be worn for mourning. It is a very somber color denoting humility. Because of this association, it is also the color for women's burkas and the cloaks worn by the ayatollahs.

Hinduism

Hinduism is the third-largest religion, and may be the oldest religion still practiced. It is extremely diverse, ranging in its perceived concept of God from monotheism to polytheism. Hinduism doesn't have a specific unified system of beliefs. The majority of Hindus accepts some tenets of the faith; however, it is difficult to identify specific canons with universal acceptance among all denominations. Prominent themes in Hindu beliefs include Dharma (ethics/duties), Samsara (the continuing cycle of birth, life, death, and rebirth), Karma (action and subsequent reaction), Moksha (liberation from Samsara), and the various yogas (paths or practices).

Followers of Hinduism often practice yoga. Meditation and tranquility are prevailing themes, as well as aligning the charkas or spiritual centers, each of which is represented by a color. Those hues influence Hindu color symbolism, and the color palette contains predominently spectral hues. The festival of **Holi**, also known as the Festival of Color, is a Hindu religious event observing the coming of spring and good over evil. In the central ritual, celebrants throw colored powders and colored waters at each other in joyous celebration (Figure 10-14). This celebration has deep mythological basis representing both Krishna's love for Radha as well as the triumph of Prahlada over his evil father to worship Vishnu. It is a time when Hindus' caste differences are set aside and all sects are allowed to freely mix with one another.

One of the most popular Hindu colors is red. It is a color associated with happiness and joy. The red dye of henna is also associated with joyous occasions such as weddings. There is an old proverb that says wherever there is henna there is joy. Deities who are benevolent, protective, and courageous wear red. It is a color that destroys evil. Because of its more passionate and prosperous associations, many brides wear red saris. Ending the cycle of life, a woman's body may be wrapped in red cloth for the cremation.

Yellow is the color of saffron, one of the most expensive and prized spices. It represents the fire that burns out impurities. Wearing yellow symbolizes the quest for light and personal enlightenment and it is often worn by holy men, signifying religious abstinence.

The working class is associated with blue, similar to the western concept of the blue-collar worker. High-caste Hindus avoid this color because of its association with the fermentation process for producing this hue, which was considered impure. Those of the lower caste, including farmers, weavers, and artisans, commonly wear blue. Conversely, blue is also associated with the protectors of humanity, Rama and Krishna. Closely related to this aspect of blue, purple indicates one's oneness with god, peace, and wisdom.

Originally, the merchant classes wore green. Today, the hue has become more closely associated with fertility and nature. Because of this many Hindu brides wear green garments, a practice also popular among many Muslim groups as well. The association between the color and fertility has become so strong that widows are forbidden to wear any green-hued clothing.

White is represents purity and is worn during rituals and for mourning. It is considered a very solemn color. Black is viewed as a reflection of sorrow and bad omens and is, therefore, usually avoided.

Figure 10-14.
The Celebration of Holi. As part of the Holi celebration participants douse each other with brightly colored powders and waters as a central rite in the celebration of spring.
Photo © AJAY VERMA/ Reuters/Corbis.

Buddhism

Buddhism is a religion and philosophy founded 26 centuries ago in what is now Nepal and northeastern India on the teachings of Siddhartha Gautama. He is more commonly known as "the Buddha," meaning, "awakened one." The most prominent color concept in Buddhism is that of the rainbow body, which is the highest level of meditative achievement wherein the body is transformed into pure light (Figure 10-15). The rainbow body is the highest achievement other than Nirvana, which is the essential end goal for Buddhists. Since the "pure light" on the spectrum contains all colors, and is white, to possess a rainbow body means to possess all colors.

Light and wisdom are associated with the color blue. In Buddhism there are two shades of blue, light and dark, which are represented as turquoise and lapis lazuli. The light blue or turquoise is associated with the earth and a safe journey. The stone embodies the two ends of life, living and dying. This is because turquoise can change color from blue to white

Figure 10-15.
Gonkar Gyatso, *Buddha@hotmail*, 2006.
A Tibetan native, Gyasto creates the image of Buddha using stickers, pictures of cars, superheroes, and many other images gathered from the Internet to highlight the complex world of the modern Buddhist. It may also reflect the difficulty in today's world associated with one's personal quest to rid themselves of pride, greed, avarice, and elements of the material world.
Photo courtesy of Gonkar Gyatso.

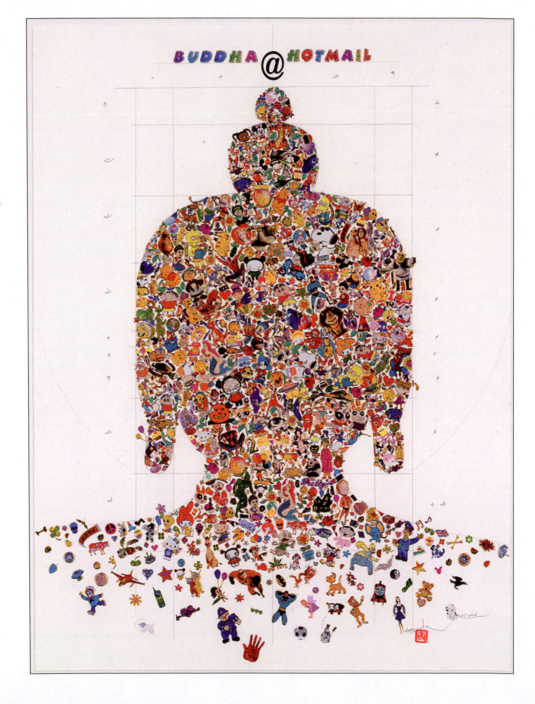

or even black with exposure to light or skin oil. It is therefore considered a reminder of human life. Wearing it is believed to give the wearer long life as well as absorbing sin. Since lapis is a rare gemstone, it represents purity and healing as seen in the Blue Buddha, also known as the Medicine Buddha. Its dark color signifies the endless expanse of the night sky.

Karma, harmony, action, youth, and vigor are all associated with green. It is the color visually seen in foliage. Since it is the color at the middle of the spectrum, it also represents balance.

Yellow is the color of saffron. It has the highest symbolic qualities of humility and separation from materialistic society. It denotes stability and a grounded nature. Closely related to yellow is orange, which symbolizes the Buddha's teachings and wisdom (Figure 10-16). Achievement, wisdom, virtue, and fortune are represented by red. It is the color of good luck. At Chinese New Year, children receive red envelopes with money for a prosperous coming year.

Global Color Usage

Assimilating all of the information on global color and using it intelligently is part of the role of the artist and designer. It is important to understand how people in different countries, regions, and ethnic and religious groups view color and its usage. There is no universal color scheme. Hues that may work with one group may not work for another.

Remember, color has underlying cultural, religious, and psychological connotations. After you have developed a color scheme, review your choices and think about the context in which it will be used and what associations the viewing public may bring. Lastly, don't just concern yourself with the color; remember to consider value and saturation. With that noted, here are some ideas to stimulate your thinking and discussions regarding global color usage.

- Green is a hue that many groups associate with fertility and regeneration. Therefore, it may not be an appropriate hue to use in advertising or packaging for birth control (contraception). Since the hue has these intrinsic associations with life and growth, in what other ways could you use the hue and what other products or services might also convey this underlying message?

- Blue is the color of water and air, life giving entities. Because of this association it could easily have become the color for the environmental and sustainability movement. Everyone is concerned with the quality of the water they drink and the air they breathe. From the Medicine Buddha on, the hue has underlying associations with health and devotion. This may be one reason why early medicine bottles

Figure 10-16.
Kazuaki Tanahashi, *Sun Within*, 2001.
The "Ensos" is a calligraphic Zen circular motif that represents enlightenment. It is drawn or painted in one decisive brush stroke, with no retouching. The single stroke and its accompanying movement are part of a Buddhist meditative tradition.
Photo courtesy of Kazuaki Tanahashi.

were cobalt blue. Any product that refreshes, quenches, cools, or heals could be associated with this hue.

- Red is a passionate color. It is the color of many intense elements including fire and blood. Because of its relationship to blood, red can represent life, but it also signifies death in many cultures and regions. It is a great hue to use when you want to inflame the audience with strong emotions or passionate feelings.

- Yellow and gold are very energetic colors. In many areas and in many religions, it represents the color of the energy of the sun and light, but more specifically God's light. This can be a powerful underlying attribute or characteristic to work with. Moving past the common associations of sunny and happy, what more evocative emotional connotation could you develop with yellow as a dominant hue?

- Because it is so difficult and expensive to produce a saturated violet hue, it has higher-level connections and in numerous cultures signifies status and royalty. It may be the only hue that is universally accepted, free from negative associations, and is, therefore, defiantly the above-average hue.

What other individual hues or color combinations can you think of that would have the best global acceptance for a design, product, or artwork?

Summary

No matter one's religion, nationality, or sex, color plays an enormous role in our lives. A single hue can represent a person's religion or birthplace. Color can distinguish one people from another. Ethnic and religious groups are identified by their color choices, for example, orange for Protestants, green for Islam, and so on. Much of our adult color preference can be traced to the colors we grew up with as influenced by religion, where we lived, and even our socio-economic status.

The most basic colors are those found in natural elements, the flora and fauna. Each indigenous group has exploited their surroundings to produce the hues most closely associated with their tribe or group.

More than anything else the artist or designer must not rely on stereotypic color concepts of a particular group. There are no universal colors for any continent. Each indigenous group of people, even if they live in proximity to one another, will have their own color code, symbolism, and use. The artist and designer's role is to find the right hue for their audience and intended message.

The future of color is now. Color is a part of our ever-changing world. The ways we create and use color are constantly evolving. New technologies bring advances in our application and use of color, and the Internet and progress in such divergent areas as virtual realities and cybernetics are changing our ideas regarding the very nature of what color is and can be. But it is not just through high-tech research that innovation occurs. There are low-tech and no-tech advances in theory, practice, and convention. Even our courts and the rule of law play a role in how we work with and use color.

Figure 11-1.
Winsor & Newton water-mixable oil colors. Turpentine is no longer required—they clean up with just soap and water. Photo courtesy of Winsor & Newton.

Environmentally Friendly Paints

Not all advances in color involve digital technology. Even in traditional media, new advances are being made. The push for nontoxic, environmentally friendly materials will continue. Artists want to try to minimize the health-related illnesses caused by the materials they work with and that have historically plagued the art and design fields. Nontoxic inks for etching and printing have grown in popularity. In the last few years, Winsor & Newton has introduced water-mixable oil colors to the market (Figure 11-1). Their advantage to traditional oil paints is that they do not require turpentine to clean brushes and other materials—they clean up with plain soap and water. This eliminates the fire hazard of oil- and turpentine-soaked rags, as well as the noxious smell. According to the manufacturer, hog hair brushes are advised for a heavy impasto of paint, while thinner coats normally used for glazing require a soft-haired brush.

The interest in new safe materials is only one part of a larger sustainability movement. It extends beyond the art world, encompassing every facet of contemporary life. One thing is certain—everyone has become conscious of our environmental footprint.

The Color Green

Today the word *green* has more significance and deeper meaning than just the name of a single hue. It represents much more. It has come to signify a movement, a way of thinking as well as a concern for the environment and the earth.

Green represents nature and the growth of the earth's flora. It symbolizes fertility and life. In some religions the color is associated with resurrection, regeneration, and paradise. Worldwide it is used to represent safety. It's a word and hue with positive connotations. So it's only natural that it would come to symbolize the environmental movement and concern for the sustainability of the earth. The **"green movement"**—or as it has been called, "the green revolution"—is a global phenomenon. It has influenced virtually every aspect of our lives, every profession and discipline.

Green Art

Green art, environmental art, or eco-art is hard to define. It encompasses many things including conceptual art, earthworks, found object, activist art, and more (Figure 11-2). Working "green" means that artists and designers employ the use of non-toxic media, using organic, natural, sustainable, or recycled materials. It can even incorporate the use of renewable energy and resources. Many of the works created are ephemeral, with the end product designed to degrade or erode back to their natural state. Above all, the work should in no way have a negative effect or harm the environment. It is a socially responsible art and design practice.

One gray area is the use of digital media. Some would say this qualifies as a green practice while others believe that the toners, chemicals, packing material (such

Figure 11-2.

Nils-Udo, *Clemson Clay Nest*, Botanical Garden of South Carolina, 2005. Pines tress, Bamboos. Fuji flex on aluminum, 111×125 cm. Bavarian artist Nils-Udo has been working directly with nature for more than three decades. His lyrical pieces, what he refers to as "potential utopias" are of giant nests, misty forestscapes that all have an air of mystery and playfulness. He works in response to the surrounding landscape, using materials found locally including berries, leaves, sticks. Photo © NILS-UDO.

Figure 11-3.
Stitched Painting on Silk entitled "Puzzle of Salt" by Linda Gass
Part of the Green Quilt tradition, Gass' work is a comment on issues of sustainability of our waterways. Her though provoking work engages the audience to begin to reflect on these concerns.
Copyright © 2005 Linda Gass.
Photo credit: Don Tuttle.

as Styrofoam), and even the hardware itself constitute a negative environmental impact.

The Green Museum

The Green Museum has no buildings or art collection. While its offices are located in northern California, the museum exists online in the virtual world of cyberspace (green-museum.org). The museum does not back any single approach or concept; it exhibits a vast array of work from earthworks to more traditional paintings, sculptures, textiles, and prints (Figure 11-3). The museum considers itself an umbrella organization, seeing itself as a giant collaborative "art-making tool." It currently has a long waiting list of artists that would like to have their work posted online and exhibited on the museum's Web site.

Corporate Green

The green movement has spread from the fields of art and design to the mainstream. Some companies undertake eco-friendly practices as an act of social responsibility; others may be more concerned with the appearance of being socially responsible and the customers that they might garner by do so. One of the first corporations to try to rehabilitate their image as a major oil conglomerate by changing their public face with a new logo was BP (Figure 11-4). They

Figure 11-4.
BP Logo
British Petroleum selected the floral motif and analogous color scheme of yellow, yellow-green, and green to portray themselves as an environmentally conscious energy company.
Photo © ANDY RAIN/epa/Corbis.

understood that by changing their logo, the visual element the public saw on a daily basis, they could begin to affect how they were perceived. Their new corporate symbol was a stylized floral sunburst incorporating various green hues. The company understood that using this new color scheme would send a subliminal eco-friendly message.

Mickey D's Goes Green

Other companies have seen that going green can have a huge impact, generating good press and PR as well as a significant financial benefit. After years of some negative press surrounding their packaging and other practices, McDonald's is moving toward trying to become a good corporate and world citizen. They have started to experiment with green practices. The company has modified their logo, interiors, and architectural décor to reflect this new direction. The traditional red background of their logo has been replaced in these new establishments with a green background (Figure 11-5). The décor has also undergone a change to more than just the new hue (Figure 11-6). The new "green" franchises employ many sustainable elements including LED interior and exterior lighting, skylights, water-conserving toilets, vegetated green roofs, and electric vehicle (EV) charging stations in the parking lot. So far this experiment has been limited to a handful of locations in Brazil, Canada, Europe, and, in the United States, Chicago and Cary, North Carolina. This has been seen by many as a positive first step. It is expected that many more companies will follow suit.

Green Building and Architecture

Architecture has been one of the leading disciplines moving toward a more ecological and environmental consciousness. At the forefront of green design has been architect Renzo Piano. His design for the California

Figure 11-5.
A McDonald's green logo
A restaurant in Achim, northern Germany has changed the company's traditional logo from red to green to signal its respect for the environment. The golden arches, which is the heart of their branding, has not been altered.
Photo © Nigel Treblin / Getty Images.

Academy of Sciences has earned it the reputation as one of the world's greenest museums (Figure 11-7). The museum received a platinum rating for Leadership in Energy and Environmental Design (LEED), a green building rating system developed by the U.S. Green Building Council. This commitment to sustainability extends to all

Figure 11-6.
McDonald's New Green Décor
The interior from the "green" McDonald's in Chicago uses recycled and natural materials. The green hue used in the furnishing subtly reinforces the eco-friendly theme.
Photo © McDonald's.

Figure 11-7.
Renzo Piano, *California Academy of Sciences,* 2005.
The planted roofscape creates a visual continuum and acts as a unifying element between the building and its surrounding landscape.
Photo courtesy of the California Academy of Sciences.

facets of the facility, from the bike racks and rechargeable vehicle stations outside the building to the radiant sub-floor heating inside the building to the energy-generating solar panels on top of the building.

Color Ownership: Color and the Law

In a sense, there are really only a limited number of colors or hues, or at least ones that can be reproduced in printing, packaging, and products. As advertising and product branding increasingly encroach on daily life, people are bombarded with advertisements and product placement in everything from movies to elevators, as well as all of the pop-ups on the Internet. The colors and names of products are so closely associated that consumers often reach for a product by the visual color cues of its packaging. With each company seeking to claim colors for themselves and their products, legal disputes are bound to arise. The question of whether a color can be so closely associated with a specific product that no other manufacturer can use it is litigated regularly.

Colors are used to identify products, and certain hues can become synonymous with a particular brand of merchandise. If companies were allowed to wholly copyright colors and their usage, the remaining few left for new products would be sorely limited. Notice the minute differences between the colors used on labels and packages. These slight variations are enough for your eye to distinguish the color differences and therefore for the manufacturers to be happy that you will not reach for the wrong product. So why do some products use the same basic coloring for their labels? Take, for example, Banquet frozen fried chicken and Ore-Ida frozen toaster hash browns. The basic body of the box on each is the same shade of bright red. The main differences are that the boxes are in vastly different sizes and each has a large image of the product on the front of the package. There is very little chance you will pick up the wrong item by mistake. Additionally, since they are completely different food products, they are not in competition with each other.

Most of us remember LifeSavers candies from our childhood. That distinctive multi-colored package with the red, yellow, orange, and green bands of color hinted to the fruit flavors inside (Figure 11-8). The Curtiss Candy Company came out with a similar, multicolored stripe package for a round disk-shaped, fruit-flavored candy. LifeSavers sued Curtiss, saying they had the sole market use of the multicolored striped package and that the colored bands were synonymous with their candy. The courts ruled against LifeSavers, saying that there was no trademark infringement. The ruling stated that the use of this type of multicolored packaging was the "general practice of the trade" and the coloring was descriptive of the flavors of the candy. Since the coloring of the package directly related to the flavors of the candy inside, it could not be trademarked.

In another case, Dap, which makes building and construction supplies, sold ceramic tile adhesive (as well as many of its other adhesives) packages with red labels (Figure 11-9). When rival Color Tile Manufacturing, Inc. came out with a similarly colored packaging for their version of the same type of product, Dap "saw red." They filed suit, and the courts ruled in their favor. So how was this different from the LifeSavers case? The decision said that red was not intrinsically related to that product nor was it descriptive of its function or use. Flavor was not an issue here. Therefore, when Color Tile used a similar red for their product packaging, they were infringing on the "secondary meaning" of the color red that was associated with Dap in the minds of consumers. The use of the color red was not related to the color of the product, its use, or its flavor, as in the LifeSavers case, so there was no valid reason for the another company to choose red for their package.

A specific color may receive protection, but the courts realize there should be limits.

When a color is so closely associated to a specific brand of a product, it may be protected. However, colors such as green are associated with a vast number of products, from citrus to mint flavors and even peanut butter. Therefore, a company trying to trademark a specific green hue would have a much harder time stating their case for trademark protection. The courts have also said that if the use of a specific color was related to the "functionality" of a product, it could not be

Figure 11-8.
LIFESAVERS®, a roll of fruit-flavored candies. The multicolored stripes on the LifeSavers package shows the consumer the flavors of the candies in the roll. The company uses different-colored packaging depending upon the flavor of the candy.
Photo © Wm. Wrigley Jr. Company.

Figure 11-9.
Dap adhesive
The color of the red package has nothing to do with the product inside. It was selected for visibility and product identification and not product function.
Courtesy of DAP Inc., Weldwood® is a registered trademark of Champion International.

trademarked, as in the case of fertilizers that use blue packaging to show they contain nitrate. But even in these cases, the manufacturer of the color in question must be able to show that it has used that particular hue for a long enough and extended period of time for the general public to wholly associate that color to the specific brand of the product. The trademark laws are just vague enough when it comes to the issue of color to keep lawyers busy for years to come.

Will you be able to use that particular hue in your painting, animation, or game? Or will you have to check with a legal clearinghouse before you apply the paint to the canvas or select a hue with your computer's color picker?

It's doubtful it will ever come to this and that things will go so far afield. It is certain, however, that color will no longer be the sole purview of the artist and designer. We are going to have to share our palette with a wide variety of folks because color is one of the most defining elements of our life and universe.

While owning a specific hue may not be possible, selecting a specific hue has become easier. Pantone now has a cell phone application that uses the camera in the phone to capture an image and its color. The color is compared to a database of PANTONE colors and the corresponding hue appears on your screen. For those without smart phones, Pantone makes a handheld device that works in much the same manner.

New Territory

Digital technology will remain an ever-increasing influence. At its inception in the early 1980s, many people sought to write off this new technology as a fad and said it would never catch on, let alone last. Now the only question is: what's next? New fields have been created—from computer animation to games to virtual realities—that are so sophisticated that the images on screen could pass for the real thing.

Artists and their ever-inquisitive search for new forms to make art have grabbed onto the computer and other new media such as lasers and holography. For some, technology is used as a tool to create their work, while to others the technology itself has become their principle medium.

This combination of high technology and art has not really produced a new movement or "-ism." However, it has opened up the boundaries of what it is possible to make art with. It is not one single medium, but a host of mediums mixed together to form a new means of creating art. Artists are now able to make art and interact with the viewer on a new grand scale. In the past, the audience has played a passive role in viewing art. Now with the use of motion-capture devices and sensors, the audience becomes an important element of the artwork itself.

In these new ways of visualizing space, the computer becomes the pigment for this type of artist in the same way da Vinci used oils. The artists creating these works do not consider themselves techno-artists, but simply artists who are working in a new medium and who mix mediums. These artists have not completely abandoned traditional concerns. They are still involved in figure/ground relationships as their traditional media counterparts, but now the ground is the screen or actual space.

Lasers and Holography

The term *laser* stands for light amplifications by stimulated emission of radiation. The basic principle of a laser is that light can be intensified and made to amplify itself to such a degree that it could burn a hole in a diamond. The first lasers were created in 1960, and the technology has been advancing steadily ever since. To create a laser, a beam of light is shot through a hollow gas-filled tube. The ends are reflective and the beam of light bounces back and forth between the ends of the reflective chambers until they develop into a wavelength of tremendous intensity.

The color of the laser beam is related to the gas used. Red is the most commonly used and is created using helium-neon gas. Krypton gas can produce the widest range of colors, including red, green, yellow, and blue. Since laser beams can travel great distances without spreading out, they are used in outdoor shows and have even been experimented with to replace fireworks. Once lasers were expensive, but today they are used in pointers and many other devices.

Another use for lasers is in holography. The term comes from the Greek word *holos* meaning whole or complete, and *gram* meaning message. The image itself is referred to as a hologram, while the complete process is called holography. It is the process of holding and displaying a three-dimensional image on a photographic plate or light-sensitive media. Holography is composed of two parts: creating the hologram and illuminating it to show the image. To do this, a beam of laser light is reflected off the subject onto a light-sensitive media. Then another laser beam, known as the reference beam, is shined onto the plate. Where the beams cross, they create a complex pattern of stripes and illuminate the image. The hologram changes the direction of the light waves in the beam so that they seem to come from the original subject. This creates a three-dimensional image that appears to float in space.

Katalin Sallai is one of a number of artists who use lasers in the form of holography in their artwork. She feels that the color the laser produces in the hologram is very unique and that she cannot achieve it in any other media. In *His Story* (Figure 11-10), Sallai feels that the bright green color of the

hologram represents terror, while the lighter greens and blues of the outer image represent a poisonous atmosphere that works in a homogenous manner with the deep intense green of the cross. The cross itself is made up of several images of Christ and Mary. Mary is slightly out of focus to symbolize what Sallai believes—women are treated as second-class citizens in society.

Web Art

John Weber calls the Internet the "wild card" in the world of art. Egalitarian by its very nature, there is no admission charge or need to fly to a distant land to see an individual artwork. The art is wherever you

Figure 11-10.
Katalin Sallai, *His Story*, 1994.
Sallai feels she can only obtain the deep acid green she wanted for the figures inside the cross by using holography and chose it first and foremost because of the intensity of the color.
Photo courtesy of Katalin Sallai.

are—online and hooked up to the Internet. Mark Napier is one of a number of new artists who are producing artwork specifically for the Web. Napier's Web site *Potatoland* (http://www.potatoland.org/) is a vast collection of all of his online artworks. It includes projects from *USA* to the *Digital Landfill* to name a few.

Fall of Rome, Part II, which is a part or subsection of the large work, starts out with a somewhat blank screen, which then begins to fill with white lines of color placed on a red background. The screen continues to fill with these, creating one, then two, then three wireframe buildings. This color shift spans the full range of the hue, working in an analogous scheme from yellow to red. The color then continues to shift to a green hue as seen in Figure 11–11. The hues grow darker, moving from green to its complement of red. The buildings begin to shake and are almost reminiscent of the World Trade Center disaster on September 11, 2001. The work is a powerful analogy as evidenced by its title. The complexity of Web-based art continues to push the bounds of this growing art form, with the works created becoming more thought provoking and grittier.

Figure 11-11.
Mark Napier, *Fall of Rome, Part II,* 2005. URL: http://www.potatoland.org/kk2/kk3_line
Since his images are reproduced for the viewer on their home monitor, a more intimate space created. The image has an overall dark blue-green hue with a hint of yellow-green in the wrier frame building on the top left. Napier also uses a complementary red hue in the center to help balance out the image and bring out the darker green wire frame element of the building.
Photo courtesy of Mark Napier.

Virtual Reality and Interactivity

Virtual realities have been around for a number of years, but they are still in their infancy. In the past they have been used as simulators and trainers for pilots, the military, police, and doctors. Newer uses include theme rides at the nation's top amusement parks. But they have also long been the area of exploration for artists. They are a place to experiment with visuals, sound, and interactivity. In this type of art, the audience is no longer merely viewing, but is actively participating in the artwork. Without the audience interaction, there is no art. The art is in the interaction.

Char Davies has completed several major interactive artworks. *Ephémère* is a fully interactive visual and aural virtual artwork. The work uses real-time 3-D computer graphics and interactive 3-D sound. The immersant (no longer merely a viewer as in traditional forms of art) dons a stereoscopic head mounted display and real-time motion tracking, which is based on balance and breath. During the immersive experience, visual and aural elements develop, linger, and then transition out in response to several variables, including pace of movement, length and duration of gaze, passage of time, and more.

The piece works on three levels: the landscape, earth, and interior body. It suggests the symbolic relations between body and earth. As a Canadian, the work was inspired by an actual place on the mountain slopes of rural Quebec. This inspiration was evident in the color used in the work. Her use of strong neutrals in an analogous range of warm colors can clearly be seen in Figure 11-12. These hues bring viewers back to the natural world and are evocative of nature.

Second Life

Second Life, also known as **SL,** was launched on June 23, 2003. Created by Linden Labs (who still controls the domain), it has become one of the fastest growing virtual entities.

Figure 11-12.
Char Davies. *Seeds,
Ephémère,* 1998.
Digital still captured in
real-time through HMD
during live performance
of immersive virtual
reality environment
Ephémère.
Additional credits:
Custom VR software,
John Harrison.
Computer graphics,
Georges Mauro.
Sonic architecture and
programming, Dorota
Blaszczak.
The artist becomes a
creator and manager in a
work of this magnitude,
which takes several
individuals with diverse
specialties to be able to
present it. This type of
art experience literally
envelops the viewer (now
a participant) in a unique
visceral encounter. After
several minutes within
the work, the color and
sound fade in one of
several endings in which
naturalist hues—neutrals
of either autumn leaves,
embers, or ashes—float
in an empty space.
Photo courtesy of
Char Davies.

It is a domain in which everything is resident-created, with a fully integrated economy where goods and services are developed, purchased, sold, and traded. As part of this economic system, one can buy SL cash and even trade it in for real currency. With SL cash or a line of credit, a person can purchase land, start a business, or anything else that can be done in real life. Its interesting that even in SL there is no free ride, and without money virtual life is as bleak an existence as anywhere poverty exists.

SL may be considered part of the Web 2.0 phenomenon in that the residents, not Linden Lab, create most of the content of the world. Residents retain intellectual property rights to their digital creations; they can buy, sell, and trade with other residents. User-generated content comprises the largest portion of the activity within SL. Built into the client is a 3D modeling tool that allows any resident to construct virtual objects.

Since it uses an HD color space, users have millions of colors to work with.

SL inhabitants in this vast online social network are known as **avatars**. An avatar can be human in appearance and may be of either gender with an extensive array of physical attributes, or may take on a variety of humanoid and other forms. Many people are secretive regarding their avatar and may change their appearance, sex, or even humanoid form to more closely match their inner fantasy, psyche, or desires (Figure 11-13). In an example of this, artist Cassandra Jones

Figure 11-13.
Cassandra Jones, *Tricky
Reifsnider,* Second Life
Avatar.
The butterfly winged
being that Jones uses as
her avatar reflects her
personality. The orange
dress is a complement to
the blue-hued figure.
Photo courtesy of
Cassandra L. Jones.

Figure 11-14.
Second Life Gallery at
Ball State University
Student, faculty, and
guest artists can exhibit
their work in this venue.
Photo courtesy of Ball State
University.

created her avatar, *Tricky Reifsnider*, as a blue, bald, freckle-cheeked woman with wide set eyes and a uniquely shaped body that could only be achieved in the virtual realm of SL. Its wings reflect the ability in SL for one to fly or teleport from place to place. The wings draw attention to the possibility of flight even while grounded.

Artists and designers are producing works solely for SL to be exhibited only within this virtual realm. Commercial galleries are exhibiting and selling these works. There are even numerous virtual museums. Many colleges and universities now not only own property in SL but also offer classes in this virtual domain (Figure 11-14). SL will continue to be a driving force for many years to come.

Summary

None of us can quite know the future of color. It will change and evolve as technology and science continue to move forward. But it is certain to say that advances will continue. Low-tech inventions have helped refine the existing art media and have made them safer to work with and use. This may open up art to new experiments from hobbyists to professionals. Legal issues will also continue to shape graphic design and advertising. Since there are only a finite number of hues, the rush to claim their providence will continue and may become more contentious.

Concern for the earth and issues of sustainability will continue to be at the forefront of art and design. Green issues affect us all. From the materials we use to the artworks and design produced, everyone realizes that our resources are finite and must be cared for.

Whether it is finding new uses for materials or exploring the realms of new technology, color never stands still. But it is not only technology that will shape the future of color, but our desire to find new modes of expression and communication.

As we have seen throughout the text, color may be one of the single most important design elements. Its future is now in your hands. Where will you take it? How will you use it? What new forms will you be able to create?

Glossary

A

absolute threshold—the minimum amount of light needed to cause a discernable visual sensation.

achromatics—also known as neutrals, they have no chroma or color and include black, white, and gray. Since they are not hues, they cannot be found on the color wheel.

additive color—mixtures of light. The additive primaries are red, green, and blue.

afterimage—a fleeting false image that is seen after prolonged exposure to a specific hue. The afterimage seen will be the complement of that hue.

aliasing—the jagged edge or stair-step effect seen in a digital image. What you are seeing are the actual pixels that make up the image.

analogous colors—three hues that are next to each other on the color wheel. On very large color wheels (48 steps or more), four hues that are next to each other may be used.

atmospheric perspective—a visual effect caused by the diminishing light. As elements recede into deep space, they dissolve into a middle gray.

avatar—digitally created inhabitant of online social networks such as Second Life.

B

Blu-ray (short for *Blu-ray Disc*)—an optical disc formatting system using blue laser wavelengths that allows for five times more data storage on a standard CD.

C

candelas—unit of measure for the brightness of lamps.

chromophobia—fear of color and the use of color.

colorimeter—a device that measures hue, luminance, and saturation.

color management profile—a computer-generated and assigned value or record of the color mode used in creating the image.

color modes—models that enable us to express color in terms of numerical values. CMYK, HSB, LAB, and RGB are examples of color modes.

complementary contrast—the effect created when two complementary hues of equal value and saturation are placed next to each other in a design.

complements—hues that are directly opposite each other on the color wheel.

D

dermo-optic vision—alternative color perception where the skin literally sees or senses the color.

double split complementary—two hues that are next to each other on the color wheel and their complements or opposite hues.

F

fovea—the photoreceptor area in the retina that contains only cones.

fugitive colors—colors (paints and pigments) that fade over time due to exposure to sunlight.

G

gamma—the measurement and mathematical formula of the relationship of voltage input to the relative brightness of the image seen on the screen.

gamut—the range of color that devices such as monitors, scanners, and printers can display or reproduce.

giclée—a high-end inkjet printing process for archival output.

green, green movement—a contemporary movement concerned with sustainability and concern for the environment.

guerilla artworks—unsponsored artworks put up without permission.

H

heightened color—the use of color without regard to the natural or local color of the object, usually used by the artist for dramatic or emotional effect.

Holi—Hindu spring observance known as the Festival of Color.

hue—the actual name of a color.

I

image-based lighting—a computer algorithm that emulates how light reflects off of an object and scatters over surfaces used in animation.

incident beam—the beam of light coming from the light source and striking the object.

inherent value—the actual value of a given object.

intermediate color—a synonymous term for tertiary color. The two terms are often used interchangeably.

iodopsin—the light-sensitive chemical agent in the cone that is believed to be involved with our ability to see color.

L

light emitting diode (LED)—a type of monitor that offers brighter color and more contrast for richer color levels.

liquid-crystal display (LCD)—a type of backlit monitor that uses a series of color cathode-ray fluorescent lamps at the rear of the screen. It produces darker hues and blacks by twisting, which blocks the light, or untwisting, for whites and bright colors.

local color—the actual color of an object.

luminaire—the proper name for a light fixture, or what we normally call lamps.

luminosity—the perceived light given off by an object; it goes hand in hand with value.

M

megapixels (MP)—a megapixel is equal to one million pixels.

metamerism—the visual phenomena that occurs when two objects or hues appear to be the same when viewed under one light source, but appear visually different when viewed under a different light source.

monochromatic—a single color that includes the full range of tints, tones, and shades of that color.

monochromatics—people who are color blind (those who have an extremely rare vision abnormality that prevents them from seeing color). People affected by this disorder can only see black, white, and shades of gray.

N

neutral—the opposite of a hue. Black, white, and grays are considered neutrals and do not appear anywhere on the color wheel.

O

opponent–process theory—associated with the cones in the eye, it is the theory that when complementary colors are viewed, pairs of receptors cause one color to be inhibited when the other one is viewed.

P

PANTONE—a proprietary formula of inks or pigments used in printing and manufacturing to insure color accuracy and consistency.

perception—the ability to make sense of or understand visual stimuli.

pigments—the finely ground minerals, oxides, and chemicals that give paints, pastels, and other art media their color.

pixel/pixilated—the square two-dimensional picture elements of light that make up images in raster-based programs such as Photoshop.

plasma display panel (PDP)—a type of monitor that uses tiny cells, located between two panels of glass, which hold an inert mixture of noble gases (neon and xenon). The gases are electrically turned into plasma, exciting phosphors to emit light.

PostScript—a page description language developed by Adobe that tells the printer specifically how to create and print an image on the page.

primary colors (hues)—there are two different primary groups. For subtractive color (pigments) the three most basic hues are red, yellow, and blue. The additive primary system (light) is RGB or red, green, and blue. They are considered primary hues because they can be added to make up all of the other colors.

Q

QuadPixel technology—Sharp's proprietary technology which adds a yellow channel or filter to the standard three-hued light primary range, resulting in a RGBY color filter system that can reproduce a trillion hues.

quaternary colors—hues that are made up of a tertiary and a primary or secondary color.

R

radiance map—a special algorithm that is used to predict the reaction of light falling on an object, creating the proper color relationship to the quality of light on a given surface. (*See also* **image-based lighting**.)

raster image processor (RIP)—works hand in hand with the PostScript language and interprets the data or code translating and the instructions to the printer. A RIP is built into most desktop printers, but is a separate module for imagesetters.

rasters—rows of pixels.

reflected beam—the beam of light reflected off a given object that shows us its color.

render/rendering—the process by which the computer collects all of the data from the digital animation program, the lighting, effects, and specified camera angles, and compiles all of the information to videotape or film.

resolution—the number of pixels per inch making up a digital raster-based image.

retinex theory—theory developed by Edwin Land that states that no matter what the lighting conditions are, we expect an object to retain its color.

rhodopsin—the light-sensitive chemical agent in the rods in the eye. Also called visual purple.

S

saturation—the lightness or darkness of a hue. Also referred to as chroma, intensity, or brightness.

Second Life (SL)—a virtual world created by Linden Labs.

secondary colors (hues)—colors made by mixing equal parts of two primary hues together.

sensation—the response or reaction to a stimulus.

separations—plates made to be used in production printing, which correspond to the four colors (CMYK) of inks used in the printing process.

shade—a hue plus the addition of black.

simultaneous contrast—the effect of complementary colors to influence each other and the adjacent hues.

site specific—works of art that are developed for a specific location and may become part of that environment when finished.

split complement—a hue plus the two adjacent hues to its complement.

standing waves—electromagnetic waves that remain in a constant position.

successive contrast—color phenomenon seen when the same hue is placed on differing background colors to visually change the color of the original hue.

synesthesia—a form of color perception in which people perceive their environment by using a combination of two or more senses.

T

tertiary color—color made by combining a primary and a secondary color.

tetrad—four hues that are of equal distance from each other on the color wheel.

texture map—a skin that an animator applies over a wireframe, which consists of texture and color information.

tiled/tiling—also referred to as page tiling. An algorithm that pieces together a print from smaller segments.

tint—the hue plus the addition of white.

tone—the hue plus the addition of gray.

triad—three hues that are of equal distance from each other on the color wheel.

trichromatic theory—states that there are three types of cone pigment each for sensing a different wavelength of light; blue-violet for short range, green for middle range, and red for the longest wavelengths.

trompe l'oeil—visual deception, from the French meaning "to fool the eye," in which objects are rendered in extremely fine detail.

truth in materials—Constantine Brancusi's philosophy that materials should not be painted or disguised, and that the natural beauty of the material should be displayed.

twain acquire (TWAIN)—the image-scanning software built into Adobe Photoshop. It stands for "technology without an interesting name."

V

value contrast—the concept of how a color may appear when placed on a contrasting background.

vector-based programs—software programs that use a mathematical formula to create the art or graphics. Examples of vector-based programs include Illustrator, Freehand, and Flash.

vehicle—the agent used to suspend the pigment and aid in the flow of water colors, oils, and acrylic paints.

W

wax bloom—a white waxy buildup that can occur in crayons and colored pencils. It happens when the wax base or binder of the medium begins to separate and bead up on the surface of a drawing.

wireframe—a structure on which an animator can apply a skin that contains texture and color information called a texture map.

Index and Illustration List

Illustration List by Artist